ALSO BY GLENN BECK

Liars

The Immortal Nicholas

It IS About Islam

Agenda 21: Into the Shadows

Dreamers and Deceivers

*Conform: Exposing the Truth About Common Core
and Public Education*

*Miracles and Massacres: True and Untold Stories of the
Making of America*

The Eye of Moloch

Control: Exposing the Truth About Guns

Agenda 21

Cowards: What Politicians, Radicals, and the Media Refuse to Say

*Being George Washington: The Indispensable Man,
as You've Never Seen Him*

Snow Angel

The Original Argument: The Federalists' Case for the Constitution,
Adapted for the 21st Century

The 7: Seven Wonders that Will Change Your Life

Broke: The Plan to Restore Our Trust, Truth and Treasure

The Overton Window

Idiots Unplugged: Truth for Those Who Care to Listen (audiobook)

The Christmas Sweater: A Picture Book

Arguing with Idiots: How to Stop Small Minds and Big Government

Glenn Beck's Common Sense: The Case Against an Out-of-Control
Government, Inspired by Thomas Paine

America's March to Socialism: Why We're One Step Closer to
Giant Missile Parades (audiobook)

The Christmas Sweater

An Inconvenient Book: Real Solutions to the World's Biggest Problems

The Real America: Early Writings from the Heart and Heartland

ADDICTED
TO
OUTRAGE

HOW THINKING LIKE
A RECOVERING ADDICT CAN
HEAL THE COUNTRY

GLENN BECK

Threshold Editions / Mercury Radio Arts

NEW YORK   LONDON   TORONTO   SYDNEY   NEW DELHI

Threshold Editions / Mercury Radio Arts
An Imprint of Simon & Schuster, Inc.
1230 Avenue of the Americas
New York, NY 10020

Copyright © 2018 by Mercury Radio Arts, Inc.

First Threshold Editions/Mercury Radio Arts hardcover edition September 2018

THRESHOLD EDITIONS and colophon are trademarks
of Simon & Schuster, Inc.

GLENN BECK is a trademark of Mercury Radio Arts, Inc.

For information about special discounts for bulk purchases,
please contact Simon & Schuster Special Sales at 1-866-506-1949
or business@simonandschuster.com.

The Simon & Schuster Speakers Bureau can bring authors to your
live event. For more information, or to book an event, contact the
Simon & Schuster Speakers Bureau at 866-248-3049
or visit our website at www.simonspeakers.com.

Interior design by Paul Dippolito

Manufactured in the United States of America

1   3   5   7   9   10   8   6   4   2

Library of Congress Cataloging-in-Publication Data is available.

ISBN: 978-1-4767-9886-8
ISBN: 978-1-4767-9892-9 (ebook)

*To those who are willing to step out in front of the crowd,
to question, reason, and have the dangerous conversations.
Men with whom I may strongly disagree at times, but will
always consider Refounders of Reason and contemporary heroes:
Ben Shapiro, Dave Rubin, Jordan Peterson, Bret Weinstein,
Sam Harris, Jonathan Sacks, Penn Jillette, and Joe Rogan.*

There are things that I believe that I shall never say, but I shall never say those things I do not believe.

—I. Kant

Silence in the face of evil is itself evil . . . Not to speak is to speak.

—D. Bonhoeffer

Question with boldness even the existence of a God; because, if there be one, he must more approve of the homage of reason, than that of blind-folded fear.

—T. Jefferson

Contents

Prologue

Wrath Makes Him Deaf

The floor of the United States Senate was mostly deserted on the afternoon of May 22, 1856. Republican senator Charles Sumner was sitting at his desk, dutifully scribbling some notes. In an angry speech a few days earlier he had attacked South Carolina senator Andrew Butler, claiming, "The senator from South Carolina has read many books of chivalry, and believes himself a chivalrous knight with sentiments of honor and courage. Of course he has chosen a mistress to whom he has made his vows, and who, though ugly to others, is always lovely to him; though polluted in the sight of the world, is chaste in his sight—I mean the harlot, slavery."

Then he had added derisively, "[He] touches nothing which he does not disfigure with error, sometimes of principle, sometimes of fact. He cannot open his mouth, but out there flies a blunder."

It was a satisfying and, Sumner believed, absolutely necessary response to Butler's own recent attempt to race-bait him by making sexual innuendos concerning female slaves.

As the gallery finally emptied, Butler's cousin, South Carolina congressman Preston Brooks, hobbled onto the Senate floor. His wounds from a duel earlier in life forced him to rely on a heavy cane with a gold head. Like so many Americans divided by the issue of slavery, Brooks's hatred for the opposing side had reached the boiling point. Sumner's speech, he decided, was a scurrilous slander on both his cousin and the state of South Carolina. It had to be answered. He had considered challenging Sumner to a duel, but rejected that because the senator was not a gentleman. Instead he intended to humiliate him by beating him in public.

Brooks calmly accused Sumner of a public slander, and then began beating him savagely with his cane. He smashed him over and over, across his face, back, and shoulders. Sumner was beaten onto the floor, pinned under his desk, which was bolted to the floor, but still Brooks kept striking him. Sumner managed to rip the desk free and tried desperately to escape. Blood was pouring from his wounds. Several other senators tried to stop the attack but were held away by two other members of Congress wielding a cane and a gun. Brooks's cane snapped into pieces, but even that didn't stop him. He continued hitting Sumner with its remnants until the senator lay unconscious in a bloody heap on the floor.

While Sumner was rushed into the cloakroom for medical aid, Brooks walked out of the building and the pieces of the broken cane were collected. No charges were ever brought against the Democratic congressman, and Sumner eventually recovered. The attack made both men heroes to their supporters. Remnants of the cane were shaped into rings, which southern lawmakers wore proudly around their necks. Brooks received hundreds of replacement canes. In northern cities thousands of people attended rallies, helping to transform the new Republican Party into a political force, and more than a million copies of Sumner's speech were distributed and prized as souvenirs.

Five years later the hatred between the North and South erupted into a civil war that was as close as this country has ever been to being ripped apart. An estimated eight hundred thousand Americans died during that war, 2 percent of the nation's entire population. The end of the fighting in 1865 did almost nothing to stop the hatred, which continued to be felt throughout the country for decades. It seemed impossible that the situation would ever again reach that point, that hatred between Americans who share the same basic constitutional rights would threaten to destroy this country.

But then Al Gore invented the Internet. And made it available to all Americans, and provided social media platforms like Facebook, Twitter, and Instagram that allowed people to anonymously express their opinions. And today we spend countless hours each day virtually beating each other with canes into bloody compliance.

PART ONE

We Have a Problem

And Jesus knew their thoughts and said unto him, Every kingdom divided against itself is brought desolation; and every city or house divided against itself shall not stand.

—Gospel of Matthew, 12:25, King James Version

"So now you'd give the Devil benefit of law?"

"Yes. What would you do? Cut a great road through the law to get after the Devil. . . . And when the last law was down and the Devil turned round on you—where would you hide, the laws all being flat? This country's planted thick with laws from coast to coast . . . and if you cut them down d'you really think you could stand upright in the winds that would blow then? Yes, I'd give the Devil benefit of law, for my own safety's sake."

—Thomas More in Robert Bolt's *A Man for All Seasons*

1

Hello, My Name Is Glenn, and I Am Addicted to Outrage

And unless you've been living under a rock for the past twenty years, chances are you're addicted to outrage, too. If you don't believe you are part of the problem, I recommend you start with my last book: *Liars*.

I know it is tough to even think about being part of the problem, but the truth is, we all are. Believe it or not, I have good friends across the entire political spectrum. We actually all like each other and respect each other. Over the years I have really tried to listen to those with whom I don't always agree. I have learned a ton. Not just about the other "side" but also about me. My biggest mistakes always revolve around my thinking "I am right and they are wrong." The moment I begin to feel that, I begin to believe that "the other side has nothing to teach me." I have made this mistake many times; I have failed to listen, and it always creates problems. I did it in the 2016 election. I was so sure about Donald Trump that I failed to listen to what half of the country was actually saying. I had become so blinded by him that I failed to see the who and the why supporting him. Did you know that over 20 percent of Donald Trump supporters consider themselves Democrats and voted for Obama? Of course not, because if you know that, you begin to see deep flaws in not only the GOP but also the Democratic platform and candidates.

When I am listening, really listening, I discover something truly game changing. We many times—not always, but much of the time—are saying almost the same exact thing, just with different words. This is not true with Live-or-Die Demopublicans. Nor am I suggesting that those who believe in the republic under the Constitution and Bill of Rights will agree or perhaps even like a communist revolutionary. But if we actually listen to each other, we may find that one of us is mistaken on what we believe, what we think others believe, or what is separating us in the first place.

Many times we are not even aware of what the real divide is. For instance, let's dip our feet into the outrage pool and see if we cannot quickly see how our vision is being blurred intentionally on both sides:

The border issue over the summer of 2018.

It began in the opening weeks of June, with the outrage of pictures of border kids being "abused" and kept in "cages" by the Trump administration. The problem was it was a story from 2014. Many on the left were quickly embarrassed that they were "outraged" by something they all ignored under Obama. The editor of the *New York Times*, who tweeted the photos, quickly responded that it was "the weekend and the kids had distracted him." But the speed at which these pictures circulated and the outrage they drew was powerful. So, I believe to turn their humiliation into a righteous cause, they quickly changed "the outrage" to the fact that these kids were being "separated from their parents." Now, with all of the press on the same page, the fact that Obama not only had the same policy but defiantly defended the same policy in 2014 didn't seem to matter. This is a problem that began under the Clinton administration. In 1997, the Flores v. Reno Agreement set formal policy for the detention of minors in the custody of the U.S. government's Immigration and Naturalization Services. It included the guidelines that both the Obama and Trump administrations were following, which did include the detention of illegal-alien minors until a suitable adult relative or guardian could be identified.

However, as is the case with every "Band-Aid," this only created a bigger problem: human trafficking. Drug cartels realized that if they could smuggle children over the border, they could "conscript" fourteen- to seventeen-year-olds to bring children over the border who would then be released, and the "children" would be given to "relatives." The children were being sold into slavery. Thus, the Wilberforce Act was passed under George W. Bush to try stop the human trafficking problem caused by the Reno decision. Back to square one and a half. When Obama had a massive influx of "refugees," the system quickly became overloaded. I know, because I was one of the few "reporters" there. The government was paralyzed, and because it did not see the crisis, the press never showed it to the American people. The very same ICE agents whom Americans are now publicly "stoning" are the people who quietly came to me and begged me to bring attention to what was being done to these kids. Their biggest problem then, as it was mainly underage kids without parents, was the fact that the children were all being separated by age. So, if a group of brothers and sisters came over together, for example, a fifteen-year-old son, a twelve-year-old boy, and a six-year-old sister, they were all placed in different "rooms," "areas," or "cages." The trauma that these children were undergoing was beyond understanding. At one point under President Obama, more than 25,000 children were held. When Trump took over there were still 10,000 in custody. At the time of the media outrage that number had grown to 12,000. Some of the additional 2,000 had been separated from their parents. The vast majority had not been. Had they been ripped apart as brothers and sisters? Most likely the majority of them. But still today, the press doesn't care about that part of the story. Why? Because the outrage of children being taken by men with guns near barbed wire is more than enough to begin to evoke images of a Nazi concentration camp. CNN actually aired an interview with George Takei, who did a grave disservice by distorting and dishonoring the truth of what FDR did when he interned all Americans of Japanese descent. These were Americans, some of whom were held for months in horse stalls at California racetracks. These citizens, many if not most of whom were born here in America, spent most of the war in American "concentration camps," without trial or charges. In the end we treated them shamefully, and when it was all over, sent them back "home" here in America with no money, house, or property returned and most likely to hostile neighbors.

But this idea of American concentration camps is a powerful enough outrage to blot out all reason. If you dare say anything but dismantle the SS, which now is ICE, you are for these camps and are a monster. Hitler versus Jesus.

Yet if we can strip away the outrage, let's look at the facts. Did you know that 70 percent of Americans agree, both right and left, that breaking up families on the border is wrong? Only 4 percent agreed with the Obama or Trump policy. FOUR. That is three times smaller than the number of Americans who deny we actually landed on the moon. That is a small and insignificant group of people.

So what is it that we are fighting over? Well, the media and the left present America with a false option. No borders with no immigration enforcement, or Gitmo. This is not a serious solution for any country.

We need a balance between justice and mercy. Justice meaning if you break the law or cut in line, you are punished, corrected, or at least simply returned to "Go" without collecting $200. Justice is essential in society. Without it, civilizations break down. But it also must be balanced by mercy, or the state devolves into a communistic, Stalinist state. Mercy, in this case, means that we do all we can to ensure that those who need help and are true asylum seekers are given a fair hearing. We must protect the most vulnerable. So, how do we do this? Actually, in this case it is fairly easy. The first thing to do is to secure the border as we hire a butt-load of judges to hear cases at the border in as short a time as possible and find those who are true refugees and those who are not. This would require about five hundred judges in a "night court" sort of system and could turn the cases around in ten to twenty-one days. Refugees stay, as always, and the rest go home. If you do not have valid paperwork proving that these are your children, and refuse to submit to a DNA test, then your "children" are kept here in foster care. (Warning: This is a Band-Aid and a point of failure, but we cannot send them home to foster care, as these places in foreign countries are many times engaged in human trafficking.) At the same time this process is being put into place, the State Department should run ads in Latin America reinforcing the idea that people should NOT send their kids alone to America or come to America as "illegal." If they need protection, they should immediately go to the U.S. consulate in their area.

Crisis is caused by chaos. The first thing a nation must do in a crisis is to bring clarity. The media and special interest groups are doing the opposite.

Meanwhile, the left and right are left arguing something that only 20 percent actually want: full amnesty and open borders. Which provides neither justice nor mercy. So, why do 80 percent think that half the country is an enemy of freedom or refugees or that the other half wants chaos on the border? Because we are being painted a picture of MS13 gang members gladly being welcomed by the left, or David Duke holding the first Klan campfire on the right. Neither is true. We are all being used.

This is part of the problem to which this book hopes to bring clarity. But it begins with us and our willingness to suppress the "outrage" and look at all sides. A willingness to see how the problem is amplified by each of us. It is easy to see the problem in the other person, or "political team," and the urge to scream "hypocrite" no matter which team you play for is almost overwhelming at times. But let us, for just a minute, consider that perhaps the other side has a valid reason for calling us names, or we them. Forget about the past, who started it, or even "they are sooo much worse." Let's just examine our thoughts, words, and actions. Then, stop listening to the "outrage" and begin to look to the facts on each side. Isn't the entirety of man's freedom worth seriously considering this thought? If I am wrong, we may find ourselves fighting in the streets. But if I am correct, it just might mean that if enough of us on both sides begin to drop the outrage and anger, we just may stand a chance and heal this nation.

Millions of us have spent the last several years engaged in our new favorite national pastime, expressing outrage at everyone and everything that is different from ourselves. It's an epidemic worse and more insidious than our growing crisis of opioid addiction, far worse than our addiction to caffeine, sugar, or fast food, because our Outrage Addiction is destroying our nation. Unlike addictions to so-called vices and chemicals, which are universally recognized as bad for us and therefore carry negative social stigmas, Outrage Addiction adds the enabling element that makes it almost impossible to overcome: It is viewed as a virtue and as proof of our social value. Being constantly outraged is inherently reinforced by everyone around us; it is seen as a demonstration of our moral, cultural, and intellectual awareness, as proof that we are, in fact, "woke." It's like your mom finding out you're using cocaine and then buying you an eight-ball and giving you a pat on the back. With Outrage Addiction, each of us has become a massive enabler of the addiction of those in our tribe, because we provide Outrage Addicts the very real physical, social, and psychological rewards that feed and reinforce their addiction.

Our Thumbs-Up or Like or LOL make each of us an unwitting dope dealer. Thumbs-up? Dopamine surge. Retweet? Serotonin hit. Kicked off a new subreddit thread? Splash of oxytocin. "Dopamine" is the root word of the slang: "dope." Make no mistake, our addiction to outrage is as real and as chemically rich as the latest street drug, but even worse because it's 100 percent legal and is being reinforced by the press, social platforms, celebrities, and political leaders.

I say all of this as an admitted and recovering addict myself. Look, I've been there and done that. In fact, it's fair to say that identifying things to be outraged about and expressing that outrage to my audience is part of my day job. And there are certainly things deserving of outrage, though they're not nearly as prevalent as the media would have you believe.

If you listen to my show, you know that my outrage generally isn't directed at specific people. I don't despise any particular Democrat. (Well, maybe Woodrow Wilson.) They all make me furious and have for a long time, but it's not because I don't like them as individuals; in fact, I count many who identify on the political left as personal friends. They make me frustrated because I believe their ideas on policy and government are so bad. In fact, I've found most of the Democrats whom I've known over the years to be downright good, likable people, despite their fanciful, utopian, irredeemably bad ideas. I thought—I knew!—I was CERTAIN that they were all corrupt; I was frustrated by the belief they were terrible liars and they were doing horrible damage to my country. Make no mistake, I still think they are corrupt, but so are the Republicans. As far as the Democrats are concerned, the party as it was even of Obama is now dead. It has been fully hijacked by the über left, and until they begin to listen to the Democratic voters in the center of the country, they are going to have a hard time winning elections. I may be wrong on this, but I still do not believe that the average Democrats in the center of the country believe what is happening in our universities is good, healthy, or right, nor do they agree with partial-birth abortion or that the Second Amendment should be abolished as now almost all of the leadership does. My problem is not with the people who are working hard every day and not living or breathing politics—it is with those who actually are a part of the system, who truly believe that it is best for our schools to pay teachers to sit out their contract and remain on the payroll after they have been wildly inappropriate with children.

But somewhere we began judging people not by their character or their actions but by their political affiliation and beliefs. A person who had different opinions than you wasn't just wrong but suddenly became a bad, deplorable person, someone not to be trusted. Someone who must be ostracized, isolated, and destroyed. In today's America, we deem that person a "traitor." We seem, nowadays, to use that word more than at any time in my lifetime. Does no one see that we are becoming the America of the McCarthy hearings? There were communists in the government in the 1950s, but McCarthy, unfortunately, was a deeply flawed messenger. The real problem was the fact that we believed, as a people, that if you believed in communism, you should be in prison and should have no part in society. How does a country where freedom of speech, freedom of association, freedom of assembly, and freedom to petition our government is OUR FIRST AMENDMENT yet try and jail those who believe differently?

This is the path we are on. One where the mistakes of the past will be made all over again. If you do not agree with whomever is in power, you can and will be targeted. You will be targeted by the IRS, the EPA, or the NSA, or by the David Hogg–type of professional outrage peddlers who live their lives in a state of perpetual moral outrage inviting mobs of mindless addicts to join their latest boycott, die-in, or corporate bullying campaign. If you cannot be tried and jailed, then you will be smeared and blackballed. Your name and reputation will be forever destroyed. If you are white, straight, male, and Christian, you will be treated as those who were black, homosexual, or communist were treated in the 1950s. And if you own a gun, eat meat, and express doubt about your truck being the cause for climate change? Huge numbers of your fellow men are literally wishing for your death right now, my friend. Outrage targeting isn't a weapon used exclusively by those on the left. Just ask any number of celebrities who've been the target of a Trump tweet-storm and ended up receiving death threats as the outrage wave crashes over them on social media.

How is it that "progressives" (on both left and right) who believe in the concept that man progresses as a collective do not see that humans are taking giant leaps backward? Those in the past who were called un-American for what they believed, who were treated as second-class citizens simply because of their skin color or forced into the closet for who they were, now support leaders who are deciding which views are un-American, judging people by skin color, and forcing others into a closet.

America is in trouble. We are facing challenges in the near future that literally will change the world. A century of technological advancement will take place in a decade. There are going to be massive shifts in every aspect of society that will cause tremendous upheaval. Entire industries are going to disappear; according to some, we are looking at 30 percent unemployment by 2030.

Think about how blessed we are to live in this country at this time. Both in Obama's and Trump's America. Life has literally never been better for humans than it is right now. Never have a people been more free, or better fed, educated, wealthy, and healthy, or had access to information and communication than right now. And yet, if one listens to the media or browses our social media platforms, one would think that we were royally screwed. But what are we all so outraged about? Most of the time, not much.

For all of eternity, man was able to stay alive without a refrigerator, electricity, radio, microwave, or color television. It might have been hot, sticky, and a lot less entertaining, but survival was possible. Today, each of these self-evident "luxury" items (when measured against all of human history) are owned by between 96.3 and 99.3 percent of households.

Take the computer. When Bill Clinton was elected, only 20 percent of American households had one. When Barack Obama left office, more than 80 percent had a computer, more than half had a tablet, and almost everyone had a smartphone far more powerful than any computer used in the Clinton years.

The average piece of land that produces corn now yields 8.6 times as much corn as it did during World War II. This is only one example, and only positive if you like corn, but you get the point. Among other things, these increases in food production have led to a sixty-point drop in the percentage of our disposable income that we spend on food.

The portion of the U.S. population that is homeless and unsheltered is less than 0.1 percent. I'm not saying that doesn't mean we have more work to do, but in the rest of the world that number is over 20 percent.

The homicide rate in the United States has dropped by about half from the levels of the 1970s, 1980s, and 1990s. While the media constantly warns us of the epidemic of "rape culture," the rate of forcible rape has dropped by over 30 percent since the 1990s. Even in Hollywood.

Perhaps most surprising is the fact that even the number of school shootings has dropped dramatically. The rate of students killed per million in fatal school shootings has dropped by over 75 percent.

Read that sentence again. Heard that on CNN? Or even Fox?

Researchers at Northeastern noted that this means "four times the number of children were killed in schools in the early 1990s as today." Their summary would shock any modern cable news fanatic: "There is not an epidemic of school shootings."

In 1952 there were 57,879 cases of polio in the United States. In 2017, there were zero.

Among men in the U.S., death rates from colon cancer have dropped by 30 percent, lung cancer by 40 percent, prostate cancer by 45 percent, and stomach cancer by almost 50 percent, all since 1990. Among women, the death rate from breast cancer has dropped by 35 percent.

Does all that mean we don't keep trying to improve things? No. Does it mean we should take a moment to review things and gain a little perspective the next time Pundit A or Newscaster B tries to keep us from changing the channel with a headline that says "School Children Under Attack Daily In the U.S."? Yep, it sure does.

Don't get me wrong—there are times when the outrage is justifiable, but all too often we seem to be screaming about existential issues like whether Kylie Jenner is ignorant, racist, or both for braiding her hair into cornrows without acknowledging the cultural origin of the style, or whether the *Simpsons* character Apu is the most racist character in recent history. Geez, if we can get this worked up over issues like this, what happens when we actually hit real problems?

What level of outrage will exist when a third of our population cannot find a job and doesn't have enough money to pay the bills?

Instead of being outraged about the nation's ballooning debt, we're focused on shaming Chance the Rapper into an apology for having the audacity to tweet: "Not all black people have to be Democrats."

Instead of celebrating the triumph of the first scientist to land an Earth-sourced spacecraft on a comet, we choose to excoriate the guy and label him as a sexist, misogynist pig for wearing a Hawaiian shirt featuring scantily clad women.

A white teenage girl wears what the Internet determines is a Chinese-style dress (it wasn't), and more than one hundred thousand posts accuse her of cultural appropriation.

When Miss Nevada (in the final year of Miss America that still featured a swimsuit competition) suggests that one way for women to deal with the #MeToo movement is to get self-defense training, feminists attack her for validating rape culture.

When a liberal sex-education instructor had the temerity to refer to "male" penis versus "female" vagina in her descriptions of sexual anatomy, she was attacked relentlessly on social channels. She now refers to these as gender-neutral sexual organs.

Our capacity for outrage has reached the point of the ridiculous.

2

The Story of Outrage

I often describe myself as an optimistic catastrophist. I am optimistic because I believe in Americans; I have seen what they have done in the past. I have seen them rise to the greatest challenges the world has ever seen. I have seen us come together against all odds. I am optimistic because I know who we can be when the chips are down. I am a catastrophist because I see all of the places where the structure is weak, the arrogance of those in charge, hiding behind shields of moral superiority that are born of nothing but an expression of outrage at some claimed victimhood or other. Worst of all, I see our interactions with one another. I can see the icebergs in the water, and I have counted the lifeboats. It doesn't mean the *Titanic* will sink. It just means that the odds are not in our favor unless we are vigilant and actually steer around the icebergs in front of us.

The good—no, the GREAT—news is that we can do this. Actually, we have a very simple formula to implement, one that our forefathers found self-evident and implemented and proved works to build a powerful, productive, and prosperous nation. And because we have the model and proof the model works, I'm very hopeful that we sit in a place to be able to move, as a culture, back toward civility, reason, and cooperation.

And that starts with first admitting that we have a problem. I do believe grave danger is on its way, and I'm afraid that we've become too weak to deal with it. And if we don't stop and figure out how to work with each other America is going to lose her place in the world. This demonizing of the other side is destroying our democracy. So my harshest words are reserved for the people who have put us in this precarious position—on both sides. Those people who day after day beat into us the concept that we are right and they are wrong, that we are the good guys and they are our enemy.

Oh. Wait. Just wait a second here. Elephant waltzing around the room.

I know what you are thinking. Especially if you are a Democrat. "I can't take it anymore! This guy?! The Fox News blowhard? The guy who would and did say anything for ratings! The tinfoil-hat conspiracy guy who said Obama was a racist is telling me that he hates when people divide us?" Okay, you know what? You're right. I accept responsibility for my part in all of this. Yes, I played a role in helping to set this country against itself. I said what I believed and I said it in the most entertaining way possible. Jon Stewart once criticized me as "a guy who says what people who aren't thinking are thinking." Good line. But we were thinking, he just didn't care to understand the point we were trying to make.

It is funny, because much of what I said then is being said by the left today: "The president has too much power." "He could easily become a dictator." "The president is a liar." "The president is a racist." The last was said by me about Obama—and corrected on the spot: "I don't think he is a racist; he has a deep-seated hatred for the white culture." I was cornered on "What is the white culture, Glenn?" by Katie Couric. I don't think she could even ask that question now with a straight face. "The same culture that our children are now being taught is evil, Katie." It is the white culture—and specifically the white male culture—that is apparently responsible for all the ills of the world. This is the problem I was sensing at the time; I just didn't know how to express it, as I hadn't been schooled in postmodernism yet. I recognized the feeling of something amiss, I knew racism wasn't quite right, but the language of the neo-Marxist professors was still foreign to me.

Now, Don Lemon and others say Trump is racist and they are applauded for it by the left and vilified by the red-state voters. What Don is saying is very much what I tried to express. Something is not right here, and because I am not sure what it is I will use the most basic word to describe what I am feeling. The feeling that Don cannot pinpoint, or perhaps even understand, is the loss of heritage and national identity. Many Americans feel that every good that this country has done is being erased or ignored by the elites. "The white culture" or "white male cisgender hierarchy" really just means, to many on the left, "the Western Judeo-Christian culture." It has been attacked on every side, and those who are comfortable with "cis-gender" talk are not comfortable with "Judeo-Christian talk." But, believe me, we are talking about the same thing. Maybe it is racist to some, but deep-seated hatred of the white culture seems to fit. Perhaps Don Lemon, whom I know and like, does hate the Western world (I highly doubt it), but what we all fail to see is that we are talking over each other. Neither side is willing to recognize that our verbiage is doing as much damage as our belief system.

I believe what Obama and those in the Marxist, gender, race, and inequality studies world spoke of as "fairness" was and is understood by many Americans as racist and sexist. And when Trump or his supporters speak of the loss of traditional values, the left hears, "I hate Mexicans, and them gays, too." On both sides what we "hear" may be accurate at some level. But it is the level of those who mean it this way that makes all the difference, and at this point we don't trust each other enough.

But, in my defense, and in Don's as well: No matter which way we actually meant it or how the audience took it, it works! It works incredibly well. Mind-bogglingly well. People watched my program, first on CNN and later on Fox, as much to see what I might do as to hear what I was saying. In 2009 I was pictured on the cover of *Time*, my tongue out derisively above the caption "Mad Man: Glenn Beck and the angry style of American politics!" "For conservatives," the story read, "these are times of economic uncertainty and political weakness, and Beck has emerged as a virtuoso on the strings of the discontent." Very much the same thing could be said of Rachel Maddow today for the left.

Unintentionally, I fed their addiction to outrage by giving in to my own. And it worked. And there is a clear and obvious reason why it worked—for me, for Don, for Rachel, and for millions of social media users every day: Addiction to outrage is real, widespread, and (almost) fully ingrained in our cultural identity.

3

Here's Why Outrage "Works"—and Why It's More Addictive than Heroin

Part of what makes outrage so addictive—and useful—is that it fulfills several key social and psychological functions. As a tool for social interaction, it checks an awful lot of boxes:

OUTRAGE SIGNALS VIRTUE

One of the most effective ways to demonstrate one's own social value is by wearing the trappings of outrage on behalf of others, especially if the others are of a minority social group. The earlier you are and the more loudly you demonstrate you are outraged that some other group has been wronged, the more virtue you demonstrate. November 2016 provided an excellent case in point. In the aftermath of the Trump election-night triumph, millions of social media posts began to appear with users posting safety pins, apparently in a show of support for "minorities." Post a GIF of a safety pin? Worth two virtue points. Post an identifiable pic of yourself wearing a safety pin? Five virtue points. Post a picture of yourself dressed as a safety pin, holding a protest sign and shouting random curse words at a Republican mayor's town-hall meeting? Well, they don't even have the algorithm yet to assign enough virtue points to that (though a social scoring system similar to this has actually been implemented in China), but you're sure to feel good about yourself for a few days.

OUTRAGE AS A SHIELD FROM MORAL JUDGMENT

Moral outrage is also effective as a shield from judgment. Being morally outraged seems to function very effectively as a mechanism to protect the purveyors of outrage against any evaluation of their actions, tactics, honesty, or morality. After the horrific shooting at Parkland High School in February 2018, parents, students, and teachers were excused for accusing all gun owners, NRA members, and civil-rights advocates of being baby killers, because they were (justifiably) traumatized by those events. Never mind that they were caught lying, exaggerating, engaging in verbal bullying, and invoking violence against NRA leaders and congressmen. They were outraged, and outrage excuses one from having to tell the truth or exhibiting moral behavior.

OUTRAGE AS A WEAPON

Outrage is also an exceptional weapon that can pierce the armor of nearly any foe. It's like a bow with three magically tipped arrows: shame, guilt, and fear. Moral outrage expressed against opponents can strike them with any one or all three of these instruments at any given time. The instant that someone outside of your tribe slips up and says or does something that you might have the slightest chance to paint as insensitive, racist, politically incorrect, outdated, judgmental, or insulting to a protected class or group, that person has opened up an opportunity to attack with a weapon they cannot possibly resist.

Shame almost always comes first, a form of stripping the subject of attack of any normal form of moral defense by replacing rational argument and discussion with a disarming sense of betrayal—betrayal of the group, the tribe's trust and code of behavior. Shame leads to a reduction in the offender's social status or, worse, outright banishment from the social circle.

As a tribe begins using shame and guilt more brazenly as a

weapon, fear begins to overtake each member's normal sense of morality and reason. Fear of being shamed and ostracized can eventually paralyze a culture and prevent constructive dialogue, reason, and the free flow of ideas.

OUTRAGE AS IDENTITY

By far the most destructive aspect of Outrage Addiction is that over time it tends to overtake and replace the addicts' identity. They surrender the responsibility of developing a caring, rational, human persona. Hallmarks of a genuine and healthy human personality tend to be smothered below a facade of impulsive, manic emotional responses driven by the addiction. Rather than actual empathy for the misfortune or suffering of others, addicts respond with oversized and obnoxious levels of self-righteous indignation, always scattering blame against the alleged perpetrators of the crime, against some victims, or against humanity itself. Rather than quiet, reasoned introspection, addicts instead make a grossly obvious, grand spectacle of their sympathy and protestations that bespeaks their inner disquiet and self-loathing. Wrongdoers didn't simply make a mistake, they have acted in a subhuman manner and must be castigated by the tribe, fully and wholly shamed in the public square, ostracized from the group, and ultimately destroyed. Only this victory will fill the void, the hole that has been left in the moral outrage addict—the hole left by the absence of an actual human soul.

This is why Outrage Addiction is so dangerous to our culture and to mankind: It deprives human beings of genuine humanity, replacing it instead with an outwardly facing caricature of a virtuous human being wrapped around a rotting corpse.

Look, it's not that all outrage is wrong all the time. There are times, of course, when outrage is a perfectly appropriate and reasonable response to actions we see in others. As with any addiction, the problem isn't the chemical or the behavior itself. America isn't having an opioid crisis because opioids are inherently bad or evil. It's the abuse and the involuntary need of the object of the addiction. The unhealthy dependence upon the thing in order to feel, to function. Expressing moral outrage has become the automatic, compulsive response to anything we see or hear that challenges our tribe's beliefs. And instantly and automatically supporting the outrage of others is even more important. That's the concerning thing. Moral outrage is simultaneously a badge of honor and a shield against any objective judgment. And that makes it destructive and divisive.

Outrage Addiction has replaced constructive dialogue and suppressed genuine empathy and warmness. It's no wonder that suicide has become the tenth leading cause of death in America—we don't have authentic conversations anymore. We don't express actual sympathy when others are suffering or being abused; we express outrage instead. As a result, we don't know what's real anymore. Do people really care about women being sexually harassed or assaulted in Hollywood and the Arkansas governor's mansion, or are they just following the crowd because to avoid doing so would be to aid and abet rape culture?

4

Chemistry Class

*Did you ever see an unhappy horse? Did you ever see a
bird that had the blues? One reason why birds and horses
are not unhappy is because they are not trying to impress
other birds and horses.*

—Dale Carnegie

In May 2018, former New York City mayor Mike Bloomberg delivered the commencement address at Rice University. His theme
was the "extreme partisanship" that is dividing the country and the
willingness of both ends of the political spectrum to believe anything
that depicts the other end in a bad light. "This is what is fueling and
excusing all this dishonesty," he said. He described it as an infectious
disease. "But instead of crippling the body, it cripples the mind. It
blocks us from understanding the other side. It blinds us from seeing
the strength of their ideas—and the weakness of our own. And it
leads us to defend or excuse lies and unethical actions when our own
side commits them."

Americans are becoming more loyal to their political party than
to the country, Bloomberg warned, with their objective being gaining power rather than making progress. "Bringing the country back
together I know won't be easy. But I believe it can be done—and if
we are to continue as a true democracy, it must be done. . . . Because
bringing the country back together starts with the first lesson you

learned here at Rice: Honesty matters. And everyone must be held accountable for being honest."

This country is more divided between right and left, Republican and Democrat, conservative and liberal right now than at any time at least since the Civil War.

I've spent a lot of time and effort the last few years admitting I have been wrong. It was difficult at first, but once I got the hang of it, it came a lot more easily. And with it, I found, I became a lot more understanding of the other side. The "other side" in this case being anyone and everyone who didn't agree with me. Unexpectedly, the anger I had kept inside for so long slowly dissipated as I accepted the fact(!) that the right and the left are both responsible for the situation we're in. And that as long as we can't even talk to each other civilly, there is no possible way we're going to figure out how to maintain our country's standing in the world.

I have said in as many different ways as I know how that in order to protect your rights you have to defend the rights of others, especially those with whom you disagree. It turns out, I finally understood that the Bill of Rights is fulfilling its purpose when it helps the side you wish it didn't. We all agree that we can't talk only to those people with whom we agree, but here's the kicker: We can't just listen to people we agree with either. We have to listen to them and, like Bloomberg said, at least be open to the possibility that on some tiny level, in one little way, they actually might have a pretty reasonable point.

Of course, there are many people who have criticized me for doing that, telling me—sometimes angrily—that I was wrong to admit that I was wrong. And the more they told me how wrong I was about both sides being responsible for this growing anger, the angrier they became!

But the inescapable truth is that our casual disregard for truth and honesty has already corrupted our system. When was the last time, for example, that you heard a politician, any politician, admit he or she was wrong? Certainly it hasn't happened very often. For

fun, I googled "Politicians admitting they were wrong" and in return got a pretty short list. Near the top was Florida senator Marco
Rubio acknowledging he was wrong when he said, "Welders make
more money than philosophers. We need more welders and less philosophers." Three years later he tweeted, "I've changed my view on
philosophy. But not on welders. We need both!"

Just imagine how incredibly lucky we are in this country. We have
100 United States senators. We have 435 representatives. We have 50
state governors. And apparently all of them are right all the time! We
seem to have forgotten the fine art of being honest. I'd like you to
just stop here for a second, look away from the page, and remember
the last time you were wrong and wouldn't admit it.

Okay, 100 senators, 435 representatives, 50 governors . . . and you.

Somewhere we began regarding an admission of being wrong
as a weakness rather than an admirable act of courage. A 2012 study
published in the *European Journal of Psychology* found that refusing to
apologize can have psychological benefits (and we issue no mea culpa
for this research finding) and reported that when people refused to
apologize, they felt more powerful and more in control, as well as had
higher self-esteem. In other words, even when we know we're wrong,
we don't want to admit it.

How in the world are we ever going to deal with the coming
crises if we can't even face the truth? How can you respect anyone
else—or yourself—when they refuse to deal with reality? We have to
begin by teaching our kids critical thinking. We have to be able to
teach people how to think and how to teach kids not what to think
but how to think.

The facts are out there for us to look at and use to form our opinions. Unfortunately, those facts don't often square with our opinions,
so we have to cut them down and shape them so that they support
our beliefs, whatever they are. There was an old Cold War story told
about a two-horse race between a Russian horse and an American
horse. The American newspapers reported accurately that the American horse won by ten lengths. The Russian newspapers reported

just as accurately that the Russian horse finished second while the American horse finished next-to-last.

It would be impossible for me to overstate the danger of the loss of our grasp on truth and facts. Giving the commencement address at Virginia Military Institute in May 2018, the recently fired Secretary of State Rex Tillerson warned,

> If our leaders seek to conceal the truth, or we as people become accepting of alternative realities that are no longer grounded in facts, then we as American citizens are on a pathway to relinquishing our freedom. This is the life of non-Democratic societies. . . .
>
> A responsibility of every American citizen is to preserve and protect our freedom by recognizing what truth is and is not, what a fact is and is not, and begin by holding ourselves accountable to truthfulness and demand our pursuit of America's future be fact-based—not based on wishful thinking, not hoped-for outcomes made in shallow promises—but with a clear-eyed view of the facts as they are, and guided by the truth that will set us free to seek solutions to our most daunting challenges.
>
> When we as people, a free people, go wobbly on the truth, even on what may seem the most trivial of matters, we go wobbly on America.

That's my point; that's exactly right. I wrote once, "Is it a stretch to say that freedom of speech is under attack in the United States of America? Well, I could point to evidence that if you question this president, his administration and policies, you come under vicious attack—that much is certain."

There are a lot of people, most of them on the left, I suspect, who would agree completely with me. Well, at least they would until they found out that I wrote those words in 2010 about President Barack Obama and his administration. I had exactly the same objection about Obama. He would say things that I knew were not true, and his side would attack anyone who disagreed with him. Now that the lies are coming from President Trump's administration, the left acts as though they've just discovered there was gambling going on in Casablanca!

The divide between the political factions is now so wide that every day each side presents its own version of the news. Every issue becomes that proverbial two-horse race. Special Prosecutor Robert Mueller, for example, is either trying to save America from Russian interference in our elections or trying to destroy America with his unfounded attacks on the administration. There is no middle ground. We get our news and opinions from different sources, networks, and newspapers that exist primarily to reinforce the positions we already hold. When we're told over and over in many different ways that the other side is tearing down America, it makes it impossible to accept the fact that the other side may actually have a point—that they may not be 100 percent wrong about everything. As hard as it is to accept, it might make sense to listen to them.

Mostly, though, Americans distrust anyone or any source that disagrees with them. We live in partisan wind tunnels. There are few things more dangerous to our future than the Trump administration's threatening to take away credentials from legitimate news outlets. That attempt to threaten the media should frighten every American, but it doesn't. Instead, a large number of people are cheering for him to do just that. They don't agree with the reporting coming from those sources, which too often attack their beliefs, so they have no qualms about shutting them out and allowing the news to be reported only by media outlets that agree with their position. Thomas Jefferson warned more than two centuries ago, "When the speech condemns a free press, you are hearing the words of a tyrant."

When we no longer know what we can believe, we'll start believing anything. For example, I'm sure most readers believe Jefferson actually said that because it showed up on the Internet accompanied by a really somber drawing of Jefferson looking extremely sincere. And the fact that I quoted him here. The fact is, there is no record that Jefferson ever said that. It's a handy tool to use, though; when you quote Jefferson it makes it feel real, and the unknown person who created and posted that knew it would be believed.

Unlike Trump, though, Jefferson was a staunch defender of a free press, even when he was being attacked. In a 1789 letter acknowledging the importance of a completely free press to the future of this then-new country, he wrote, "The way to prevent these irregular interpositions of the people is to give them full information of their affairs thro' the channel of the public papers, and to contrive that those papers should penetrate the whole mass of the people. The basis of our governments being the opinion of the people, the very first object should be to keep that right; and were it left to me to decide whether we should have a government without newspapers or newspapers without a government, I should not hesitate a moment to prefer the latter. But I should mean that every man should receive those papers and be capable of reading them."

Okay, here's a little test. True or false: Thomas Jefferson was a staunch defender of our free press.

Not so quick. He absolutely was—except when he wasn't. Several years after his stirring defense, he wrote in another letter, "[N]othing can be believed which is seen in a newspaper. . . . Truth itself becomes suspicious by being put into that polluted vehicle."

That's the problem with facts: They can be used by intelligent people to support almost any argument they want to make. It is factual to say Jefferson was passionate in his support of the media, and it is equally accurate to say that Jefferson was a bitter foe of the media. The point is that the people on the other side of your debate may have facts on their side, too. Their position may be just as valid as yours. In other words, two rights don't necessarily make one of you wrong.

No wonder you get so upset. But the source of your outrage isn't the other side, it's you. It's your frustration. It's your anger. It's outrage. And it makes it easy for other people to manipulate you.

The reason the sources of information you watch tend to support what you already believe is that they know it will bring you back for more. Who doesn't want to be told they're right? Maybe instead of the chicken and the egg, the question should be what came first: Strong political opinions or partisan news sources? Roger Ailes figured out how to build loyalty, and the other networks followed. Your loyalty is valuable to them. You're a statistic, that's all you are. A number that is used to generate income for them. A number that can be used to win elections.

What's true? What's real? Among those other things I have in my collection of artifacts is the microphone used during World War II by Tokyo Rose, supposedly to demoralize Americans fighting against Japan. The nickname "Tokyo Rose" became synonymous with traitor. But after buying this mic I did my own research and discovered that much of what we had been told wasn't accurate.

Tokyo Rose actually was an American citizen who was visiting Japan when the war began and got stuck there. The Japanese government used her to broadcast propaganda, but there is considerable evidence she also used that platform to convey life-saving information to the Allies.

In 2013 we rejiggered the wiring in that mic and I used it on my radio broadcast. That was the first time it had been turned on since the 1940s. We didn't test it; we didn't know if it would work at all, but I had decided that if it did, I was going to use it to talk about the truth. And while in this broadcast I focused on truth and the government, I could just as easily have thrown the media in with it. Here's what I told my listeners: "America, tell the truth. Tell the truth, even if it means in the end it hurts you. America, don't believe everything that your country and your government tells you. Because while many times, most times, it's true, in many critical times it's an out-and-out lie. And it's not an American problem. It is a government problem. It is a human problem. People want power, and they will do anything to keep that power or enhance that power. It's incumbent upon you, if you want to remain free, to do your own homework. And if you don't, you will lose your freedom. And because of that, innocent people will suffer. Truth and justice is the American way."

The American way. How quaint that sounds. Remember when there was an American way, not a Republican way, not a Democratic way? I learned an important lesson several years ago when I took my family to Poland. Among the people I met there was a lovely ninety-year-old woman named Paulina. She was honored as a Righteous Among the Nations, which is a phrase used by Israel to describe non-Jews who risked their own lives to save Jews during the Holocaust. My family sat down with her and listened to her story. She was sixteen years old, she explained, when she saved her first Jew. During the course of the war she was credited with saving about a hundred Jews. She told us harrowing stories in the most matter-of-fact manner. When my kids finally got up and wandered away, I said to her, "Paulina, I see storms coming in America. I hope I'm wrong, but I see them coming. And I believe this, I believe the tree of righteousness is in each of us, but how do I water that tree? What do I do to make it grow?"

She looked at me as if I were an alien. Then she smiled and shook her head. "You misunderstand," she finally said. "The righteous didn't suddenly become righteous. They just refused to go over the cliff with the rest of humanity."

Well, there's a place to start, I thought. What she was explaining to me was that people didn't have to change to deal with changing circumstances, that doing the right thing didn't require being a hero: You just have to do what's right. The basic principles of decency don't change. What was right yesterday is right today and will be right tomorrow.

How do you know what's right? How do you know what to believe? For some of it, at least, you have to trust your gut feeling. You wouldn't be reading this page today if you weren't concerned about our country, and that concern alone is evidence to me that you have a fundamental understanding of right and wrong.

That's the place to begin. You know the right thing to do; the hard part is doing it.

C'mon, let's be honest. It's just you and me on this page right now. Let's not kid each other; we both know how good it feels to attack political foes, to score points in a debate, to point out their contradictions or when they cite some erroneous "fact." Let's not pretend it doesn't. It does, it feels good. But we also know that at times some part of us is a little embarrassed by some of the things we say or write. It's probably not something we would do in person. We sure wouldn't want the people we work with to find out about it. The reality is we know we can get away with it because no one knows our screen name or who we really are. But it's time to cut it out. It's time to stop it.

Okay, Glenn, you talk a good game; now tell me how to do it. Let me quote the wonderful Mr. Mark Twain here, who remarked once about overcoming an addiction, "Giving up smoking is the easiest thing in the world," he said. "I know because I've done it hundreds of times."

As any addict will tell you, wanting to break an addiction is a lot easier than actually doing it. Overcoming your outrage is both a physical and a psychological challenge. As someone who has found himself lying on a floor almost in a fetal position to try to stop drinking, I know how hard it is. The Chinese philosopher Lao Tzu got it right when he said, "A journey of a thousand miles begins with a single step."

Within the science of behavior modification there is a strategy called chaining. Chaining is something a lot of us do on a daily basis without realizing we are following a scientific principle. The basic concept is that every behavior is the result of a series of small actions. For example, it's incredibly hard for alcoholics to look at a glass of their go-to choice sitting in front of them and resist picking it up and taking just one sip. But there were a lot of steps that had to be taken before that glass got there. The alcohol had to be bought and carried home. It had to be opened and poured. The glass had to be placed on the table. Each of those actions is a link in the chain, and you can lengthen any chain. And the fact is, some links are a lot stronger than others. The longer a chain is, the easier it is to break the weakest link. People using this method to cut down on overeating, for example, don't buy prepared foods or even keep food in the house. That forces them to go to the store for whatever they want to eat, bring it home, and go through all the steps of preparation. It's a lot easier to resist going to the store and shopping than it is to stare down a slice of chocolate cake.

Think of it this way: Try to resist eating the second Oreo Double Stuf in the package! I have a hard time not eating the entire sleeve.

Most of use some version of social media to fuel our outrage. We're generally okay face-to-face with people who disagree with us; our good manners usually kick in to prevent us from confronting them. But our behavior is quite different on social media. For something so amorphous, the Internet is the most powerful tool ever invented. Here's an interesting fact: It's estimated the Internet weighs about the same as a single average strawberry, about two ounces. I know that is "true" because I learned it on the Internet. (Actually, I don't have the slightest idea if it is true or not. But I like it, it's fun, so I'll use it!) According to the source I found on the Internet, the Internet actually consists of several hundred trillion electrons, which cumulatively weigh about fifty grams, or two ounces. And yet too many of us allow something with the weight of a strawberry to dominate our attention.

There is a great deal of data demonstrating that the massive amount of time we are spending on social media has changed, in fundamental ways, how we relate to other people. Americans spend an estimated 10 percent of our time on the Internet, and that has led to a massive shift in behavior. A study published in March 2017 in the *Archives of Sexual Behavior* reports that even in our sexualized culture Americans had less sex than two decades earlier. That's incredible; even with the availability of all those meet-up sites and the acceptance of casual sex, Americans—especially millennials and Generation Xers—are having less sex than in the 1990s. They suggested several possible reasons for this, but, not surprisingly, the amount of time spent on social media is considered a primary culprit. Apparently, many people prefer Angry Birds to loving people. That's one powerful strawberry.

So what is it about the Internet that makes it so hard to quit, or even, in so many cases, to just reduce the amount of time we spend on it? Categorizing addictive behaviors is a complex undertaking. There are some things we get addicted to because they make us feel good, while we embrace other addictions because they allow us to feel nothing. Believe me, it doesn't feel good to black out when you're telling your kids about bunnies. That addiction becomes an escape mechanism. The director of the Semel Institute for Neuroscience and Human Behavior at UCLA refers to the computer as "electronic cocaine."

When the Internet and social media first became ubiquitous, it was sort of the Wild West of technology. Remember, in the early days people paid by the hour for access to the Internet. When that format disappeared, advertising became the source of income, and advertisers pay for audience exposure. So how to attract the largest audience spending the most time on a site became the objective. But as it became monetized and the battle for "visitors" began, researchers began searching for hooks guaranteed to bring people back to a site or a game. Just as the tobacco industry had done decades earlier, they began to look for ways to get people addicted to a specific experience.

Media and news websites have also begun to leverage this technique, with sites like Buzzfeed, Axios, and Politico paying content writers based on the eyeballs they are able to capture and keep coming back. Just as Hearst and Pulitzer instructed editors to use eye-catching headlines and racy images to sell papers in 1900, now "information architects" build web pages designed to captivate (root word "capture") a surfer's attention.

It's been known since the 1950s that the neurotransmitter dopamine is sort of like the barn door to pleasurable experiences. Apparently, dopamine performs numerous important functions in our body, but its claim to fame is that it is the precursor to something we believe we are going to enjoy. It has been referred to in scientific literature as "the chemical in the brain that controls mood, motivation, and a sense of reward," and in popular media as "the Kim Kardashian of neurotransmitters." When we sense we are going to be rewarded, the brain releases that chemical into its pleasure centers. It opens the door to a good time! But it's an anticipatory release rather than being responsible for that feeling of pleasure. There is some evidence that the brain becomes accustomed to the release, and, just as with other drugs, repeating that same feeling over and over eventually requires an increasingly larger dose of the chemical.

In fact, in the 1970s, street drugs—especially heroin—were commonly referred to as "dope," supposedly because of the high dopamine content. More recently, dope has become a slang term used to describe almost anything that's great or excellent. I sort of like that, and now when people call me dopey I take it as a compliment.

What happened is that marketers figured out how to use dopamine to attract and keep an audience coming back. "We may appear to be choosing this technology," Tony Dokoupil wrote in *Newsweek* in 2012, "but in fact we are being dragged to it by the potential of short-term rewards." Every ping could be social, sexual, or professional opportunity, and we get a mini-reward, a squirt of dopamine, for answering the bell. "These rewards serve as jolts of energy that recharge the compulsion engine, much like the frisson a gambler receives as a new card hits the table," MIT media scholar Judith Donath recently told *Scientific American*. "Cumulatively, the effect is potent and hard to resist."

While dopamine is associated with pleasure, the much-better-known adrenaline is released when someone is afraid. It's the yang to dopamine's yin. It's the chemical that causes your heart to start beating quickly, your skin to become flushed, and at its extreme, it even affects your breathing. And it also plays a role in your addiction. Solis Arr, the former director of the Student Center at UC Davis, described how this "Micro-Aggression" plays an important part in keeping us hooked: "[Y]our different ideas are not merely offensive to me—they are now creating a mental health crisis for me, and how could you? My hope for anyone addicted to outrage is that they come to find there is a chemical phenomenon that occurs with this feeling. Adrenaline."

Mr. Arr continued, "Adrenaline makes me feel powerful. It's far better than showing my fear." Showing our fear is rather terrifying, actually. He concluded, "I'd rather show strength by attacking your position and showing you outrage."

These marketers eventually discovered that political debate—although it's probably more accurate to describe it as political ranting—was as irresistible as an oasis in the desert. Several years ago, Andrew Park wrote about his "obsession with Glenn Beck" in *Psychology Today*: "I disagreed with everything he said, but somehow I couldn't get enough of the red meat he was serving up to his fervent audience. I loved to hate it."

Park continued, "The futurist and novelist David Brin argued that what I was doing . . . is more than just a guilty pleasure. The outrage we feel when we listen to these rants is a 'bona fide drug high' and we are addicted to it." He then quoted Andrew Sullivan, who agreed, "You go into the bathroom during one of these snits and you look in the mirror and you have to admit, this feels great! 'I am so much smarter and better than my enemies. And they are so wrong and I am so right!'" I think all of us have felt that high, whether we were willing to admit it at the time or not.

Sullivan went further: "Is there anything wrong with letting this addiction guide our politics? Insofar as it distracts from engaging the issues, the candidates, and each other at a more civil and meaningful level, then yes." Sullivan continued, "If the sum total of our political activity is waiting for the *Huffington Post* or the *Drudge Report* to serve up another sound bite . . . then we are shortchanging ourselves and our democratic system." Very nicely stated.

After the horror in Las Vegas, *Washington Post* columnist David Von Drehle wrote that he was not at all surprised that the media focused on a stupid comment made by a CBS lawyer about the victims being mostly country music fans, so she didn't really regret the shootings. Sullivan noted that as evidence of the issue with addiction to outrage, stating, "Addiction compels you to chase a high that only makes you feel worse. It reduces you to a lesser version of yourself. And you can't stop, because deep down you really don't want to change. . . ."

Sullivan went further too, in discussing the role the media plays as well: "The [controversy peddlers] know that, rather than endure the misery of withdrawal, the junkies will return again and again for future fixes. This is a business. An ugly business, but a lucrative one." He's right; believe me, I know. He continued, "Controversy, real or manufactured, juices ratings at cable 'news' networks. It drives readers to partisan websites and listeners to talk radio. It pumps up speaker fees and inflates book advances." Couldn't have said it better myself. Sullivan even identified early on how it makes our country vulnerable to attack: "When Russians wanted to mess with the heads of American voters, they trafficked in hyped conflict, Facebook informed Congress this week. . . . The oversupply of controversy is bottomless, because some human somewhere is always indulging a thoughtless blurt, and social media seduces us to publish our blurts for the world to overhear." Amen, brother.

Social media websites have been the final nail in our proverbial cultural coffin, fulfilling yet another desperate weakness and addiction for human beings: a sense of belonging, validation, and acceptance by the tribe. When you are validated by your peers, friends, and loved ones, your brain is flooded with a potent cocktail of chemicals led by serotonin, which is known as the "Confidence Molecule" among neurochemists. Social validation by way of thumbs-up, shares, likes, and emojis is among the most addictive of neurochemical processes because it directly feeds our precious sense of ego and confirms that we are of value to the tribe.

In a very real way, you're being used. You're being manipulated. On a chessboard you would be a pawn, easily sacrificed for the good of the king. I guess you can take some solace in the fact that it isn't completely your fault, that you are a victim of biology, neurochemistry, and marketing.

Once we're hooked—or in this case charged up, plugged in, or battery operated—it isn't easy to stop. In 2010, for example, the International Center for Media & the Public Agenda asked two hundred University of Maryland students to detach themselves from all social media for twenty-four hours. One full day. One student summed up the results when he wrote, "I clearly am addicted, and the dependency is sickening. I feel like most people these days are in a similar situation, for between having a BlackBerry, a laptop, a television, and an iPod, people have become unable to shed their media skin."

The one thing I would ask you to do now is take a little personal inventory. Just take a guess how much time you spend involved in political thought and debate and how much time you spend reading, researching, or debating political material weekly.

I'm not even asking you to admit you're wrong. As we've pointed out, in many cases there is no right or wrong, just a difference of opinion—and it doesn't make the slightest difference what side of each issue you're on. We don't have to agree on everything. Heck, we don't have to agree on anything—other than the fact we are ready to stop splitting this country into two enemy camps. Advertisers and content managers don't care about your political beliefs. In some cases, as we've learned from the Russian investigation, sometimes there actually isn't even a human being disagreeing with you; it's a bot! Whatever position you take, it's going to take the opposite position to provoke you, to get the adrenaline flowing, to get the dopamine flowing, to get you outraged, and to keep you engaged.

OUTRAGE-AHOLISM

"I am sure I don't have a problem."

When I first began studying AA, I wondered if there was a test you could take that would help you determine whether you were an alcoholic. Turns out there is.

I have adapted those questions to America's current addiction. See how well you do. Now, remember, it does no good to lie to yourself and not answer honestly. It's not like I am keeping track while you read this book. Unless you are using a reader. I still will not be tracking, but the NSA will. But don't worry, they already have "everything they need on you."

1. Do politics or social media occasionally make you say and do things you regret afterward?
2. Do people often recommend that you cut down or stop consuming so much news or social media?
3. Do you speak in absolutes more often than you did five years ago?
4. Have you avoided friends, places, or events because of politics?
5. Would you be disappointed if your children treated others the same way you do in your political interactions?
6. Does your circle of online political allies include people you aren't completely comfortable being aligned with?
7. Do you feel great when someone attacks your political opponent?
8. Do you find yourself defending your political allies by pointing out that the other side does the same objectionable thing?
9. Have you ever decided to give up social media, only to fail within a few days?
10. Have you defended behavior in others that you would never accept in your own life?
11. Is the way you treat people online inconsistent with the way you treat people in person?

12. Have you often taken actions designed only to trigger the emotions of someone you disagree with?
13. Have you said things you would have been uncomfortable hearing someone else say five years ago?
14. Would your life be better without all the political arguments or comments on social media?
15. When answering these questions, did you use the importance of the political cause to justify your negative behavior?
16. Have you reevaluated your standards and are you supporting or defending actions or ideas that you would have never supported five years ago?
17. Do you definitely believe that all or most of the media sources on the (right/left) rarely tell the truth (knowingly or unknowingly), and that they are dangerous and perhaps should be shut down or regulated by the government?

If you answered YES 1–5 times, you might be approaching a problem. Your concern over important issues is admirable, but you're crossing the line a bit too often.

If you answered YES 6–10 times, you have a problem. Politics dominates your life in a way it should not, and it's changing who you are. Get a hobby. Something outside.

If you answered YES 11 or more times, most of the people you interact with don't like you. They might not say it, but it's true. Immediately burn your computer and throw your phone off a bridge that crosses a body of deep and treacherous water.

5

So What Makes You an Expert?

In Gallup's 2010 poll of the Most Admired People in the World, Pope Benedict and I tied for fourth place, barely trailing Nelson Mandela. In May that year I organized and hosted the Restoring Honor Rally on the Lincoln Memorial mall, which drew several hundred thousand people. Those who attended say that it was a life-changing event. But in another poll taken only a year later I was voted one of the most hated people in the country. About half of the country hated me.

That list the pope did not make.

I earned my place on both lists. I was passionate about my beliefs. At times I did and said controversial and ignorant things. I did my thinking out loud. I was convinced that "we" were right and "they" were wrong, and I knew how to get my message across. I was a radio guy doing television and I thought that if I could make people smile, if I could entertain them, I could draw a crowd and people would listen to the questions I was raising. How did I do that? I put on a pair of lederhosen and sang "Edelweiss." I drew frantically on my blackboard. I gave 'em the old razzmatazz; a little song, a little dance, a little seltzer down my pants. I did whatever it took to draw, entertain, and—I hoped—educate my audience. I did it all with a specific objective: I honestly believed that I could take those people who came for the circus and move them with my intellectual brilliance! I believed if I could make a strong factual case, people would listen to me and think about the points I was making. More important, I always said that I wasn't a journalist but rather a guy who was trying to figure out what was happening and how we got there. I really believed that if I had enough facts, journalists who were watching every night would say "Wow, that is a good point. I hadn't thought of it that way," or "That can't be right," and follow up on it. Not my theories, but the FACTS I was presenting.

Yes, Obama wanted single-payer health care. He spoke about it openly before the election. Yes, he knew that the vast majority of Americans couldn't keep their health insurance. The math spelled it all out. And don't get me started on death panels. He knew about death panels because of the Complete Lives System, which spelled it all out. Written by Zeke Emanuel, the brother of the president's chief of staff at the time. We are seeing them now in England with Charlie Gard and even here in Texas with the Advance Directives Act, which empowers hospital boards to condemn patients to death if they deem treatment would be futile. We are now seeing this in action in Sweden and in England. It is again not a crazy concept, it is merely math. Why can we not be honest about something that will affect all of us?

But I was wrong about one thing: Many people who came to my circus only wanted to see the dancing elephants. Not everyone, and I don't think even anywhere close to approaching the majority. But there were a number of Americans who only wanted to hear the latest "outrage." At the same time, the press didn't care. They had made up their minds about the administration and those who questioned it. The more I tried to get people to listen to the warnings by upping the theatrics, the less inclined the "other side" was to hear or, better yet, really listen. The press had decided the truth. But they found that if they wanted to increase their click rates and Nielsen ratings, all they needed to do was talk smack about me, and the left, too, took sound bites, twisted them or left out context, and raised millions to fight their new monster. Presto, two Americas, neither one able to listen to the other. So, in the end, very few outside of the core audience actually heard the message. Everyone else, left and right, wanted me to feed their new and growing addiction: outrage.

And that realization in 2012 and again in 2016 was soul-crushing to me. As I have tried to speak to others in the press about this over the last five years, it has only made the despair worse. Can't anyone see what is happening?

I have to admit, at the time, I felt justified. I often felt that I was watching someone strangling something I loved. That was emotionally terrorizing to me, and I discovered a lot of other people felt the same way. I was crying out for them to help me save it. They love this country as much as I do, they understand and appreciate the freedoms we have and saw them slowly disappearing. And I was outraged. So I spoke up loudly. I defended my beliefs.

Just as Jimmy Kimmel did in 2017–18. He believed in something and fought hard for it using his show. He even wept as I did. We both wept because what we spoke about hit too close to home and we were passionate about it. People on the left right now act like we did under Obama, and too many of us are treating them like they treated us. Those on the left can't hear me say this because they automatically go to "How dare you say Trump is as bad as Obama?" And so the merry-go-round continues.

But for those on the left, try to see this from the other side. Because you and the press didn't see Obama in the same light, you mocked, ridiculed, and called families who stood together and peacefully protested un-American, fake, abusive, unstable, revolutionaries, and terrorists.

Jimmy was applauded and made into a hero for his emotional rants. He was brave to be so outspoken. While I had a leftie photographer "set me up" to make it look as if I used Vicks to cry on TV, Jimmy was "groundbreaking."

But was he accurate? This was what I wanted someone to do. Look at the facts—not the opinion or even the conclusion, but the facts. I refused to do to him what so many did to me, ridicule the messenger and dismiss the message. As it turns out, his talking points were misguided at best. You might claim he knowingly lied or distorted the facts; you can choose to believe he made an honest mistake or didn't do enough homework; but the one thing we cannot do, if we are to survive as a republic, is ignore the message or the inaccuracies or truth it contains.

I've always led with my mistakes. I even went to so far as to install a private phone line to my studio so the White House could call and correct anything that was inaccurate. Only the White House had the number. They never called. However, they did come and meet with Roger Ailes to try to get me fired. He told them that he wouldn't fire anyone for their opinion unless it was based on false or misleading facts. He asked them to prepare a list. A week later, the only thing the White House objected to was that I had said Van Jones had gone to prison, when in fact he had only gone to jail. I quickly corrected it on air, and reminded them that the problem I was concerned with was the fact that he was a self-declared communist who had said "green is the new red." I thought the American people should know whether he still believed that, as he was now the president's green jobs czar.

No matter the cause, the result was that I was a contributor to the outrage competition that has consumed this country and is now threatening to destroy our democracy. So yes, I take responsibility. In fact, I will happily take more than my fair share if others in the media will join me in deep self-reflection on their role. I don't need the apology or to place blame, but I do think it is an important step toward humility, which will lead to our hearing each other clearly.

For those who want to hang on to their anger, understand that if Glenn Beck, Jimmy Kimmel, Obama, and Trump were all hit by a bus while re-creating the *Abbey Road* album cover, none of our problems would be gone. Our troubles were not caused by one man, one party, or even one generation. Nor will they be solved by the same. The moment we realize that no "one guy," group, or party will solve our problems, this generation can begin the long journey of fixing things that the next will complete. In this book I'm going to guide you through a series of steps that, if we follow them, can lead to change. They aren't exactly the same steps that I was taught in AA; don't worry, they won't require anyone to go to meetings, and you won't get a coin to celebrate each year. But if we do follow them, there's a good chance we'll learn to be friends again—or at least cordial neighbors.

HOW OUTRAGE DISMANTLES CULTURE

Our problems are not about presidents or even about parties. Our problems center on the loss of what brought us together in the first place. Without "it," we have no reason to come back together, and no chance to do so either.

When I decided to leave Fox News, "Can you imagine," I said on one of my last shows there, "the difference we could have if we could put our differences aside, and put the past in the past and say, 'Let's learn from each other'?" Since that time I have tried my best to douse the anger and outrage that has divided this country. Some days I succeed and no one notices; sometimes I fail and it is all anyone notices. That is okay. I am doing the best I can to get it right. All part of my recovery process.

As I once told a reporter, "Obama made me a better man," although I don't think that was his intention. Because he was so radical, to me, it forced me to really look at who I was and what I believed. I learned so much about our founding, the documents, and volumes of sheer knowledge I would not even have looked for had he not been president. Since then, I have tried to find ways to bring the two sides together. It hasn't been easy. I have been on this mission for at least the last five years, and until very recently I haven't had much success finding partners to join me in this effort. But it hasn't been completely hopeless. I began by looking toward anyone I could find who was even willing to have a conversation. Most would not, but as I have learned, it wasn't just the willingness to really listen—they needed to sincerely be motivated to act.

6

Samantha Bee

First, my apologies to Samantha Bee, as what follows is my perception of our relationship. She may have perceived all of this very differently. I do not mean offense by claiming we are friends, nor do I mean to hold myself up as some mentor or genius whom she had turned to for wisdom and advice. After all, I learned a ton from Samantha Bee and her journey over the last couple of years, and most of it was painful to me personally. Mostly because I see both the struggle of the good intent and the failure of the execution due to media blindness.

I believe Sam is a good person. I know there are many on the right who are shouting at me right now, but hear me out, because I believe in this case, I don't have just an opinion, I have perspective. I have walked in her shoes; very few have.

When Sam first called me it was before the election of Donald Trump, and I knew all she wanted was someone from the right who might say some bad things about Trump. I wasn't going to be a pawn for her agenda. I told her I would consider it after the election, but I would not make it about Donald Trump. She agreed.

I never thought I would hear from her again. But apparently, I was still an enigma to the left, or at least someone who they thought was fun to watch, who they thought was a guy who'd come over to their side. I hadn't. I told her that if she wanted to come to Dallas, we could spend the time to do an interview, but it was to be a real conversation, as I was a real person and not a prop for her to use. To be honest, I had watched very little of her work, but it wasn't as if she was building the first suspension bridge. She mocked almost everything I held dear—I knew this—but I have a sense of humor and I thought she was smart.

When her crew arrived the day before she did, I spoke a bit with her staff. Just enough to know that at least the staff had every intention of doing what they do best. I called her after her flight arrived around ten that night and told her that I no longer wanted to do the interview, as I just didn't believe they were even capable of having a real conversation. I am not sure if it was her tone or her words, but something told me that there was more to her than a comedy hatchet.

The next day, sitting in my office, fifteen minutes into the interview, it sadly was going exactly as I had guessed it would. After I had answered one of the rhetorical comedy questions, I told her that I thought they had enough to make me look like an idiot and her like the champion who speared the evil giant. To which she responded honestly, "No, we don't. I mean, that isn't the intent, but if it were, we still wouldn't have enough." I laughed and turned to her producer and said, "Please, are you telling me that you don't have enough to make me look ridiculous? He looked at her, honestly, and, smiling, and said, "Oh, yes. Really, we have more than enough."

I loved that guy. He was honest.

Sam then said something unexpected. "Okay, but really that wasn't my intent. And I don't want to do that, but I don't know how to do it any other way."

I believed her. She then turned it over to me. "How do we do this right? Show me."

It took only one question: "Can you tell me what you really care about, beyond politics?"

For ninety minutes we talked like actual human beings. A mom and a dad, an American-born man and a woman who had just become a U.S. citizen. Yes, we had different backgrounds, educations, and experiences, but we both cared deeply about many if not most of the same things. She even hated Woodrow Wilson almost as much as I did. And on that front, it wasn't lip service—she really knew many of the reasons he was a monster. I really liked her, and I think she liked me.

Here is the part, as I recall it, that I have not shared before. Later, she came to my dressing room. We sat, just the two of us, one who had been in a Cat 5 political hurricane and one who was about to go into one. She told me that she was frightened because the election had changed everything for her. She thought so poorly of Donald Trump. It wasn't political; she is a hard-core feminist. She truly thought he was a despicable guy. Agree or disagree, it was something that she deeply felt. She didn't understand how people could dismiss his flaws. But what made her so human was that she understood the pain of the people in the middle of the country. She, unlike most in her shoes, knew the center of the country. She had traveled for the *Daily Show*, spending time in the little towns and state fairs in between the coasts, and really liked and admired those she had met. When she spoke about them it was warm and genuine.

She told me that she wasn't even sure she could do the show now, or even wanted to; the election had changed her comedy into something deeply personal. I felt for her. I had been there.

Most people outside my audience don't know this, but I used to be funny. In fact, early in my talk radio career, stations weren't sure they wanted a funny, not-all-political show on before Rush. I traveled a ton and would do a forty-city "comedy tour" every year. But then we went into Iraq, which I had supported, and when I saw we really didn't have a plan that would work, I soured; I began to understand the Patriot Act was anything but patriotic, I saw the Republicans betray everything they said they believed in, the economy collapsed, and I saw us "abandon the free market to save the free market."

I, too, wanted hope and change. Just not from a guy who had been a good friend of Jeremiah Wright and an active member of his church. Things began to change for me, and I knew how to draw a crowd, how to make people laugh, but it was important to me to expose, and convince the country that many Americans were horribly and dangerously wrong. It became a mission. When that happens, your world changes.

I explained to her my journey, my mistakes and regret. I think, perhaps, for the first time she had a little understanding of me and what I had tried to do. Perhaps not. In fact, if she didn't, it explains the path that she took.

I told her that her audience would cheer and grow the more she took on "the king." The more she fed their outrage with her coverage, the more they would cheer. But in the end, even though she was not doing it for ratings but because she honestly had something to say and she thought it would help, she would do damage that she didn't recognize at the time and would divide us even further, even if it wasn't her intent. I tried to explain how I had really believed, and in some ways still believed, that I was acting as a pressure valve that was releasing steam that my own side needed released. What I hadn't seen is that by making my own side laugh, I was inflicting deep wounds on the other half. These wounds she would also inflict, and she would, as time went by, regret them more and more. Because I believe she is a smart and deeply compassionate person who happens to be tasked with making "her tribe" laugh and at the same time being an activist for what she believes in. This is new territory for most, and people who can do it are paid a great deal of money and are encouraged by those who pay them and watch to "keep going," "don't give up," and "get 'em." You feel responsible to speak to power without fear . . . and the spiral down begins.

She asked me, and I'm paraphrasing here, "So, then how do I do this?" I told her, I am not a comedian but an opinion guy who moonlighted at being funny on the side. But if I had to do it all over again, with the knowledge I have now, "I would probably end up mostly doing it the same way I did it the first time." I told her that as a student of history I hadn't yet found any examples of anyone in media, comedy, et cetera, who had ever charted a successful course through these waters. But if she ever wanted an understanding ear, I was here.

A few weeks later, I called her to discuss coming with me to

Detroit to do a service project together, with the caveat that our audiences were not allowed to talk politics. We could then end the weekend at some theater and discuss what our audiences learned by working side by side. She was interested but said, "I am not sure how to make that funny."

My next suggestion, a few months later, to come with me to Asia or Africa to rescue child slaves, was even harder to make funny. I told her that the "funny" would be her being locked in a plane at forty thousand feet with nothing but ocean underneath for hours. She didn't take me up on the offer. I would still text her from time to time. She would text back something short but meaningful. But eventually we fell out of contact. The more I would see in clips and stories, the more worried I became for her. She had chosen a course, or perhaps, like me, it was the only one she knew or understood how to work, and it was a path that I felt she would soon regret.

When she finally called Ivanka the c-word, I cringed. It was her "Obama is a racist" moment. But unlike that moment for me, this was scripted. It was planned and approved in a comedy room and by producers. Somehow, this feminist had gotten to the point of calling another woman a name that even Donald Trump hadn't used when he described where celebrities could grab women.

It was degrading and an insult when he referred to that as locker-room talk. But without justifying it at all, it is who he is, and you don't change when you are successful. You have no motive to change; everything is working. What's more, everyone around you at that time is incentivized to boost you up, to empower and enable you to go even further. No one around Trump or Bee provided any kind of real pushback. They had both surrounded themselves with like-minded people who had seen the success and so provided no help to the talent or the person, because it was all a part of what made them successful.

This was her act, and what was she doing that was so different from what others were doing? People had called Sarah Palin that same name, and Trump supporters had printed T-shirts with that word under Hillary Clinton's face.

The problem was, Ivanka was likable.

Political correctness does not have consistent or static rules. It isn't what you say, it is also about whom you say it to or about, who you are, how much of an impact you are making for "your team," and which team you are playing for.

This is antithetical to American justice and thinking. It was the Enlightenment that changed all of this. For as long as men have had rulers meting out justice, there has been man-made injustice. And social justice returns us to the Dark Ages when rulers, the mob, or the powerful try to balance some mythical scale of justice for the collective. So, in many ways, it doesn't matter if you did it or not; if your tribe is the source of some perceived injustice of the past, you are to be condemned, even if innocent, as it serves to balance the scales.

We must once again return to reason, and what matters is the integrity of the thought, and not the personality.

Samantha recently learned the hard way that even a darling of the left isn't immune from the outrage brigade. She said something grossly out of bounds and was called out for it. But in our day and age, an apology, no matter how sincere, isn't enough. From the right and left, calls have come for her head and her career on a platter. Even her apology has caused a round of outrage from the militant feminist left, who are outraged she didn't stand by her demeaning expletive!

I genuinely believe Samantha Bee is a good, compassionate person. Like all of us, she is navigating very frothy waters, as our Outrage Addiction can be triggered by any slight error or omission that violates the values of one tribe or another.

Because all of us, on both sides, so firmly believe "our side" is right, we cannot see the mistakes we each make are exactly the same. I haven't been especially successful at bringing both sides together.

One truly hopeful sign that has appeared over the last couple of years has been the appearance and popularity of the New Enlightenment movement that has begun to reach younger people on the "Intellectual Dark Web." Ben Shapiro, Dave Rubin, Jordan Peterson,

Bret Weinstein, Joe Rogan, Jonathan Sacks, and Penn Jillette. The last two names on the list aren't generally recognized as part of this group, but they should be. These men are not always right—for all I know, they will turn out to be pedophile car thieves—but they are at least actively engaged in rational, civil discussions and are seeking to use reason to find the truth. To me, they set a good example of the right way to engage with readers, colleagues, and opponents online.

7

Divisions

Sadly, the members of the New Enlightenment are largely unheard across mainstream media's constant and ongoing rage-fest. In early 2018 Sean Hannity warned that things had gotten so bad that "this country is headed toward a civil war in terms of two sides that are just hating each other," a battle that would be ignited if prosecutor Robert Mueller went after President Trump. Although later he explained that he wasn't predicting a real war, he was just pointing out that the "two sides of this are fighting and dividing this country at a level we've never seen." I believe he is wrong. If things don't change, we will be fighting a real civil war.

Rocker and NRA board member Ted Nugent went even further, claiming liberals are "rabid coyotes running around. You don't wait till you see one to go get your gun. Keep your gun handy, and every time you see one, you shoot one."

The left has been no better. During the 2016 campaign, Hillary Clinton described Trump's supporters as "a basket of deplorables." The would-be assassin who attacked a group of Republican members of Congress on a softball field, shooting House Majority Whip Steve Scalise, made certain they were Republicans before opening fire. In 2013, Oprah Winfrey, clad in the impenetrable cloak of the moral outrage afforded by society solely to African Americans, famously stated that she believes the only way for racism to be solved is that "older Americans . . . who were born and bred and marinated . . . in that prejudice and racism . . . just have to die."

If you want to investigate this theme further, just do a "Trump supporters are subhuman" search on Twitter or Reddit. You can find thousands and thousands of relevant results, retweets, and upvotes.

In 1856, a congressman beat a U.S. senator nearly to death on the floor of the Capitol Building. We aren't that far off from that. When Senator Rand Paul was attacked and badly injured by an irate neighbor with whom he'd had strong political disagreements in the past, social media erupted with an avalanche of taunting, celebratory posts that a firebrand of the right had been attacked and put in his place. Most don't even talk about the day we almost lost several congressmen at a shooting on a baseball diamond in Virginia in the spring of 2017. The shooter was a Bernie Sanders volunteer who had written much about his hatred of Republicans. He had plotted and planned, and when he arrived at the ballpark, he asked if those were the Republicans on the field. When he was told yes, he moved into position with a rifle. The media covered it, but with not even a fraction of the coverage for a school shooting. Where was the CNN town hall? One can't help but ask, would the media coverage have been the same had it been Democrats on the field? If it were a Republican Donald Trump volunteer, do you think everyone would now know him, including his middle name? Lee Harvey Oswald, John Wilkes Booth, and Mark David Chapman. I remember the name of the woman who tried to shoot President Ford: Lynette Alice "Squeaky" Fromme. That happened in 1975. I was eleven. Now, let me ask you, do you remember the would-be mass assassin's name from the baseball game? Even just the first name? Why is that, do you suppose?

He is identified as a self-described "left-wing activist," James Hodgkinson. The Virginia Attorney general, speaking of his act, "concluded it was fueled by rage against Republican legislators and was an act of terrorism."

The media claimed it was NOT politically motivated.

There has been no let-up since then. In June 2018 numerous

pundits and politicians, wearing the trappings of outrage, called upon the public to begin a campaign of "protest" that formerly might have been known as bullying. Congresswoman Maxine Waters called followers to a grand "resistance" wherein any Trump administration officials were fair game when it came to forming a mob and confronting them in public to ensure they knew they were not welcome "anywhere." Several cabinet members have since then been harassed in public, being physically chased out of restaurants or shouted down by mobs in the street. Outraged that Justice Kennedy had dared to announce his retirement during the Trump administration, Michael Moore, apparently eager to demonstrate that Trump Derangement Syndrome is actually a thing, suggested that he and a million people should form a human "wall of flesh" around the Supreme Court building to prevent any Trump nominee from taking a seat on the nation's highest court. Given the fact this occurred before Trump had even released a short list of potential names to go through the Senate review process, it would seem that insurrection against the U.S. government might be a little extreme.

Continuing the irrational narratives born of everything-Trump-does-is-pure-evil outrage, Bette Midler went a step further still, claiming, "Every single institution or agency in our government is being dismantled by this administration. Congress, gone; SCOTUS, gone; the executive branch, in the hands of a madman; the FBI, DOE, etc., etc., etc. And you thought it couldn't happen here."

Perhaps Bette misunderstands what fascist dictators do. They build giant government agencies. If you don't like the dismantling of a giant state, you may not want to march or support those who want to abolish ICE. The real problem here is that there are many people who are not actually on the side they think they are.

"INCONCEIVABLE" has become today's "FASCIST."

"You keep using that word. I do not think it means what you think it means."

We can't go on like this. We can't. This country will not survive as the world's great democracy if we don't learn how to work together again and tell the truth. I know there are some readers who are smiling as they read this and thinking, "Oh, that's just good old Glenn putting on his catastrophist hat again." But it isn't just me saying that, it's history. Roy Williams, in his groundbreaking marketing book *The Pendulum*, has traced the history of society back to the time of Christ, and concluded that all empires swing like a "pendulum" every eighty years from a Me generation to a We. He said that he was trying to find out how a society defines what is acceptable and what is not. What he found was remarkable. He writes: "Me" and "we" are the equal-but-opposite attractions that pull society's pendulum one way, then the other. The twenty-year upswing to the zenith of "We" (1923–1943) is followed by a twenty-year downswing as that "We" cycle loses energy (1943–1963). Society then begins a twenty-year upswing into "Me" (1963–1983), then the downswing (1983–2003). We are currently headed for the zenith of the upswing of "We." Historically, the place of maximum discord and danger is the apex of the "We" cycle (2023). And then, if we're lucky or well-managed, the cycle begins again. Neither cycle is good nor bad, but too much of anything isn't healthy. Strauss and Howe have done complementary work and describe the generations as the Idealist Me and the Civic We.

Think of the things that we have spent the last ten or twenty years craving. We have been looking for someone who is real, experiences that are authentic. Politicians who will just say it as it is. This is because in the "Me" cycle, the zenith goes too far and creates people and situations that ring hollow, people who are "posers," phonies. Self-centeredness, guru worship, and depravity. Think Michael Douglas in the original *Wall Street*. At the other extreme, the height of the "We" cycle, the distortions become self-righteousness, oppressiveness, and obligations to conform to the collective. If you play this cycle back and rewind time, you can see that the big movement of the West (for some reason the East is on the opposite swing) always comes at the zenith of the "We." The year 1943 was the height of World War II, when almost the entire West was swept up into totalitarianism, fascism, communism, and, even here at home, collectivism/

socialism. We had collectivized ourselves under the New Deal and had rounded up Japanese Americans for the good of the collective, even though all studies done at the time told the progressive president that they were no threat. The "We" before that was the American Civil War, which was horrid in its bloodshed but righteous in its cause. But if you look overseas, it was at this same time that Europe had been set on fire in what is called "the Spring of Nations," a revolution started by Marx and Engels after the publication of *The Communist Manifesto*.

If we rewind time again, the next "We" moment produced both the American Revolution and the French Revolution.

With any real understanding of the impact of this swing, you may begin to grasp how critical it is to find our way back to our principles and each other. If we are rooted in decency and service to a noble cause, we will do great things. If we are just slightly off, we will fall prey to nationalism, fascism, or communism, as Europe did each and every swing to We. It is the We generations that divide, categorize, and exterminate those who are deemed unworthy, dangerous, or out of step with the collective. You can see this everywhere now—even in Sweden, where the people are turning on their own inclusive values and for the first time dividing into an us-versus-them community. Unfortunately, the line between life and death, noble and evil is so thin that it can easily be missed. It certainly will be missed if we are all outraged and in "fight or flight" mode as our reason centers shut down in outrage, anger, and fear.

In 1926, in a study requested by Joseph Stalin, who wanted reassurance that communism was superior to capitalism, Russian economist Nikolai Kondratiev wrote that nations went through economic waves lasting about sixty years. He had studied the life and death cycles of the great empires throughout history and concluded that these waves consisted of roughly a decade of depression, followed by several decades of technological innovation that led to economic prosperity, then another decade of uncertainty. These changes are inevitable, he wrote, and therefore capitalism will crush communism. You must not ignore the natural cycles of man and life.

As a result of Kondratiev's work, Stalin had him shot by a firing squad in 1938.

THE "WE'RE DIFFERENT" DENIAL

I am sure there are a lot of Americans saying with great confidence that this can't happen to us. We're too strong, too powerful. We're the economic engine of the world. Currencies are based on the fluctuations of our dollar. We have so much technology and access to energy. When America sneezes, Europe and Asia catch a cold. And I'm just as certain that Romans once said the same thing. And the Greeks and the Portuguese and the Spanish.

Remember when the sun never set on the British empire? Of course, that was followed by what Winston Churchill referred to as its Darkest Hour.

America took its place as the most powerful country on earth following World War I. That was just about a century ago. We're at the beginning of the next cycle, and we're being challenged economically, militarily, and even morally. A great disruption is coming, and if we can't deal with it together, it will rip us apart. History tells us what happens to those civilizations that fall into these patterns.

If we can't even figure out how to have a civil conversation with our neighbors, we certainly aren't going to be able to determine how to successfully integrate the coming revolution of technologies—supercomputing and artificial intelligence, for starters—into a functioning society.

Here's something to think about: How can we possibly have a serious discussion about weaponizing outer space or preventing another depression when we're spending so much time arguing about whether the president had sex with a porn star, and whether we should care? How can we teach a machine to police hate speech or teach military drones to respect life when we can't even agree on the most basic definitions of those words?

8

The Pushers

Let me just address the media, party players, and politicians on their daily hysteria over what used to be called "childish" behavior.

Stop with the so-called outrage about the stuff your guy did in the past that never bothered you until the other guy did it. Suddenly, now it's a crisis in your life and you are going to start a campaign, knit a hat, and hold rallies to stop "the injustice."

Stop with outrage that CNN, *The New York Times*, MSNBC, et cetera have lost touch because they can't stop talking about Trump in negative ways "all the time, every show!" (Remember when I was on Fox?) and the cries: "It is outrageous! CNN is all fake news." Stop it.

"No!" says the left. "You don't even begin to understand OUT-RAGEOUS! I just can't believe how Fox covers for this president. They worship him! He can do no wrong for them! They aren't a news organization because they refuse to even admit the president has scandals." Stop it!

Is there any self-awareness? None? From either side?

If you are on the left and in the press, stop pretending you are so outraged because it hurts the credibility of the press when someone accuses you of being nothing more than "fake news." Any chance you remember "faux news?" Remember how funny you all thought that was back in the day? Harmful? Of course not, because you knew that your side was right and they were wrong.

Also, I am having a tough time with your newfound outrage that "the president would target the press." Maybe you should speak to James Rosen or Sharyl Attkisson. I tried to get you to join me or anyone else in protecting freedom of the press. You didn't seem to have any outrage back then.

If you are on the right—stop with the fake outrage that the press won't leave a sexual scandal alone, or perhaps you should recall what made Matt Drudge "Matt Drudge." Does no one remember the early days of Fox or talk radio on Lewinsky? Oh, really, lefties, now? Really? Now, you feel it is your duty to warn about how much of a predator Trump is, when it was an open secret about Harvey Weinstein and none of you even warned Michelle or Barak not to send their daughter to intern with him? Or did the Secret Service already tell them, and everyone knew "she would be safe"— after all, she is the president's daughter. Where were the predator warnings for everyone else? Wow, with friends like you, who needs Woody Allen?

Can you imagine if anyone dared call DJT "The third black president"? I mean, he would have to be the third, as we all know Bill Clinton was dubbed the first. May I ask, because I am still a little fuzzy on the rules: Doesn't that fall into cultural appropriation? Or is that one legitimately just racist?

I find myself sometimes now being outraged by the lack of outrage. There are so many things to be outraged by that sometimes we miss a few really outrageous outrages.

Can someone draw me a road map, because this cis male author is so lost I feel like I need to stop to ask for directions. I would make a joke here about my wife telling me to stop and ask and I just never will do it, but that would be sexist, and I might get in trouble with a feminist.

Now, preachers, I wish I could send your younger self "back to the future" to knock some sense into you. Forgiveness requires repentance. You should never sell out the fundamentals of the teachings of the one YOU call Christ for access to the Oval. It is okay that Trump sins; we all do. But like everything, when he sins, he sins BIG.

You can still respect him as the president, but please don't tell people that an unrepentant man is "okeydokey and in line with the teachings of Christ." That ain't in the Bible. That isn't even in Jeremiah Wright's Bible, and there seems to be a lot of extra crazy stuff in his.

Give the American people—and, frankly, God—a little more credit than not seeing through that butt kiss.

Left: Stop with the fake outrage that Trump is cozy with Russia or may have secret deals with Russians.

Right: For those who were apoplectic about Clinton's dealings with Gazprom, check your outrage at the media trying to hype Russian relationships.

For those who thought presidential powers were fine to hand out like candy under Obama, does your current and justified outrage about the same powers being used by Trump signal that you now get it, or that you will be fine with it once it is your turn again?

The Tenth Amendment—still racist or now a good idea? Californians who talk about leaving the Union, crazy like Texans were under Obama or totally fine and justified?

If you were fine with the president doing the Iran deal without oversight, why should this president have to have oversight with North Korea?

While I appreciate the outrage, sincerely, about children being slaughtered in the safety of their classroom, it might seem more sincere if you had been a tad upset about Planned Parenthood harvesting dead children for organs.

Stop being outraged that cities won't enforce UNCONSTITUTIONAL gun laws while you run sanctuary cities, and perhaps the right can stop faking outrage over the spending habits of Nancy Pelosi, Chuck Schumer, and the Democratic Congress while they rack up another trillion in debt and at record speed.

Do you ever get the feeling that all this outrage is fake? That those in positions of real power or influence are not really that outraged? Has anyone thought, gee, maybe they are just using this outrage to get us to fight against each other to help them raise money or gain more power or use it as misdirection? Nah. They would never do that because that would be an outrage!

We seem to be outraged ALL THE TIME.

Those are just the party players! What about the university professors, or those on campus without a safe zone, or the teacher who called the police because her autistic eight-year-old student was "brandishing" an "imaginary rifle" and there she stood, armed but still unwilling to draw and use her "class-two look-alike weapon" (formerly known as a "finger gun"—batteries not included).

Yep, America, as it turns out, it seems a few people here and there in our communities are a little "ticked" themselves on a few things. Can we all admit that we have a problem?

PSST, WANT TO BUY SOME OUTRAGE?

Politics has practically become a blood sport. The system has been set up to divide us. It has been designed to ratchet up our emotions until we're practically living in attack mode, ready to respond angrily at the slightest provocation. We have been polarized by design. Both political parties not only encourage that, they depend on it to build loyalty—to get you to donate and get you to vote. It's no longer enough just to be right; you have to grind your opponent into the cyberdirt. The anonymity of the Internet allows people to release all their pent-up hostility without any consequences. Whatever is happening in your life—your spouse is giving you a hard time, the boss is treating you like an idiot, your kids won't stop whining, the dog pooped on the floor, whatever else is making your life terrible—you can get it all out on the Internet. At work you may feel disrespected, some of your coworkers barely notice you, but online you're SuperBadMama1024 or ToughPatriot11. And it feels good. Good? It feels great! It's fun. People who disagree with you aren't just wrong, they're idiots. They're dumb, they're trolls, they're racists and bigots, they're the enemy or whatever clever name you want to call them. It doesn't take long before your adrenaline starts flowing.

Energy just surges through your whole body. If they respond, you double down on the name-calling. It gets as personal as two strangers using made-up names can get. It isn't intellectual, it's physiological. Trump figured that out, which is why anyone who opposes him isn't wrong, he or she is a crook or "little" or crazy or talentless. That was the point of his "search" for Obama's birth certificate. The evidence didn't make any difference; it didn't matter if it was true or completely made-up; it reached people emotionally.

We've become like mice in a Pavlovian test lab: hit the pedal, get the cheese, hit the pedal, get the cheese. We have literally become chemically addicted to the social rewards we receive online, through digital thumbs and text-message acronyms and emoticons. Virtue-signaling our friends and trolling our foes have replaced actual virtue and spirited debate with our peers.

When I was getting famous for saying outrageous things on Fox, the Internet and especially the social web were fairly young. People fed their addiction by tuning in to my show and watching me feed my own addiction. But today it's everywhere, across Facebook, Twitter, Instagram, text messages, and memes.

The Russians also figured it out and have become masters at using it to divide us. I have no idea if they actually wanted Trump to be elected in 2016 (Putin doesn't confer with me), but I do know that what they really wanted to do was rip the country apart. They wanted to solidify the growing hatred in this country. Their bot and troll campaign was incredibly successful at creating dissent. It was a highly sophisticated program meant to ignite arguments and inflame passions. It was designed to trigger moral outrage. It wasn't just Democrats against Republicans, it was Democrats against Democrats. The divide between Clinton supporters and Sanders backers was as bitter as that between the two parties, and Republican campaign fights among Ted Cruz, Jeb Bush, Marco Rubio, and Trump were just as bitter.

As a result, people have made such deep emotional investments in whichever side or candidate we support that we won't easily give that up. We have been personally empowered, our voice matters, people are finally paying attention to us, each of us is part of a great movement, and together we are changing the world! We belong, and we are right!

Oh my goodness! Can you hear those trumpets blaring triumphantly? Do you see how many shares my meme got? Did you see the likes my picture of Trump with devil horns got? Ha, I'm awesome, people like me! I know that feeling. It's euphoric! It's amazingly powerful. Once you experience it, it's very difficult to give it up. You've become addicted to it. You want more of that feeling. In fact, you don't just want it, you need it.

Hit the pedal, get the cheese. Hit the pedal, get the cheese.

And then someone like me comes along and tells you listen, you've got to give it up. It isn't good for the country. Well, the response to that is obvious: What is wrong with you, Beck?

People on the right think I'm betraying them, that I've gone crazy and joined the enemy, while those on the left already know I'm crazy and this is just an obvious, devious attempt to make them lower their guard.

I guess the good news is that I've finally found something on which both sides can finally agree.

I know what they are feeling. Believe me, there are many days when I have completely different monologues planned for the show, but instead, I see something in the news that I just "have to mention this first," I think to myself. They next thing I know, it is forty minutes in and I have been ranting the entire time, and it feels good. But here is the rub: I also know what it means to be an addict.

Probably the very first thing an addict knows for sure is that he or she isn't an addict. The substance isn't controlling me, I'm controlling it. There's nothing wrong with it, and it makes me feel good. I can live without it. I can stop anytime I want to. It's my life; as long as I'm not hurting anyone else, what difference does it make? Stopping is easy, but I'll do it slowly. I'll do it at my own pace; I just have a little, then just a little more.

For me, this book begins at the end: My name is Glenn, and I am an addict currently recovering from social-media-driven moral outrage. Years ago, I was certain that my side was right and the left was wrong. I didn't have any doubts about that. They couldn't be more wrong, in fact, which made them dangerous to me and the country that I love so much. It turned out that I was the dangerous guy; dangerous because I was so certain about that. I knew that if we were given the reins of government we would curtail the power of the presidency, we would restore the traditional constitutional barriers, we would deliver real and affordable health care to the sick and elderly without the fat cats getting richer. I knew we would have a sensible foreign policy that defended American interests. I began every conversation with one of "them" knowing that they were so wrong, so misinformed and naïve, that I didn't need to waste my time listening. I knew that they had nothing to teach me, and it was useless for me to try to explain reality to them because they just wouldn't listen to reason. I was absolutely certain about that; that's what I said on my broadcasts, and as a result my popularity continued to rise.

Big oops.

I was certain about Obama and isolated millions of good Americans. In 2016, I was certain about Donald Trump and alienated millions of good Americans who felt no one was listening to them.

Well, we all make mistakes. Unfortunately for me, they tend to be huge and very public. So perhaps I should begin this book with the only thing I am now certain of: I shouldn't be certain of anything—except that I'm tired of this meaningless fight that is keeping us apart.

Look, the more I learn, the less sure I am that I know very much. About a lot of things. But this is a topic I do have experience in. I've lived this.

Understanding how we've gotten to this point and accepting what the dangers are to ourselves, our children, and our country if we don't change, all of us, will make a difference for all of us. Right now, both sides know for certain there is nothing to be learned from the other side, and knowing that, as I did, makes it easy to ridicule and dismiss "them." And as each side draws sharper lines, it becomes easier and easier to ratchet up the rhetoric and dehumanize the other side. That eventually grows into hatred for "them" and the belief that all of our problems are caused by "them" and helps to justify physical violence against "them." As Yoda taught us, "Fear is the path to the dark side. Fear leads to anger, anger leads to hate, hate leads to suffering." The left is quick to point out anytime Trump uses language they claim dehumanizes immigrants, but in the same breath they have no problem referring to his supporters as "callous," "racist," "deplorable," or "subhuman." And we wonder why adults feel justified in physically assaulting teenagers wearing MAGA hats in public.

We can do this. We just need to learn to accept and love ourselves and each other for the very real, very human people we all are.

The stop starts now.

9

Sorry, Not Sorry

This is not an apology book. Mine or yours.

But that doesn't mean I can't admit when I've been wrong. In fact, I'm delighted to do so.

Let's have an adult conversation about President Donald Trump. It seems to be the only conversation people want to have these days anyway. It's important to be able to have nuanced, balanced, and forthright dialogue, even about a demagogue we don't necessarily like for whatever reason. We need to be able to call balls and strikes without having George Brett come flying out of the dugout throwing haymakers every time he disagrees with a call.

Trump doesn't need defending, not by me or by anybody. He is single-handedly crushing the media—or single-thumbedly, since he's mostly using Twitter to do it. I don't like it, but I also don't like the response from the media.

Both sides are trying so hard to get us involved in their fight. I say we just sit back and let the Titans fight it out. Personally, I'm putting my money on the Kraken.

Let me make it very clear: It appears that on many of his policies that I thought he would never implement, he has come through. In recognizing Jerusalem as the capital of Israel and in his Supreme Court and appeals court appointments, he has shown the bravery shown by Truman and the consistency in constitutional adherence conservatives have been hoping for my whole lifetime.

He quickly and cleanly defeated ISIS, while reversing the Iranian expansion in the Middle East. With his unwavering commitment to the stability of Israel and the effortless defeat of ISIS, which he followed with his standing against almost the entire world to withdraw the United States from the disastrous Obama/Iranian Nuclear Agreement, as well as his quiet diplomacy bringing stability to Saudi Arabia while destroying OPEC in the same move, he may in the end be responsible for a realignment of regional power that greatly diminishes the influence of the mullahs and the psychopathic religious butchers. This alone, if successful, could save the lives of millions and become the greatest achievement in the Middle East by any president in the last seventy-five years.

While his tax cuts, to me, left a lot to be desired, that is an issue with Congress, not the administration. It was much better for the people and the economy. Once coupled with the massive reduction of regulations (cutting regs and the budget of the EPA by one-third) he has given employees, companies, and entrepreneurs a chance to be competitive once again on the world stage. At the time of this writing, America is experiencing the lowest unemployment rate since 1969. In June the Fed announced "Wage Inflation," which simply means your wages are going up. Because fewer people are looking for work, which means more competition for those companies that are looking to hire. Think of it this way: Inflation is caused by too many dollars chasing too few products.

Just replace the word "products" with "workers" and presto, "wage inflation." Most Americans have not seen a pay increase greater than inflation for close to three decades. The last administration felt that the only way companies would pay more is if the government dictated things like a mincome or a fifteen-dollar minimum wage. The wage inflation and low unemployment numbers have happened because the president understood that the free market works.

On these issues I am thrilled to tell you, as during the election I promised I would: I was wrong. Very wrong.

With that said, his tariffs could undo all that he has accomplished.

I am hoping that it is all nothing more than a short-term negotiating tactic, but with every passing day, I grow more and more concerned. I am also sad to say that my biggest concerns about POTUS, his character flaws as a man, continue to disappoint me. But he is the president, and we all must be honest enough to point out the good and not just the bad. Likewise, Trump supporters must be willing to point out the bad, not just the good.

I am, however, more concerned by our character flaws at this point, as we know who he is and we have already "baked those issues into the price."

What is crazy is that we are so under assault from all directions that we have lost all ability to differentiate between friends and foes. We now require 100 percent acceptance of every policy, statement, and haircut a politician has ever had. We now consider people "traitors" if they are not in total lockstep. When did this happen? I love Baskin-Robbins and Cold Stone Creamery, but not every flavor. It is why they give you the little plastic spoons. Even then, there is stuff, I know, even without the pink spoon test, that I just will not like. If it were the rum, I would be out. But it isn't. It isn't 5 Baskin-Robbins's flavors that mean I hate the whole store. They have 31. Perhaps I don't like 20 of them, I hate 3 of them and I am out-and-out hostile toward all sherbets because you and I both know they are a mockery of ice cream and healthy food. It just pretends to be healthy. I hate it. But I am not a traitor to Baskin-Robbins for not liking sherbet, even if I am suspicious of the sherbet. As if this section of the counter is where I think either Mr. Baskin or fathead Robbins is going to take the company after the other one dies. I am pretty sure that I am still welcome in all 7,800 worldwide locations, and while that Baskin bastard may be a little hostile to me himself, it is only because he knows that I know his deadly sherbet scheme, which involves killing Robbins with an otter pop, as once it melts there will be no murder weapon. I promise everyone else behind the counter doesn't require me to accept, like, or sing the praises of everything Baskin-Robbins does. Why isn't it the same with President Trump or Hillary Clinton?

Also, how disingenuous is it of the press to pretend that everything Trump says or does is bad? I mean, McDonald's has some items that are at best questionable, if they can actually be labeled food. I think I was about fifteen before I realized that the milkshake was labeled "shake" on the menu for "legal reasons." Perhaps we should rethink any item that we could be sued over because we have tried to fool people into thinking it was food. They also produce food that is the most effective and consistent laxative available anywhere. Most of it will run right through a person—there are times when I think that when they ask, "Do you want that to go?" they mean it in a completely different way. However, with all that said, their french fries are the best ever. I am not sure if they are even potatoes, and I am pretty sure they aren't French, but there is no question—the best in the business, and everyone knows it. What is happening with the media is as if Donald Trump was McDonald's, and no matter what the source, every single journalist, host, and late night show suddenly hates everything about McDonald's. I mean, the big creepy clown may have been okay in the seventies, and now it is like seeing those old photos from the 1920s of the kids in Halloween costumes, so I get it, but nothing is good? Even if it isn't good for you, you can't find anything good to say?

"Well, Steve, I have to tell you, even though we did that five-part exposé on how McDonald's doesn't actually use shamrocks to make shamrock shakes, I will tell you there is something about that obscene amount of tartar sauce that hides the taste of that plastic cheese on the fish patty that makes a Filet-O-Fish one of a kind." If no one ever said anything about liking something about McDonald's, you would know that everyone was in the bag for Wendy's or Burger King.

I am so saddened by those who pretend that character doesn't matter, as we have all seen the effects of this postmodern philosophy on our kids over the last few years. The president, the media, and our reactions will distort our culture even more and shape a new generation that will think differently about morality, truth, civility, and power, in many unexpected ways. Our "outrage" over the last three or four presidents is coming with a very high price.

It may not matter to you right now, but we are still seeing the devastating effects on our culture and our children's perception in the way that oral sex is now not looked at as "sex" due to our dismissal of the Clinton scandal. In fact, according to a recent poll, our children and culture will pay an increasingly high price for the seemingly complete dismissal of virtue in our lives.

A new study showed that only 28 percent of Americans now feel that premarital sex is morally wrong. In fact, 69 percent say that it is morally acceptable. Among adults who were asked during this study if they thought sexual relations between teens were okay, only 54 percent said no. Forty-two percent claimed it was morally acceptable. That number is up ten points since 2013, and up six points in the past twelve months. It is, however, a bright spot in the poll, as it is the only kind of sexual activity that is still not accepted by the majority. Which makes the position of the left and the media even more reprehensible. Sam Bee said that she, as a feminist, often uses the c-word, as it is her effort to "reclaim the power of that word." And yet somehow you find a one-night porn-star hookup to be beyond the pale?

On the left, citizens act as though Donald Trump's personal failings are something new, which they would never have tolerated. To them he is a deviant, a possible "tyrant," and someone who may have sold us out for cash or influence to Russia.

When I point out Bill Clinton's or Anthony Weiner's deviancy or the way Obama used government agencies to target and destroy those who opposed him, and remind them that Hillary and Bill seemingly sold access to multiple countries through the "Clinton Foundation," Democrats will try to tell me, "Yes, but—you can't compare them to Trump."

As if Clinton is merely Pee-wee Herman and Trump is Jack the Ripper. Perhaps we should recognize that our standard shouldn't be "who is the lesser deviant, tyrant, or oligarch" and set a higher standard than a man who gently inserts cigars into women or just "grabs 'em." Both are accused of sexual harassment, only one has gone to trial, and both have been accused of rape. Are they guilty? We may never know, because both parties did everything they could to discredit the women and accuse the accusers of being part of either a "vast right-wing conspiracy" or a "deep state." The point, I think, is that people who make "the party" the center of their world will tolerate anything, and it will only get worse from here as we are teaching future presidents, as well as our children, lessons that will not be forgotten soon.

The takeaway, for me, is that perhaps it is not advisable to compare the worst traits of our leaders. My mother used to tell me that I should not compare myself to others but to the me of yesterday. Jordan Peterson told me the same thing recently, backstage at one of his sold-out "shows." Me versus Me. It is the only fair comparison, and it is the one comparison no one is encouraging us to make.

Isn't this what our political debates should be about? You and me? Who cares about them. They work for us. You and me. Not Us versus Them, Trump versus Clinton, Left versus Right, or black versus white. This is about each of us and no one else. We need to look at who we are, what we believe, and who we want to become.

Soon, as you will learn in the tech section of this book, we will reenter the world of "non-sense" that we thought had died with the Dark Ages. Soon, because of what are called "deep fakes," you will not be able to trust your eyes and ears. Most have no idea what a "deep fake" is, or, if they do, they refuse to see the ramifications of a people already greatly distrusting and divided against one another, who now cannot trust their own eyes or ears, and how this could be used as a "Reichstag fire" in many places all over the world, including ours. I believe we will begin to be deeply affected by these "deep fakes" in the next three to six years. When they hit, we must all know how to think critically, to debunk, to communicate effectively, to respond quickly and globally—and, most important, to respond truthfully with reach and impact. This one extra "push" may finally be the moment of overdose in our addiction.

We must sober up, restore reason and decency, and thicken our skin. Our loyalties must be to the truth, reason, and compassion. We must also bind ourselves, with those principles, to one another or we will not make it. Not just America, but this time it may be the entirety of mankind.

If we are going to kick our addiction, we need to make promises that we can actually keep. Such as "I will praise parties, politicians, and even those online, no matter which side they hail from, when they are correct—and I will speak out when they are wrong, but I will do so with facts and reason, not outrage and half-truths."

It is hard nowadays to listen to opinions. Frankly, I am sick of even my opinion. Opinions are a little bit like armpits. We have more than one, but that doesn't mean that anyone wants to smell them.

If you are sincere, you are trying to live your own words consistently, and you are willing to hear ideas different from yours without thinking about what you are going to say after "they" stop talking and would actually change your mind if someone made a good case, then great, let's be friends. If not, we can still be friends, but keep your armpits to yourself.

The twelve steps of AA work, for the same reason our system of government works, when adhered to, because they are based in human nature and truth—not political truth, but universal and eternal truth. Those things that are "self-evident." Not what we want to believe or what enablers will allow us to get away with. Enablers are the ones who are making us more and more dependent. It is sick. Frankly, it makes the Munchausen-by-proxy freaks look healthy and loving.

We have to really take a long look in the mirror as a people and ask why we are all allowing this to happen, and have we had enough. America, we are going on 250 years old and we are acting like a five-year-old. Stop it. Grow up! We are told every day of a new outrage, a new villain, and a new "rule" that we all now must obey. None of us can possibly keep up with it.

For instance, we all had to accept Bruce Jenner's wanting to be a woman. (I was proud of us, frankly. I think all of us showed great compassion toward someone who had spent his whole life hiding and feeling as though he didn't belong. It was heartbreaking.) Then, before any procedure to physically change things, we were required to call him by his new name, Caitlyn, and had to stop calling her "him." Keep in mind this happened seemingly overnight. If you made a mistake and called her "him" or "Bruce," you were publicly shamed. Then, when she did a photo spread in *Vanity Fair*, we all had to agree that "she" was beautiful. Complete lockstep. Strangely, most people did all that without hesitation. Think of this: Within a matter of weeks the entire country, and the Western world, went from knowing an Olympic athlete who was on our Wheaties box to calling him "her" and saying, dutifully, how lovely "she" was without any trouble at all. Each step of the way, there were new rules and new terms that we had never even heard of sometimes even the night before but were expected to fall in line with right then and there. How out of control are we? How self-medicated must we really be? I am actually risking my career (no exaggeration) by using this example. For multiple reasons. I am sure I am not even aware of some of them. But perhaps the biggest offense that I have committed is that in this paragraph I have "dead named" her. Once someone says that they are a different gender, as we all are being taught now, they are that different gender and we are no longer allowed to discuss anything about their life before they SAID that they were a different gender. By my recounting the story of Bruce Jenner and who he was "before," I have "dead named" him.

Who is making these rules? When did we elect them to rule like gods above us? We have gone from sincerely trying to be more compassionate by changing what we say or how we say it to ensure we didn't hurt people's feelings to living in a word cage of our own making, not even knowing who our keepers are or what, if anything, will let us out of this cage. This is not kindness, it is fascism. The words "political correctness" have become much more clear to those who are paying attention.

Say the words (Orwell called it newspeak) and only those words that the nameless and faceless who now have "political" power tell us are correct. Refuse to comply, and those with power will first try to teach you through shame and intimidation, and then by destroying your life or others' to set an example. There is no reason, nor is there any recourse. This is not democratic rule. It is mob rule.

This mob pretends to be outraged, and so many have become so thin-skinned that they perhaps truly are outraged at the slightest "microaggression" (newspeak) and whip people into a frenzy. Meanwhile, the average citizen, who is being forced to just accept and go along, is only just now becoming outraged—not about being silently forced to comply, but by equally thin-skinned microaggressions on "their side."

We have become two distinct and different cultures: Both the left and the right live in large, constantly self-reinforcing bubbles and don't even try to understand each other. We're right, they're wrong. At the very minimum, call it Starbucks people versus Dunkin' Donuts people: We don't read the same things, we don't watch the same things on television, we're not buying the same things in the aisles of our grocery stores. Some of you probably don't remember that that used to be okay.

10

The Mountain between Us

This Great Divide isn't a recent phenomenon; in different ways it has always been part of our history. The genius of our Constitution is that our Founders were somehow able to take all of the needs and desires of people living in different regions and facing different problems and somehow knit everyone together. The conflict wasn't only North and South, it also was cities and farms, agriculture and industry, different religions, languages, and levels of education. Bringing all of those constituencies together to create a nation was about as easy as fitting the Keystone Pipeline through the eye of a needle held by Al Gore. Our differences were always far greater than those things we had in common. We are the most diverse nation in the history of the world. No nation has ever even come close.

Unlike most European nations, these people had no single language or religion; there was no national newspaper. America didn't even have a national anthem until 1931. But Madison, Hamilton, Jefferson, Adams, all those great men who wrote the Constitution somehow found the common denominator, a set of bedrock principles that all of those people could agree were worth compromising their own desires to achieve.

The mountain that divides us now is the loss of those principles.

The natural rights that we as human beings are endowed with by God are not to be limited or compromised by men. The country was built on these human rights: Respect for the choices of others. Freedom to believe and speak and worship. The right to be safe in your home, both from others and from the government. The right to your own life as your own inherent possession, and the right to defend yourself and your life from harm. The power we granted to the federal government was going to be limited to truly national issues, such as our common defense, our monetary system, international trade policies, and the resolution of disagreements between the states. Honesty mattered, and personal integrity, and, maybe most important, an understanding that we might not like or agree with the choices made by other people, but it was their right to make those choices and we would accept them for the greater good, because the greater good is based in the free agency of the individual.

A system of government that was based fundamentally on the recognition of man as he is as a species. It was what set us apart from the other countries of the world. And then we lumped those principles all together in a cauldron we called patriotism. Patriotism, which was supposed to mean an allegiance to the Constitution that upheld all of these rights, but to many people it has taken on a different definition: My country, right or wrong. The Constitution doesn't seem to play a role with many on either side anymore, and, to make matters worse, it is now becoming my party or my politician, right or wrong.

If we are to save our way of life, we must find our way back to what brought us all together in the first place. It is vital to understand that the Constitution didn't grant us these rights, it simply recognized, acknowledged, and codified their existence as a means to ensure everyone understood that the government did not have the power or authority to deprive us of those things. But in addition to those bedrock principles there was a single belief that brought us all together: the acceptance that all of our rights were given to mankind by God. God isn't even mentioned a single time in the Constitution, but the belief in a Supreme Being was the spine of the Declaration of Independence. "All men are created equal, that they are endowed by their Creator with certain unalienable Rights." The Founding Fathers embraced a broad spectrum of religious beliefs, from dogmatists to atheists, but all of them accepted the importance of the idea of a Supreme Being as a universal concept. It was pretty simple: I don't have to share your beliefs—I don't even have to believe in any God—but I accept the concept of natural laws, of which some would be enumerated in the Constitution.

If you'd like a good laugh, just pause right here for a few seconds and try to imagine how our current batch of politicians would do if they had to write either document. We are so divided that we can't even agree on a way to make sure that no American child goes hungry, that we shouldn't spend a trillion dollars a year more than we have, or that a fetus is a baby; just think about these politicians trying to deal with concepts of naturally derived human rights.

The Declaration of Independence, the Constitution, and the Bill of Rights are the most divinely inspired documents perhaps of all time. They are so brilliantly written, so crystal clear, and so unbelievably empowering that they changed the world.

It wasn't always perfect, and for a lot of Americans it wasn't always fair and it definitely wasn't equal, but we managed to bumble along. When it was necessary to protect and defend the country, we came together as Americans. The states united to make the world safe for democracy in World War I. Together we struggled through the Great Depression. And then, working together, we created the arsenal of democracy necessary to win World War II.

But this time, when that work was done once again, we couldn't entirely go our separate ways. The changes brought on by FDR and the progressive presidents before him, Wilson and Teddy Roosevelt, coupled with the progressives in both parties in Congress and the Supreme Court, had changed us in fundamental ways. The Bill of Rights and the individual rights of Americans were weakened after each war of the twentieth century. Going into the 1930s, progressives on both sides of the aisle were certain that the American system was outdated and lumbering. It couldn't move fast enough with its checks and balances.

The mountain we now feel was no mistake. It is here by design. In the late 1800s, the Germans were thought to be leading the "modern world" in science and education. The true educational elites went to university, mainly Heidelberg in Germany, where all kinds new "scientific" thought was being taught. Marxism, socialism, collectivism, evolution, and eugenics. By 1900, the Constitution and certainly the Declaration of Independence looked to men like Princeton professor Woodrow Wilson like an outdated and irrelevant missive sent from the past with no connection to the here and now. Wilson, who attended Johns Hopkins University, modeled directly after the university in Heidelberg as the "model progressive university in America," was a racist who found the new science of eugenics as the solution the Civil War and Reconstruction failed to provide to his liking. His father was the founder of the Presbyterian Church in the Confederate States of America, and while he hated his father, in many ways he, as the president of Princeton and president of the United States, achieved many things his father could not have even dreamed of.

The progressives knew they had to do two things if they were to achieve this new system run by technocrats: discredit the founding documents and transform the university system into a tool of indoctrination. Wilson's words in 1909 were clear: "The purpose of a university should be to make a son as unlike his father as possible . . . as every man of established success is dangerous to [the new] society."

At first communism was the model, and then in the 1920s Fascism came into style. Remember, this was before over 100 million were killed by the fascists and, primarily, by the communists. It might be more helpful to use the word "technocracy" as what progressives saw as the new model. It called for a strong man who could wield the power of the state quickly and efficiently. After all, what good was a government if it could not steer the power of its people and industry for the good of the central plan? The difference between this new

European "left and right" really boiled down to one question: Are we globalists or nationalists? Communism in Russia and China and National Socialism in Italy and Germany in the end produced socialist states with absolute power invested in a strong man. The real divide in Europe was the workers of the world versus the workers of Germany, Italy, or Spain. Here in the U.S., the debate was whether in the end the world would be run by a UN-style body or the state would run the world from D.C., because our money and our might told the world "we could." For many in D.C. and across the country, this is still the argument. Generally speaking, Republicans want to run the world using U.S. military might, while the Democrats want to give the state's power to an international body.

The real answer is the United States is not, nor should it ever be, either of those things. We had a wholly new idea. That "governments are instituted among men for the purpose of protecting the rights of the people." Even suggesting a technocracy shows a contempt for or, at the very least, a fundamental misunderstanding of what made America different in the first place. Let England forever search for the Holy Grail of a benevolent king, like Arthur. We, instead, would allow each citizen to rule his or her own life and property and answer to no king other than his God. This, we thought, was the best way to keep wicked rulers, kings, religious autocrats, and, later, dictators from taking control here.

Just a few days after the czar was overthrown, Woodrow Wilson praised it as a "glorious revolution," saying: "Does not every American feel that assurance has been added to our hope for the future peace of the world by the wonderful and heartening things that have been happening within the last few weeks in Russia? The autocracy now has been shaken off and the great, generous Russian people have been added in all their naïve majesty and might to the forces that are fighting for freedom in the world, for justice, and for peace. Here is a fit partner for a league of honor." Wilson and his party saw the Soviet model as the future, but they needed to get there without revolution. Luckily for our freedom, Wilson suffered a stroke a year before the end of his second term. He had been planning to run for a third term, the first president to do so.

He had moved too quickly; his policies, racism, and global governance were frightening to the American people. The next election, the people moved back toward personal freedom. Over the next eight years, the federal budget was cut by more than half, as were taxes. People were once again unleashed to create and explore. The result was the Roaring Twenties.

But in the halls of government and academia, the battle of communism or fascism as the new model continued. In fact, it took a new and dangerous turn. When Edward Bernays began the Council of Foreign Relations, its stated goal was to bring these three new branches of government together: government officials, university elites, and members of the press. Here the press would be taught what the future was to look like so they could "teach the people." Remember, this was before fascism and communism had been discredited by millions of dead. Bernays called this "teaching" propaganda. Later, he would refer to it simply as "advertising."

The love of a giant state didn't begin or end with Wilson. Many who served with him went on to powerful positions. Stuart Chase, who was in Wilson's FTC and helped Upton Sinclair in his bogus "investigations" of the meat-packing industry, later traveled to the Soviet Union with members of the first American trade union delegation and was the coauthor of a book that praised Soviet experiments in agricultural and social management—the same experiments and management that starved millions. In 1932, Chase wrote *A New Deal*, which became identified with the economic programs of FDR.

During the 1932–33 Holodomor, the man-made famine-genocide in the Ukraine, as many as 12 million people died over two years. The *New York Times*, through its reporter Walter Duranty, acted as the propaganda arm for Stalin. "Conditions are bad, but there is no famine," he wrote in a dispatch from Moscow in March of 1933. "But—to put it brutally—you can't make an omelet without breaking eggs." He won the Pulitzer Prize that year. The combination of nationalism and socialism, along with some private ownership, being practiced in Germany and Italy was appealing to the progressives as well. Mussolini became the poster child for the new scientific system of government. American elites loved this new fascism. It was the model for the New Deal.

The Nazi press enthusiastically hailed the early New Deal measures: America, like the Reich, had decisively broken with the "uninhibited frenzy of market speculation." The Nazi Party newspaper, the *Völkischer Beobachter*, stressed "Roosevelt's adoption of National Socialist strains of thought in his economic and social policies," praising the president's style of leadership as being compatible with Hitler's own dictatorial "*Führerprinzip*."

Nor was Hitler himself lacking in praise for his American counterpart. He told American ambassador William Dodd that he was "in accord with the president in the view that the virtue of duty, readiness for sacrifice, and discipline should dominate the entire people. These moral demands which the president places before every individual citizen of the United States are also the quintessence of the German state philosophy, which finds its expression in the slogan 'The Public Weal Transcends the Interest of the Individual'" (*Three New Deals: Reflections on Roosevelt's America, Mussolini's Italy, and Hitler's Germany*, by Wolfgang Schivelbusch).

After Roosevelt established the National Recovery Administration, the agency produced a report for the White House detailing its strategy, stating boldly, "The Fascist Principles are very similar to those we have been evolving here in America."

Fortunately, reality is a relentless jurist, and by the end of the war, both communism and fascism had been discredited.

Later, Stuart Chase, in his book *After the War*, began to outline what the U.S. government would eventually look like. With just a few significant exceptions, the United States is almost entirely that state now. It is clearly a fascist or "technocratic" state, controlling banking, energy, transportation, communications, health care, and welfare, and, while allowing for private ownership, imposing heavy regulations on all industry and business. It has stated goals of "getting off the gold standard," to run our budgets and not ever-expanding deficits, and to become a debtor nation rather than a lending nation. In the same book, Chase claimed that this system was now inevitable, as all the pieces had been put in place and nothing could stop it. In an effort to distance this from the Italian, German, or Soviet model, he wrote that this extra-constitutional system was "unnameable," as it wasn't quite fascist or communist. He therefore called it "system X." It is 90 percent of America today. We now merely need to wait for the benevolent "technocrat" to flip the final switch in our inevitable time of national crisis.

The biggest reason we could no longer truly "go our separate ways" was due to one of the worst rulings of the Supreme Court, *Wickard v. Filburn*. An Ohio farmer, Roscoe Filburn, was growing wheat to feed animals on his own farm. The federal government had established limits on wheat production, based on the acreage owned by a farmer, to stabilize wheat prices and supplies. Filburn grew more than the limit that he was permitted and so was ordered to pay a penalty.

In response, he said that because his wheat was not sold, it could not be regulated as commerce, let alone "interstate" commerce (described in the Constitution as "Commerce . . . among the several states").

The Supreme Court disagreed: "Whether the subject of the regulation in question was 'production,' 'consumption,' or 'marketing' is, therefore, not material for purposes of deciding the question of federal power before us. . . . But even if appellee's activity be local and though it may not be regarded as commerce, it may still, whatever its nature, be reached by Congress if it exerts a substantial economic effect on interstate commerce and this irrespective of whether such effect is what might at some earlier time have been defined as 'direct' or 'indirect.' "

This one ruling changed us forever, although very few Americans realized it at the time. It gave the federal government control in all areas of our life no matter how big or small. Who would have thought that a ruling about a rural farmer growing wheat for his own livestock would have been the basis for the 1965 Gun Control Act? And yet there it is: The "indirect" impact of guns being manufactured and sold locally gives the federal government the authority to dictate how Americans are allowed to defend their own lives and property.

I believe that this is "the unnamed mountain" that divides us. Part of the strain we are feeling is the breakdown of the system, as we are now at the point of final choosing. We either return to what we were designed to be or take the final step toward "system X." What I find so distressing is the fact that today's citizens don't seem to have a problem with what a party or a president does—for instance, keeping children in cages on the border, using warrantless wiretaps on U.S. citizens, allowing the NSA to gather information, or adding to our national debt, now to the tune of ONE TRILLION DOLLARS A YEAR. Instead, each side, it seems, has a problem only when it is done by anyone but "their guy." This is a society ready for a dictator. The only questions that remain are: What is the crisis that pushes the people to cry out for the top to come down? Which side finally grabs control? And what do they do to the other half of the country that disagrees?

So many are telling us now that they just want to "burn the whole system down." But do they even know the system? Do they know that what our Founders set forth has not been reflected for decades? If you still want to "burn it down," then what? Replace it with what? Who is in charge, how does it work? This is a hope for anarchy and chaos.

If we lose what little we have left, we will regret it. Believe me, I know.

Once I sobered up, I wanted to shed it all. Get rid of the car and nice watch. Anything that I had purchased to make me feel like I was a successful big shot. I was about to donate everything I had to charity and live without all of the trappings. My wife convinced me I would regret it and that I should not do that. She made a very compelling case that someday I would look back and wish I still had it. She was right. She took most of it in the divorce, and I do "wish I still had it."

We need to recognize what we have and really evaluate its merits before we throw it out.

We are so precariously close to throwing the baby out with the bathwater. There is so much good here; the problem is, we don't even know what it is anymore.

Ask the average American to explain our system of government. What is the role of government? What is its primary job? It might as well be magic. How did it come to be? This last July Fourth, I saw a man-on-the-street poll where they were asking, "What do we celebrate on July Fourth?" About half answered with a self-conscious giggle that signaled "I don't know for sure, but . . . independence." It was all downhill from there. Independence from whom? Only two people had that answer. "Do you know where the Declaration of Independence was signed?" One said Boston. Most had no idea. The only one who answered correctly—Philadelphia—was a Russian tourist who had been in the country for only a day. By the way, what made this even more painful was that the questions were asked on the sidewalk in front of Independence Hall.

Americans don't know; they just "know" that it isn't working. But if you have no idea how your car is supposed to work, when it breaks down, let your wife bring the car to the mechanic or you stand a very good chance of paying over $1,000 to replace your "displaced defibrillator." Unless the people educate themselves and lead the way, those who are not our better angels will "fix it" for us at a cost that none of us are going to be willing to pay.

Only one in a thousand Americans can now list the freedoms guaranteed in the First Amendment, yet this is the amendment most Americans mean when they say "I've got rights." At that pace, it isn't just the defibrillator, but it looks as if the water coolant injection system for the brakes may have gone out as well.

There are thoughtful people, like President Obama, who have a problem with our system of government because it is based on a charter of negative liberties rather than positive liberties. For instance, if you look at the Soviet Marxist Constitution, it is a charter of positive liberties—or, in other words, the things that the state MUST do. But if we have no knowledge of our system of government or what the Bill of Rights is, let alone why it enumerates negative liberties, we are a society just looking for someone to be our "daddy" and tell us that everything will be okay.

So, just for fun, let's dive into this a bit. The Soviet Constitution included a series of civil and political rights. It also granted social and economic rights not provided by constitutions in some capitalist countries. Among these were the rights to work, rest and leisure, health protection, care in old age and sickness, housing, education, and cultural benefits. Today, I believe you could sell this system to much of America. You could even call it the Constitution from the Old Soviet Republic, and, because we are so historically illiterate, I believe it just might be voted in with record numbers. People love "free stuff," but as always, free stuff comes with a price.

The Soviet Constitution outlined limitations on political rights; Article 6 effectively eliminated partisan opposition and division within government by granting to the Communist Party the power to lead and guide society.

Article 39 enabled the government to prohibit any activities it considered detrimental by stating, "Enjoyment of the rights and freedoms of citizens must not be to the detriment of the interests of society or the state."

The government did not treat as inalienable those political and socioeconomic rights the Constitution granted to the people. Citizens enjoyed rights only when the exercise of those rights did not interfere with the interests of the state, and the CPSU alone had the power and authority to determine policies for the government and society.

For example, the right to freedom of expression contained in

Article 52 could be suspended if the exercise of that freedom failed to be in accord with party policies. In other words, speech that was not politically correct. Freedom of expression did not entail the right to criticize the government. The Constitution did provide a "freedom of conscience, that is, the right to profess or not to profess any religion, and to conduct religious worship or atheistic propaganda." It prohibited incitement of hatred or hostility on religious grounds.

The Constitution also failed to provide political and judicial mechanisms for the protection of rights. Neither did the people have a higher authority within the government to which to appeal when they believed their rights had been violated. The Supreme Court had no power to ensure that constitutional rights were observed by legislation or were respected by the rest of the government.

The people also had POSITIVE RIGHTS, or things and duties they MUST perform.

Article 59 of the Constitution stated that citizens' exercising of their rights was inseparable from performance of their duties. Articles 60 through 69 defined these duties. Citizens were required to work and to observe labor discipline. The legal code labeled evasion of work "parasitism" and provided punishment for this crime. The Constitution also obliged citizens to protect socialist property and oppose corruption. Violation of this duty was considered "a betrayal of the motherland and the gravest of crimes." Finally, the Constitution required parents to train their children for socially useful work and to raise them as worthy members of socialist society.

Laws also specified that citizens could not freely renounce their citizenship. Citizens were required to apply for permission to do so from the president of the Supreme Soviet, who could reject the application if the applicant had not completed military service, had judicial duties, or was responsible for family dependents. In other words, the Soviet state was Hotel California: You can check in, but you can never leave.

With some exceptions, I believe I could sell this idea to all of those who were interviewed in front of Independence Hall. The only possible exception might be the Russian tourist, as he may be old enough to remember how high the price really was.

That is a charter of positive liberties, and history shows us that it never works out well, mainly because the state decides the rights of its people. Whereas in our form of government, its people decide what the government can and cannot do, because we are only loaning the government and its agencies the rights given to all men.

This is the biggest difference between constitutionalists and progressives. This is the mountain summit. As Obama stated, "Ours is a charter of negative liberties as opposed to a Constitution that tells the government what it can and must do for the people."

This is NOT the American system. This reverses the structure and meaning of our founding documents entirely. If we decide to "fundamentally" transform the United States of America, then we should be open, honest, and have that clear debate.

The idea of rights belonging to the people was and still very much is a new and unique concept. It means that we are not only created equal but we cannot even create a body or a government that is more than equal to its life force, the people. Under our system of government, we own our own rights, and no one can take them from us, but neither can we take them from another. We always retain our rights. We loan a few of them out so others—police, firemen, congressmen and other elected officials—can do what we need done. We, in effect, hire them to do the stuff we don't want to do or simply don't have the time to do. They represent us. They are to be our eyes, ears, and advocates.

The real secret here is that we cannot loan a right that we do not have. This is uniquely American and, when fully understood, acts as self-enforcement to protect us from an out-of-control government. For instance, we can give our right to the police to patrol our neighborhood, as we hold the right to self-protection. But we cannot as a neighborhood-watch group tell the police officer to kill one of our neighbors or steal his stuff and give it to us, because none of us hold those rights. It is a truly a remarkable system, if guarded by the people, because it keeps everyone in check.

But what are those rights? How do we get them? What is government for? What if it gets out of control? Can we break away if we don't like it? Well, let's start at the beginning. Assuming you knew all of the answers to the questions asked of those in Philadelphia, then you know what our Founders wrote that summer in 1776. But it is so brilliant that it is truly worth rereading every so often.

I like to look at it as the best breakup letter ever written, but if you look at it as a statement from a group of entrepreneurs who want to begin their own company, it works really well as an appeal to possible shareholders and as a mission statement.

The Declaration of Independence, the founding document on which we base our entire system of government, is perhaps the most important document in world history. Many countries have since used it for the base or cornerstone of their government. To understand it, think of it in two ways: our breakup letter to the king and, most important, our country's mission statement.

What makes this so powerful is that just in the first three paragraphs it outlines what kind of country we are going to strive to be. Most breakup letters, or manifestos, especially between countries, just list all the reasons they need to be apart. It was of extraordinary genius and foresight to include and tell the world what we were going to build. Think of it this way: If you wanted to start a new car company, would anyone want to invest in an unknown upstart company that wanted to try something totally new but announced its formation by saying, "We are a bunch of former employees who left the VW 'Thing' plant because, well, have you ever seen a 'Thing'? Ooof! It made the AMC Pacer look sleek . . . AND they insisted that everyone who works there had to like all thirty-one flavors at Baskin-Robbins." No one would invest.

Instead, some of the greatest and best-known minds on earth at the time, akin to Bill Gates, Steve Jobs, Elon Musk, Stephen Hawking, Christopher Hitchens, Billy Graham, Jordan Peterson, and Ben Shapiro, all signed a statement that said, "We the undersigned have an idea. We know it sounds crazy, but we have really done our homework and we believe this totally new kind of car is the future, and we have standards that are going to be higher than anyone has imagined before. We are going to get rid of the dealership thing because we know and you know it is just a game, and we are not going to play it. Our cars will be made with the highest standards, they will be more dependable, all 100 percent renewable energy, and at half the cost of the car you drive today. We are building it with you in mind, because you deserve to drive what you want, where you want, in a great car that you can afford. Please, join us." Now I want a few more details, but if that is the announcement, I think many people would invest.

This is what our Founders did, except not with a car but with a country. The Declaration of Independence is who we aspire to be. This was important for many reasons, but to me one of the least discussed reasons is that most of them liked the king and being British. They wanted him to know that they weren't bad people, that they didn't just hate him; instead they said to him, in effect, you don't even know us. This is who we are, and it is why we can no longer be together.

The Constitution came later, long after we declared ourselves free and independent. We had fought a war, cleaned ourselves up a bit, gathered all of the old team who knew why we wanted to start our own "car company" plus a few new members, sat down around our kitchen table, and said, "Okay, based on what we promised we were going to be, how do we build this company? How will we treat the management, and how do we make sure that they and all the employees understand that they all work for the customer? How do we make sure they don't ever turn into the blind jerks that were making the 'Thing'?" What they drafted was an org chart and all of the mechanicals for how we were going to build our cars. It has almost zero vision, as that was the job of our mission statement, the Declaration.

Finally, the Bill of Rights was written a year later, because there were still a lot of people who didn't trust that this car company would do what it said it would do, because most of the people who helped us draw up this "org chart" had been around the block a few times; some of them, in fact, had spent years studying all of the greatest and worst car companies in history. They searched and searched for the ideas that made a company great and not so great. Where did they fail, and why? Had anyone come up with a better idea? If so, did it work, and why or why not? One of the things that they found was that almost all senior management of big companies talk a good game but in the end, they overpay themselves, underpay the employees, and totally abuse the customers. They might even start out great, but over time, human nature takes over, and greed for power and money take over 99 percent of them. It wasn't just one company; it eventually happened to all companies and people.

But these "managers" knew, before it got too much farther down the road, we were going to write down and cast in stone the things that our company and its managers must NEVER violate. Because they had found about ten things that companies always did just before they really went off the rails. So, to act as an electric fence against bad management and an early warning system for the workers, shareholders, and customers that trouble was brewing, they posted a "we will never, ever do these things" list for all to see. Remember, this was in addition to the mission statement, which was also posted, which clearly stated that the only real job of managers was to protect the right of the customer to be who they are, to never make the "Thing" or ever tell them which ice cream—if any—they needed to like, and that their right to hate sherbet should not be infringed.

But due to some old-timey verbiage, and the fact that recent management has taken those posters down and has been telling everyone that "times have changed," while we still enjoy the spirit of those words, they really no longer apply; no one reads them, and most don't even know what they meant in the first place.

Let me take you through the Declaration. But if I may, let me liken this to a Dear John letter. In our case, a literal Dear George letter. As I do speak "old-timey" and the language of the "kids" today, I will translate line by line.

TO: The King
FROM: Us

When, in the course of human events, AS SHIT HAPPENS, it becomes necessary for one people to dissolve the political bonds which have connected them with another, I WANT YOU TO KNOW IT'S BEEN GREAT BUT and to assume among the powers of the earth, WE NEED TO BREAK UP the separate and equal station to which the laws of nature and of nature's God entitle them, BECAUSE YOU HAVE BEEN KIND OF "POSSESSIVE" IN A CREEPY "IF I CAN'T HAVE YOU, NO ONE WILL" SORT OF WAY, I WANT YOU TO KNOW THAT I CHECKED WITH EVERY-ONE INCLUDING BOTH GOD AND NATURE, AND EVERYONE SAYS THAT I CAN DO THIS. BUT I DON'T WANT TO BE A JERK, NOR DO I WANT ANY OF OUR FRIENDS TALKING JUNK ABOUT ME a de-cent respect to the opinions of mankind requires that they should declare the causes which impel them to the separa-tion. SO I AM WRITING TO LET YOU KNOW THAT REALLY, IT'S NOT ME, IT'S YOU. AFTER ALL THESE YEARS YOU STILL DON'T EVEN KNOW ME. WELL, LET ME REMIND YOU WHO I AM.

We hold these truths to be self-evident, I REALLY THINK THAT I COULD WAKE ALL OF MY FRIENDS UP IN THE MIDDLE OF THE NIGHT AND ASK THEM A FEW SIMPLE THINGS, AND EVEN FROM A DEAD SLEEP—AND THEY WOULD SAY, "LIKE, YEAH," AND GO BACK TO SLEEP LIKE A GRUMP. A FEW OF THOSE THINGS WOULD BE: that all men are created equal, NO MATTER WHAT, YOU AND I ARE EQUAL. OKAY, I'M, LIKE, SMARTER THAN YOU, AND YOU WOULD HAVE TO SWIPE RIGHT BUT I WOULD HAVE TO SWIPE LEFT ON YOU, BUT that they are endowed (REALLY, WHAT ARE YOU, TWELVE? THE WORD MEANS GIVEN OR BESTOWED UPON) by their Creator with certain unalienable rights, EACH OF US HAS RIGHTS, I MEAN REALLY BIG ONES, THEY COME FROM GOD AND NATURE, NOT YOU OR ANYBODY ELSE, AND THE WORD "UNALIENABLE" MEANS THAT NOT YOU NOR ANYONE ELSE CAN CHANGE THEM OR TAKE THEM AWAY (STALKER BOY) that among these, BUT JUST SO WE ARE CLEAR, A COUPLE OF THEM, MEANING THERE ARE MORE, are life—YOU CAN'T KILL ME—YEAH, THINGS ARE PRETTY BAD WHEN YOU HAVE TO REMIND YOUR "OTHER" THAT YOU "CAN'T KILL ME" liberty ALSO, YOU CAN'T KIDNAP ME AND JUST PUT ME IN A CELL OR IN YOUR CREEPY BASEMENT, and the pursuit of happiness. OH AND ONE LAST ONE: I WOULD SAY I HAVE A RIGHT TO HAVE MY OWN STUFF AND KEEP IT, BUT YOU ARE CURRENTLY CLAIMING THAT SOME OF MY STUFF BELONGS TO YOU . . . A FEW OF MY SKIRTS, WEIRDO, SO TO ENSURE THAT NO WORD GAMES ARE PLAYED WITH THIS, I AM GOING TO CALL IT MY PURSUIT OF HAPPINESS. That to secure these rights, governments are instituted among men, JUST SO YOU KNOW, BECAUSE I REMEMBER HOW YOU TREATED ME, I GOT A FEW OF MY FRIENDS TOGETHER AND PUT A POSSE IN PLACE JUST IN CASE THE NEXT GUY TURNS OUT TO BE A DIRTBAG TOO deriving their just powers THAT ARE GOING TO DO ONLY RIGH-

TEOUS STUFF THAT I DON'T HAVE TIME TO DO, from the consent of the governed. BECAUSE I ASKED THEM. BUT YOU SHOULD KNOW, THAT I EVEN TOLD THEM, THAT WHILE THEY ARE THERE TO PROTECT US FROM YOU KILLIN' US OR KIDNAP-PING US OR STEALING MY STUFF That whenever any form of government becomes destructive to these ends, IF THEY EVER GET OUT OF CONTROL it is the right of the people to alter or to abolish it, WE ARE GOING TO FIRE THEM OR KICK THEIR BUTTS and to institute new government, AND SET OUT A NEW POSSE laying its foundation on such principles and organizing its powers in such form, BUT I AM SURE IF WE GET TO THAT POINT, WE'RE GOING TO LEARN A BUNCH OF STUFF THAT I CAN'T THINK OF RIGHT NOW TO MAKE IT BETTER as to them shall seem most likely to effect their safety and happiness. TO MAKE SURE THE NEXT TIME I AM SAFE FROM YOU OR ANYONE ELSE WHO WANTS TO TIE ME TO THE PIPES IN THE BASEMENT. NOW, Prudence, indeed, will dictate that governments long established should not be changed for light and transient causes; I DIDN'T JUST THINK THIS UP. I MEAN, WE HAVE BEEN TOGETHER FOR, LIKE, A LONG TIME, SO I HAVE SPENT A LOT OF TIME THINKING ABOUT IT, and accordingly all experience hath shewn that mankind are more disposed to suffer, while evils are sufferable, than to right themselves by abolishing the forms to which they are accustomed. AND I KNOW THAT I HAVE BEEN BITCHING ABOUT THIS STUFF FOR A LONG TIME, BUT LEAVING YOU MEANT I HAD TO FIND A NEW PLACE AND GET A BETTER JOB TO BE ABLE TO AFFORD MY STUFF, AND, FRANKLY, I AM JUST LAZY AT TIMES. I MEAN, IT STINKS RIGHT NOW, BUT, FOR A LONG

TIME, I JUST KEPT THINKING, IT WILL GET BET-
TER OR I'LL BREAK UP TOMORROW. But when a long
train of abuses and usurpations, BUT WHEN YOU WERE
CHEATING ON ME, WHILE I WAS HOME IN THE
OTHER ROOM AND IT WAS WITH MY MOTHER, I
COULDN'T TAKE IT ANOTHER DAY! pursuing invari-
ably the same object evinces a design to reduce them under ab-
solute despotism, I THINK I JUST HAD AN ANEURYSM,
I HAVE NO IDEA WHAT THAT LAST PART MEANT
OTHER THAN YOU ARE BECOMING, LIKE, A LIT-
TLE HITLER AROUND THE HOUSE, AND I HAVE
HAD ENOUGH! SO, I AM BREAKING UP WITH YOU
BECAUSE I CAN, it is their right, BUT MY FATHER
TOLD ME THAT IF I DIDN'T, HE WAS GOING TO
SHOW UP WITH A SHOTGUN—FOR ME, BECAUSE
it is their duty, to throw off such government, IF I WANT
ANY SELF-RESPECT, I HAVE TO BREAK UP WITH
YOU BECAUSE YOU HAVE DONE A TON OF BAD
STUFF TO ME and to provide new guards for their future
security.—AND, IN ADDITION, TO FIND SOMEONE
WHO HAS A JOB AND WILL MARRY ME—YOU BUM.

The Declaration is the world's greatest breakup letter. And like
all good breakup letters, it follows a pattern:

1. It's not you . . . it's me. Look, I've changed, and I have asked you to
come along, but you didn't, and in fact you made it worse. So let me
show you one more time what I have figured out, as it is who I am
and where I am going.

2. Okay, I know I said it wasn't you, but really it kinda is, because
we've talked about all these things because I am a decent person, and
it appears that every time we talk, you make it worse, which tells me
that while I am trying to be cool, you kinda suck.

This one "letter" gives the reader a ton of information on not just who we are, what we believe, and why we need to be separate but equal away from the king but also how we are going to organize our life and set up a system of guardrails that will ensure we don't get into another bad relationship—or, if we do, how we are going to handle it. If this was all it was, it would stand alone as a remarkable document. But it is also aspirational and inspirational. We need to read these words with the eyes of someone who lived in the eighteenth century. These words are literally revolutionary. This is way beyond "We are oppressed and need to break away"; this is bold, brave, and politically and philosophically way ahead of its time. This is akin to a resignation letter to an abacus and pen-and-ink company in the 1800s from Bill Gates outlining an entirely new concept of hardware (the computer) and software (Word).

This had to be laughable to the arrogant powers in England. But it is the blueprint for success. It begins with a hopeful statement of what they believed; it then shows the steps they took and that others later might take under this document, saying it was our right AND OUR DUTY to shake off the chains of tyranny.

I have heard so many people say that we just need to "burn it all down." This document shows the weight of such action, but, more important, it points to the path of success. On thoughtful examination one notices that there is no period after the words: "duty, to throw off such government (.)" It instead uses a conjunction "AND provide new guards for their future security." This is where revolutions usually fail before they even begin. I have yet to hear a plan from anyone for what we could replace this system with that would provide better security for the rights of all mankind. What we do hear is the cry of injustice, or anger. We hear the promises of redistribution, social justice, and free universal this or that. What I have not heard is how we better secure the rights that are being trampled and lost.

It is our DUTY to not take this lightly. Should America fail, who will protect the rights of man? Who is having this conversation?

With so much at stake the world over, our flippancy toward the collapse or demise of Western civilization is grotesque. In this fast-food culture, or, worse yet, a culture that actually now gets mad if there is any download or buffering time while watching Netflix on a wireless connection at 40,000 feet and moving at seven hundred miles per hour. Do we really have the stamina to even reset a system that has gone wrong over three or four generations? I am beginning to doubt that we have the patience to take the time to understand the real problems, let alone find the solutions and a plan to put us back on track.

Because I know that each American generation since this document was drafted has been entrusted with the security of the rights of all mankind and that those rights belong to God alone, I fear the day of judgment for each of us who were to stand watch at this time. How will we even begin to explain to our children or grandchildren how we said nothing as we sold them bound and gagged, long before they were born, because we wanted free universities, while we all knew those same universities were turning out citizens who couldn't read or do basic math but instead assembled themselves in mobs to silence anyone who didn't agree with the latest number of genders?

There is no such thing as "social justice," justice for a "collective." But on an eternal time scale, there will be individual justice. We should all fear the verdict, as we know the Judge has clearly stated, "To whom much is given, much is required." We have been given more than any people ever on the face of the earth, and yet we fail to do the minimum of self-education or simply actually caring about the outcome.

Honesty, reason, logic, and truth must return, as they did during the "modern era" of the Enlightenment. But there is one other thing that I believe we all must do as we enter into this "brave new world," and sadly I mean that literally. We must grow thicker skin. It isn't enough just to do our homework, think critically, and accept the responsibility of truth; we must also begin to treat others more kindly and give others the benefit of doubt, even if we don't think they deserve it. We must at least try to not give offense. On the other side of the coin, we must also "grow a set." We cannot continue down this road of offense. We see a story and are outraged, so we feel justified in saying something that we know, especially if we stop to think, others will find outrageous. We become victim and villain in one tweet.

11

Fascism—the Logical Consequence of Postmodernism

A postmodernist believes that there is no objective natural reality, and that logic and reason are mere conceptual constructs that are not universally valid. Two other characteristic postmodern practices are a denial that human nature exists and a (sometimes moderate) skepticism toward claims that science and technology will change society for the better. Postmodernists also believe there are no objective moral values. Thus, postmodern philosophy suggests equality for all things. One's concept of good and another's concept of evil are to be equally correct, since good and evil are subjective.

Postmodern philosophy—Characteristic claims, from en.wikipedia.org

We are now approaching a time when what our Founders called self-evident truth is no longer self-evident, and worse yet, we no longer even believe in truth. At the same time we have lost our self-restraint.

Most people have never read the words of wisdom from men like Ben Franklin, who, when asked for his vote on the Constitution, "confessed" that he wasn't entirely for it, but in the end, "I do agree with this Constitution, faults and all, because I believe General Government is necessary and there is no form of government but what may be a Blessing to the People if well administered, and this is likely to be well administered for the Course of a few Years and will end in despotism as other forms have done before when the people become so corrupted as to need despotic government, being incapable of any other." Has Franklin's "course of a few years" come to an end? Have we indeed become so corrupted?

"This system is wholly inadequate for an unethical, immoral, and irreligious people." To have freedoms, we must also self-govern and set internal limitations, not because a government, a group, or even a person told us to but because we are men and not animals. The fact that we can say something doesn't mean we should. The fact that we can fire someone doesn't mean we should. Perhaps if ABC's god wasn't money, fame, or ratings, it wouldn't have ignored Rose-anne's character and track record and wouldn't have hired her in the first place. For a network that prides itself on "virtue" and political correctness, their god must be powerful indeed. The problem with self-governance is that without "Nature's Laws and Nature's God," there is no "truth." So, to many, laws become mere suggestions imposed by a "patriarchal hierarchy." So, if you have no "governor" in a society that doesn't reward or even value character, who is going to stop you? We can see the answer right in front of us. If there is no "magic man in the sky," then Big Brother will watch you and correct you. He must, because you as a citizen no longer feel as though you have a duty to anything other than not getting caught. Ever received a speeding ticket in the mail? That is now man punishing you for doing something that before only God saw you do.

Someone will always be in charge. Entrepreneurs learn this quickly. "I want to be my own boss." Well, maybe, but unless you are independently wealthy, you will always have a boss—shareholders, the bank, customers, or even your car payments.

Meanwhile, while we are trapped in our addiction to outrage watching the sideshow, under the same circus tent, something much more serious is happening in the main ring. Someone is taking charge, and when they get out of school, they are going to be bringing this into the real world. Into our workplaces and our halls of government and justice. If the old rules no longer apply and there is no objective truth, you'd better pray you are in the right gang or mob. Because someone is always willing to play God and issue new rights and revoke the old ones.

What has been happening at Evergreen State College in Olympia, Washington, should have led the news for months, but instead it was quietly tolerated, perhaps in hope that it would just go away. I grew up in Washington; it is a place I thought I understood, but I remember my grandfather complaining bitterly after an increase in our population in the mid-seventies, "The people who are just too weird for California are moving up here." Well, it isn't weird that bothers me; I can happily live next door and even enjoy "weird." What is happening is fascist.

Every American, left and right, should be shocked by what was done to Bret Weinstein.

Evergreen State College is a very progressive liberal arts school. It has a unique curriculum in which students work closely with faculty teams to choose "from more than sixty fields of study to create [their] own area of emphasis."

It was the perfect place for Bret Weinstein, a self-described "deeply progressive" biology professor who supported Bernie Sanders, Glenn Greenwald, and the Occupy Wall Street movement. For years Weinstein was one of the more popular instructors; at registration his classes were quickly filled, and "Greeners" wrote glowing reports about him. But that began changing in 2015, when a new president was hired and began making significant changes. "The president took aim at what made Evergreen unique," Weinstein and his wife, biology instructor Heather Heying, wrote. In addition to tightening the budget while increasing the size of the administration, "He went after Evergreen's unparalleled faculty autonomy, which was essential to the unique teaching done by the best professors."

One result was that student protests began occurring more frequently. Students interrupted the fall 2016 convocation; they shut down the swearing-in of the new head of campus security, and even demonstrated at the dedication of a campus building to the previous Evergreen president. As Weinstein explains, the whole collegial atmosphere on the campus changed; an "Equity Council" produced a thirty-eight-page strategic plan stressing "diversity and equity" as the criteria for new faculty members.

Weinstein objected publicly, claiming that the plan would hurt minority students. In response, he was attacked online. In this new environment, he wrote, "What was happening . . . amounted to a campaign of intimidation. Dissent was impossible."

The breaking point came in April 2017. Beginning in the 1970s, Evergreen has held an annual "Day of Absence" on which students and faculty of color stay off the campus to demonstrate their contributions to the college. That was followed by a "Day of Presence," with events and workshops fostering discussion. But in 2017, organizers decided to make a fundamental change: As the school newspaper reported, "White students, staff, and faculty will be invited to leave campus for the day's activities."

Weinstein objected in an email to the school's faculty and staff, writing, "There is a huge difference between a group or coalition deciding to voluntarily absent themselves from a shared space in order to highlight their vital and underappreciated roles, and a group or coalition encouraging another group to go away."

It was a reasonable challenge to a change in policy, an invitation to discuss and debate it. Instead, he was attacked by staff and students, who accused him of being a racist who supported "white supremacy." The world was turning upside down.

Several weeks later his class was interrupted by fifty shouting protesters, who yelled at him and prevented school police from entering the building. That same afternoon Professor Weinstein joined hundreds of people at a forum. But rather than any discussion, he and the few students who tried to defend him were shouted down by mobs of students who called him a racist, sexist, and worse.

The next day a faculty meeting was interrupted by yet another mob of angry students, and the library was blockaded. A small group of radicals had essentially taken over the campus, holding faculty members hostage, not allowed to speak but forced to sit and listen as they were screamed at and chanted at by crowds of angry students. One faculty member sympathetic to the protesters warned her colleagues, "You are now those motherfuckers that we're pushing against." When the college president attempted to reason with the students, he was told to stop waving his hands in an aggressive manner and was allowed to use the restroom only with an escort. For several hours, Professor Weinstein and numerous other faculty members were effectively held hostage and forced to sit through a grotesque mock trial reminiscent of 1600s Salem, where people were not allowed to speak in their own defense. After several hours, they were "released" by the students, after having been verbally branded as if they were Donald Trump appearing in effigy on *The View*.

At that point, Weinstein was warned by the police that they could not guarantee his safety on campus. They suggested he stop riding his bike because it made him a highly visible target. He was forced to hold his biology class outdoors, in a park. The names and photographs of his students were posted online. Graffiti demanding "Fire Bret" was painted on campus buildings. The Weinsteins and Bret's class appealed to the governor for help, explaining that the campus "had descended into a state of anarchy." There was no response.

Weinstein accepted an invitation to appear on Fox, an act that might have been unthinkable to him months earlier. That caused the situation to become even more toxic. Several faculty members called for disciplinary action to be taken against him, essentially for exercising his right of free speech. But he also received more than a thousand responses from viewers, which were overwhelmingly supportive.

His continued presence on campus became untenable. A liberal professor at a liberal college was losing his job because he had dared to challenge the "establishment"—that is, if you consider the "establishment" to be outraged politically correct students threatening physical violence, unrestrained by any legal authorities. The college was shut down for three days in June, and graduation ceremonies were moved to a stadium in Tacoma. His career ruined, Weinstein sued Evergreen for $3.85 million, claiming the college had failed to protect him. He eventually settled for $500,000, and both he and his wife resigned.

"We come from the left, and our values and world view have not changed," they wrote, adding, "A democratic system needs intelligent dissent, which means that it must create and protect the conditions in which people can learn how to think critically, and how to critique ideas and proposals. Those are long-standing values on the left, but today, they are hanging by a thread."

This is where we are.

I believe those "values" Bret describes are the same values I hold dear. They are those values or rights enshrined in and protected by the Bill of Rights.

The contradictions of a postmodern world are dizzying. They are confusing and at times even funny to track. But that is only because we are only halfway to the postmodern finish line. The next steps take us to Evergreen and beyond.

We are told to be tolerant and accepting of those things, lifestyles, or even ideas that make us very uncomfortable or go against everything we feel is right or moral. But then those same people not only destroy those who will not comply, they destroy even those who have always complied but now have a slight difference. How do you take RuPaul, someone who took all of the slings and arrows for the transgender movement, and destroy her when she doesn't use the exact language you currently insist on? The formerly most tolerant have become the least.

Each time, I hope that these "firings"—a gross overreach—will wake us, but with the technology that is coming our way and the direction the entire world is heading, during the week that put Roseanne Barr, Samantha Bee, and Joy Reid on social media trial, I could, sadly, not help but think: First they came for Glenn Beck, but he was just some crazy guy on TV, so I didn't say anything.

Then they came for Bill O'Reilly, but I heard he was a bad guy, so I kept quiet.

Then they turned on Bret Weinstein and his wife, because they wouldn't fall in line, but I don't believe in the theory of evolution, so I looked the other way.

When Hillary went from saint to villain who had to be destroyed, seemingly overnight, just because she lost the election, she wasn't my candidate, so I just didn't care.

Then they came after Roseanne, who had been an outspoken Marxist and dedicated progressive her whole life, but I heard her show was pro-Trump, so I cheered when she was dragged away.

Next it was Samantha Bee, but I really didn't watch her show anymore, so I barely noticed.

That same week it was Joy Reid, for saying things in 2004, many of which were the same things that Obama, Hillary, and all the Democrats said in 2004, and hey, I also might have said them back then, and I don't want to bring that up because now "I am woke," so I looked the other way. . . .

We all know how this ends. The question is, how many more will be silenced? Most will say that Joy Reid doesn't really even belong on this list. But to me she is the canary in the coal mine for the average citizen. When will there be another virtue upgraded or redefined? Each of us now has a very long record of what we believe online. The words we used and the positions we took. All saved, all archived and kept in a central database in an NSA facility in Salt Lake City.

When newspeak decides that you were or are now politically incorrect and need to be isolated, blackballed, or removed, who will speak for you?

Perhaps now we can begin to see the truth of political correctness. It isn't now nor has it ever been about the handicapped or people's feelings. It is all about power. How foolish we will appear to later generations, when they see the term itself: POLITICALLY CORRECT. As the Weinsteins are seeing today, if you are not saying the correct things to those who hold the real political power, be they the government or just the mob, you will be destroyed. Unless you are one of the "lucky ones" who can be of value yet to the movement. Perhaps you will be given the chance to recant and announce to the world how joyful you are to see the light and the error of your former ways.

In 2010 I read a story in the *Wall Street Journal* about Google and its impact on our individual futures. It seemed almost like fiction then, but I believe I am just beginning to see how our words, thoughts, and images from the past can dramatically affect our lives and freedom.

I don't believe society understands what happens when everything is available, knowable, and recorded by everyone all the time. Every young person will one day be allowed to change their name to distance themselves from embarrassing photographs and material stored on their friends' social media sites. (Google CEO Eric Schmitt)

How did this happen?

12

Link by Link

Life is simple; it's the people who are complex.

—Someone on the internet, or me—
I can't remember the difference anymore

When I was drinking, I was so preoccupied getting through every day that I didn't waste time thinking about the future. When I did think about it, it was pretty scary. I doubted anybody would hire me if they found out I was an alcoholic. I was afraid that if I stopped drinking, my life on radio would be over, and I didn't have any idea what I would do. I was getting hammered every day, but somehow I managed to maintain an image of Mr. Goody Two-Shoes, clean and pristine. One day, though, when I was at KC101 in New Haven, a caller told me that I didn't know what it meant to struggle. "Really," I said, a little annoyed, and then to my surprise I heard these words coming out of my mouth: "You don't have any idea who I am. Let me tell you . . ." Everyone in the studio just stopped what they were doing. They had no idea what I was going to say. "I'm a raging alcoholic," I continued. "I've made mistakes, like you, that are awful and embarrassing. I've done some despicable things. And I make myself feel better by drinking." When I was done I shut off my mic, turned to my producer, and told him, "Write this down: This is the day Glenn Beck ended his career."

I finally was able to stop drinking when the consequences of continuing became greater than my fears of the unknown. In AA, an important step is believing that a power greater than ourselves could restore us to sanity. That doesn't apply here in quite the same way. In this case, that power greater than ourselves is the bedrock constitutional principles that our leaders have relied on to steer this country for the last 250 years. It's pretty amazing; if Ben Franklin popped up one day, he wouldn't recognize the physical country, but he certainly would be thrilled to learn that we have somehow managed to adhere to those basic values that he helped create. Principles that should continue to guide us as surely as that star in the Bethlehem night guided the wise men.

That's what worries me about the future. I think we agree that we are addicted to outrage, and that it has become an important part of our life. And just as with any other addiction, we derive pleasure from it. So the obvious question is, why do we need to break that addiction? And what might happen if we don't?

Apathy and arrogance: These are the real culprits that affect us all to one degree or another. Even the students at Evergreen. The arrogance is easy to see, but with all of us, apathy can quickly turn into self-imposed ignorance.

Ironically, as technology, transportation, and mass communications began offering Americans ways to be closer together, instead we grew further apart. At the same time the small farming communities began to die out. Today the average age of a farmer on a family-run farm is nearly sixty. But that hardly matters, since less than 10 percent of the food products grown in America come from family farms anyway, instead being grown on massive automated farms owned by corporate giants. As a result, we're not connected to the real stuff of life that comes from being connected, day to day, with the land, plants, and animals that sustain our lives.

13

Urban Proximity, a False Togetherness

Maybe all of this was inevitable, from the moment the ox was replaced by a diesel tractor.

The real circle of life doesn't happen in Disney movies, it happens on a farm. You didn't need sex ed or birds-and-bees speeches, because you saw your bull try to get lucky all day long. Death, life, the meaning of the earth, and how everything is used with no waste. You understand compassion, having to kill an animal that is in pain, or finding and rescuing the one lost lamb as I and my kids did a couple of summers ago. We chased and chased, on foot, on horseback, and by ATV. We are, after all, "city slickers." We must have looked like idiots. When we caught her and put her in the pen, the kids had a new understanding of a father's love and how sometimes you have to do things that the "kid" doesn't want to do or thinks are bad, but it is only because they don't understand or see the bigger picture. There is just something real about the people in a farming town. When something happens, they deal with it and move on. While we are missing that in the cities, our farming neighbors in Idaho remind us what real people are like.

Recently we were driving along near the ranch, and up ahead of us a woman hit a deer with her car. We stopped to see if we could help. She was in her thirties, wearing a dress, and got out to check on the animal and the damage to her vehicle. "Poor little thing," she said, and retrieved a rifle from her trunk to put the deer out of its misery.

Then she promptly phoned her husband to come get the carcass, stating simply, "No reason to waste good meat."

Our community is very nice. They don't judge or laugh at us, that we know of. I am sure they have had plenty of laughs at our "NYC" ranch ways, but to be fair, I would do the same; and in fact, no one can wreck our family more than our own family. We are hysterical, especially when we don't think we are. They may laugh, but they amaze us.

We have a caretaker who works on our ranch. One day while he was putting the biggest bolt I have ever seen through three huge logs that are at the front gate, the bolt snapped and split his head open. While I would have called for some sort of air rescue, he just said "Crap." When I saw him still working on the gate as I returned home late in the afternoon, I couldn't help but notice the giant, bloody bandage. As he told me the story that resulted in thirty stitches, I told him to go home and rest. He said, "Naw, I have too much to do." I asked him what the doctor had told him. He said, "Well, driving to town and back was going to take way too much time and I still had numerous chores to get done before dark, so I just drove down to the vet and had him stitch it up instead." Some other neighbors were out deer hunting—rifles, orange vests, the whole bit. While walking through a field they came upon a deer that had gotten tangled up and stuck in some barbed wire and mud from a downed fence. As they approached, the deer thrashed about wildly trying to escape, but was trapped. The three men put down their rifles, got out some pliers, and began to try to cut the animal loose. The deer kicked and bit at them as they worked, trying to hold the animal still and cut the wires loose. By the time they freed the animal, they were all covered in bruises, cuts, and scrapes. As the deer bounded away, it turned back to them and snorted, then disappeared into the brush, leaving the men cold and bloody behind them. One neighbor smiled at me and said, "Guess we had that coming."

When we first built the house in the mountains, we wanted it to feel like my grandfather's old home. All of the furniture was secondhand except for a few pieces. One of them was a black bearskin rug. When a few of the guys from town were up, one of them said, "Wow, nice bear." Well, me still living full-time in NYC and not fully prepared for this conversation, I said, "You know, I am not really sure, but I think our designer got it at a place called Good Old Things in Manhattan." The entire room stopped, and one of the other guys said, perplexed: "You bought it . . . at a store?" They have yet to return my man card.

We love our little town. It reminds me of all of the people I grew up with who would do anything for you at any time, day or night. There is a section of town lovingly called "Snob Hill." The houses are smaller, much smaller than anything for blocks in every direction in my neighborhood in Dallas. Don't get me wrong—we love our house in Dallas. Yet we now pine for the twelve hundred square feet of our home in the mountains. Simple, quiet. There's this old 1968 Admiral TV in the living room where the kids lie on the floor, like I used to do when I was a kid. I found myself saying "Kids, back up from the TV." I threw in the cancer thing, too, even though I know that is a huge lie—I think.

You even begin to appreciate—some—bugs. Allergies and honey. You even understand the why and miracle of natural forest fires. How even the burning down of a forest in the natural world, from lightning strikes and so on, actually is good for the soil and forest in the long run. And little things like the saying "When the cows come home." Actually, it isn't that long. It's about eight to ten hours at my ranch. Now my kids look at me when I say I could do this until the cows come home and respond, "So, really, not that long, huh, Dad?"

The city is great, but we all should spend some time in my little farming town. Or some little farming town. It is where my kids and I have learned a ton about life.

The one thing I have learned by spending our time in a very small community in Idaho, where I raise cattle and grow alfalfa and wheat, is how easy it is to remain grounded. Think about that word. People say "They're very grounded," meaning someone is stable, consistent, rational. You're connected to the very stuff of life (and death) on a farm or a ranch. You're connected to your community, to neighbors, to nature in a visceral, immediate way. It's also massively humbling. Mistakes are easy to make and consequential, often resulting in bloody cuts, bruises, or work that must be repeated from the beginning.

Mucking out a stable stinks; manure is heavy and cumbersome to work with. But results are immediate, and the sense of achievement is somehow extremely rewarding. Growing a field of hay takes patient, consistent work over long periods of time. It is stressful. You pray for rain and that the frost won't kill young shoots. But feeding hay you've grown to your own cows and horses is beyond joyous and rewarding. I could do without the yearly pregnancy check where someone who has only one sleeve on his shirts has to spend the afternoon with his arm up the cow's rear end while I have to buy them drinks.

Jefferson, when helping to design the justice system, was adamant that the jury box must not be filled with eggheads but rather with average people and farmers. I get it now. All of nature's laws are explained and taught to your children through the circle of life witnessed daily on every farm. But what is more, farmers still have to rely on God. They are connected, as a matter of life and death, to nature. They can be the best, smartest farmer in the world, but should the rain not come, or should too much rain come, their crops are destroyed. They also are more willing to help their neighbors when their crops fail, as they know it is only a matter of time before they are in the same condition. It is almost a community with a natural understanding of unspoken community insurance.

Part of the reason we have the Electoral College is to protect farmers and ranchers. It was designed to help ensure the populous cities and towns wouldn't end up as a ruling elite class over the rural peasants. But it's important, because our connection to the earth is vital. What is more humbling online than being publicly shamed? In a city, eating at restaurants and zipping around on electric scooters we don't even own, we can become so disconnected from the reality of human existence on this earth, how fragile it is. The farther we are from the hard work of survival, understanding where our food comes from, understanding the cost in blood, sweat, and tears of raising, caring for, and slaughtering an animal to nourish your family and neighbors, the more likely we are to take it all for granted.

Spending time working side by side with my son, driving new posts into the ground for the fence line, never would seem like something fun—and, believe me, it is not fun-type fun—but the things like that, I think even at thirteen he would say have provided us with the best father-son time and lots of laughs.

A major motivating factor for Jefferson in deciding to make the Louisiana Purchase was his vision that Americans needed to be connected to the land. He dreamed of a connected, community-oriented agrarian society of farmers and ranchers, growing food and raising livestock, tilling the soil. Deeply connected to the process of life-affirming work, never losing sight of the value of hard work and the reality of the laws of physics, biology, chemistry, and geology that it takes to keep a person and a nation alive.

Ever wonder why postmodernism isn't very popular in "flyover" country, or why humanities professors at Berkeley don't drive pickup trucks? The professor probably doesn't have much use for a truck . . . and postmodernism ain't much use in the real world.

As we moved out of the communities where our families used to live, we grew farther apart not only as families but also as a people. We began to find like minds. Literally. In his book *Coming Apart*, Charles Murray points out that in 1960, just 3 percent of American couples both had a college degree. By 2010, that proportion stood at 25 percent. The change was so large that it was a major contributor to the creation of a new class all by itself. College brings people together at the time of life when young adults are beginning to look around for marriage partners, and the college sorting machine brings the highest-IQ young women and men together at the most prestigious schools. As if that weren't enough, graduate school adds another layer of sorting. If you put people with greater educational and cognitive similarity together, you have the makings of greater cultural similarity as well. When one spouse is a college graduate in the top percentiles of cognitive ability and the other is a high school graduate with modestly above-average cognitive ability, they are likely to have different preferences in books and movies, different ways of spending their free time, different friends, and differences in a dozen other aspects of life. In 1960 there was a measure of cultural dispersion built into marriages.

This has real effects and ominous implications, as these couples, now in the broad elite, begin to pass on their natural-born intellectual capabilities, coupled with the additional educational opportunities these elites demand and need for their children. The pool gets smaller and smaller and farther apart for those who live in the small farming communities or those who do not work with those in the upper-middle class. It is a new kind of segregation, which has nothing to do with race. We are already beginning to see the ill effects of this. If your children go to college, Woodrow Wilson's dream of the university goal of "making a man most unlike his father" has indeed become a reality. It you are religious, you have a 60 percent chance of leaving the university no longer believing in God. A 40 percent chance even if you attend a religious university.

14

Into the Arms of the Arrogant and Ignorant

This country really began changing, as I have already pointed out, in the early progressive years between 1880 and 1920, when we found out what the other guys were doing and decided to try to stop them— or as the early progressives would say, "help them"—either by war, subversion, or sterilization. It started changing when people decided their values were the only right values, then tried to make other people live by them. Internally and externally. We do not have a domestic and a foreign problem. We really have only one: arrogance. Thinking we know best and forcing others, be they our neighbors here or those on the other side of the globe, to believe as we do.

As I said in an earlier chapter, our government and our universities changed dramatically around 1900. But there was something perhaps even more toxic that happened as well: We became arrogant. I personally saw the change from humble nation to superpower on a trip to the Met in NYC. I had brought my children to teach them a bit of history and the history of art, when we came across the space where *Washington Crossing the Delaware* usually hung. I asked one of the guards if they had moved it elsewhere. He told me that it had been crated and was in the museum's warehouse. "After all, it isn't the original," he casually stated. "Pardon me?" "Yes," he began, eager to teach, "the original was destroyed in the Allied bombing of Germany in 1942."

"Wait. What?" My ignorance and arrogance were on full display.

"Why was 'our' most famous painting of Washington in Germany during the reign of Adolf Hitler?"

As it turns out, Emanuel Leutze had painted the work in Berlin during the revolutions of 1848, which had begun after the printing of the *Communist Manifesto* on February 21 of that same year. It was meant to inspire liberal Europeans with the example of the American revolutionary hero. He'd painted two full-sized replicas after a fire damaged the original in the 1850s, one of which was the one I'd visited so many times at the Met. The other hung on a wall in the West Wing of the White House for more than 150 years—that is, until 2015, when the Obamas loaned it to a museum in Minnesota.

The message comes from the people in the boat. The man in a Scottish bonnet and a man of African descent facing backward next to each other in the front, Western riflemen at the bow and stern, two farmers in broad-brimmed hats near the back (one with a bandaged head), and a rower in a red shirt, possibly meant to be a woman in man's clothing. There is also a man at the back of the boat wearing what appears to be Native American garb to represent the idea that all people in the new United States of America were represented as present in the boat along with Washington on his way to victory and success.

This was the message Leutze was trying to get his fellow Germans and other Europeans to see. If you have something strong enough to unite them, people from all walks of life can come together by choice, and miraculous things can happen.

After that experience I began to formulate a theory that the painting wasn't the only major icon whose real message I had missed.

I had always known that in the old-timey days we respected the French, and they liked us. But, really, who gives a giant three-hundred-foot statue as a present? Why would the French spend so much time, money, and effort on such an elaborate gift as the Statue of Liberty?

First of all, you've got to be pretty arrogant about your taste. I mean, what if at the time we were diggin' midcentury design? I would be questioning myself all the way to my friend's front door. "Maybe it's too big." "What if they already have a three-hundred-foot lady light?" You'd better hope they like it. Because if they don't, it isn't something that they can hide and take out when someone from France comes to visit.

"So, where did you end up putting the statue we got you?" Crap.

In my house I would be panicked. "Honey, the French are coming, they'll be here in ten minutes! I can't find that stupid statue they gave us for our anniversary anywhere."

However, I should have known it wasn't really about us once I found out they just dumped it off in a New York park like a box of unwanted hot dogs, where it lay in pieces for six years until we could raise the money and find the right man to figure out the directions, put it together, and build the base. Imagine how many extra screws and bolts were left over. And the instructions were all in French. Gee, thanks. Next year for Christmas, why not get the kids the loudest, most annoying toy on the market?

Make no mistake—just like the Delaware painting, that statue was not built for us.

In 1865, Edouard de Laboulaye, a French political intellectual and authority on the U.S. Constitution, proposed that France give a statue representing liberty to the United States for its centennial. The recent Union victory in the American Civil War reaffirmed the United States' ideals of freedom and democracy, serving as a platform for Laboulaye to argue that honoring the United States would strengthen the cause for democracy in France. In our "newfound arrogance" we have come to believe it was about us, when indeed it was actually all about the arrogant French.

You see, revolution was once again on the march. With the last revolution ending with so much bloodshed and eventually Napoleon, they needed to figure out a way to show the French that Marxism, which was beginning a second sweep across the nations of Europe, was a bad idea. They felt that if they could raise money for a giant birthday gift to their buddy America, they could also make the pitch that America was on the right track in finding real freedom.

Once the statue arrived, to raise money to assemble the world's largest IKEA project, Emma Lazarus wrote the poem that now graces the bottom of the base:

> *Not like the brazen giant of Greek fame,*
> *With conquering limbs astride from land to land;*
> *Here at our sea-washed, sunset gates shall stand*
> *A mighty woman with a torch, whose flame*
> *Is the imprisoned lightning, and her name*
> *Mother of Exiles. From her beacon-hand*
> *Glows world-wide welcome; her mild eyes command*
> *The air-bridged harbor that twin cities frame.*
> *"Keep, ancient lands, your storied pomp!" cries she*
> *With silent lips. "Give me your tired, your poor,*
> *Your huddled masses yearning to breathe free,*
> *The wretched refuse of your teeming shore.*
> *Send these, the homeless, tempest-tost to me,*
> *I lift my lamp beside the golden door!"*

This is the ultimate and real challenge of the statue to the world: Keep your guilds (unions) and family names, titles, and all that your governments do to keep those whom you call the "dregs of society" down. Send those who you claim can't make it or add to society to me. I will simply set them free to create what they want to create. I will not get in their way or tell them they can't do it because of this degree, title, license, or position. And if they do make it, they earned it and they get to keep it. What's more, I will protect them, with the Bill of Rights, from people and governments that wish to steal their work or their rewards or meddle in their lives, like you!

You often hear people quote this from the Statue of Liberty, "Give me your tired, your poor, your huddled masses . . ." People often forget this part, though: "yearning to breathe free." As you can see, our humility as a nation has been gone for a while. We now make out that immigrants are all about "their needing our help." Of course, because that is the signal we now send out. But the message isn't about welfare or socialized medicine. It's about freedom.

Are we still those people? I know my neighbors in Idaho are, but closer to the urban centers of America, we are not. Not only do we not mind our own business, we don't mind our own business the world over. That idea was such a part of American society that our first coin even had that engraved on it. It wasn't "In God We Trust." On one side it said "We Are One," and the other said simply "Mind Your Business." I suppose "So we're all in this together, but we're distinct individuals with volition and free will who leave each other alone" didn't fit.

What were those principles that the rest of the world wanted so desperately? Because they certainly didn't want us to tell them how to fight, whom to fight, how to run their banks or businesses, or which church was correct. No, it was the humility of the Bill of Rights. The laws that were "unchangeable," that freed slaves and the oppressed. It is why the statue is holding the tablets, representing the Declaration and the Constitution. Notice that it says JULY 4, 1776. This is important, as it is the birthday of man's independence. Progressives will say that the Declaration is only a breakup letter and has no meaning or impact in today's America. It does, as we discussed earlier; it is literally our founding document and the document that guides the Constitution. Without it, the entire system falls apart, as we will later see.

We can argue over how those principles were lost, but it is our virtues that animate the words and breathe life into our nation that are perhaps even more critical to recognize, as they pertain to the denial that we all seem to be living in. David Bahnsen, in his book *Crisis of Responsibility*, builds on Murray's "Founding Virtues" of industriousness, honesty, marriage, and religion. He makes the point that the revolutionary threats to the American project are real and often concentrated in bicoastal capitals of anti-Western sentiment, but believing that there are external forces (external to the core American nucleus of working-class folks who value God and country) accelerating our cultural and even economic demise is not the same as agreeing that those forces are the primary cause. Indeed, the true story of our "coming apart" is this: Rather than being the result of globalization and other contemporary challenges, the unraveling of virtues within the working class is actually the root cause of our inability to properly respond. Those, I believe, are the virtues that animate and secure our nation, but it is the principles that need to be understood, lived, protected, and reaffirmed every generation to keep that industry and, frankly, religion on track.

We still might have held it together, and we might yet restore it if we still shared a belief in those basic principles. They began disappearing en masse during the Vietnam War. The damage that war did to this country has been severe and lasting, and massively underappreciated. Before that war the Greatest Generation, those people who had been born into the Depression and fought and won World War II, still believed in our traditional institutions. We believed that Americans fought wars only to guarantee liberty for all people; we believed that our government always told us the truth and that we could trust our politicians, as well as popular agencies like the FBI.

We did; we really did believe all that. It was the American myth: that because our government was elected by the people, and the Constitution was there to stop it from abusing its power, it would be benevolent and would serve the people. Boy, was that wrong. We had failed to listen to the two farewell addresses that could still save us—George Washington's and Dwight Eisenhower's. Both outline how to preserve the Republic. One warns of foreign entanglements and political parties, while both call for an enlightened, educated, and engaged citizenry. But to me, a close examination of Eisenhower's farewell address points to not the press but to us. We know the famous part, with most not even knowing why or where it came from, but look at the last part of the text and tell me we haven't failed to hear this clarion call to responsibility:

> Until the latest of our world conflicts, the United States had no armaments industry. American makers of plowshares

could, with time and as required, make swords as well. But now we can no longer risk emergency improvisation of national defense; we have been compelled to create a permanent armaments industry of vast proportions. Added to this, three and a half million men and women are directly engaged in the defense establishment. We annually spend on military security more than the net income of all United States corporations.

This conjunction of an immense military establishment and a large arms industry is new in the American experience. The total influence—economic, political, even spiritual—is felt in every city, every State house, every office of the Federal government. We recognize the imperative need for this development. Yet we must not fail to comprehend its grave implications. Our toil, resources, and livelihood are all involved; so is the very structure of our society.

In the councils of government, we must guard against the acquisition of unwarranted influence, whether sought or unsought, by the military industrial complex. The potential for the disastrous rise of misplaced power exists and will persist.

We must never let the weight of this combination endanger our liberties or democratic processes. We should take nothing for granted. Only an alert and knowledgeable citizenry can compel the proper meshing of the huge industrial and military machinery of defense with our peaceful methods and goals, so that security and liberty may prosper together.

Akin to, and largely responsible for, the sweeping changes in our industrial-military posture has been the technological revolution during recent decades.

In this revolution, research has become central; it also becomes more formalized, complex, and costly. A steadily increasing share is conducted for, by, or at the direction of the Federal government.

Today, the solitary inventor tinkering in his shop has

been overshadowed by task forces of scientists in laboratories and testing fields. In the same fashion, the free university, historically the fountainhead of free ideas and scientific discovery, has experienced a revolution in the conduct of research. Partly because of the huge costs involved, a government contract becomes virtually a substitute for intellectual curiosity. For every old blackboard there are now hundreds of new electronic computers.

The prospect of domination of the nation's scholars by Federal employment, project allocations, and the power of money is ever present and is gravely to be regarded. Yet in holding scientific research and discovery in respect, as we should, we must also be alert to the equal and opposite danger that public policy could itself become the captive of a scientific, technological elite.

It is the task of statesmanship to mold, to balance, and to integrate these and other forces, new and old, within the principles of our democratic system—ever aiming toward the supreme goals of our free society.

Another factor in maintaining balance involves the element of time. As we peer into society's future, we—you and I, and our government—must avoid the impulse to live only for today, plundering, for our own ease and convenience, the precious resources of tomorrow. We cannot mortgage the material assets of our grandchildren without risking the loss also of their political and spiritual heritage. We want democracy to survive for all generations to come, not to become the insolvent phantom of tomorrow.

Oopsie. I guess we missed that one, huh? Remember, this warning was given by what the left would now call "a man of war." Where are those leaders who are willing to hurt "their own" for the liberty of all?

The reality that our government was capable of lying to us, that we weren't always the good guys, that a lot of young Americans were being sent to die for political necessity, that sometimes the government even spied on us, and that elected politicians could be corrupt destroyed that myth. Our government was no longer the embodiment of our values and principles but had become something foreign to and at odds with the people. Progressives had used the government to try to create a super-race of white Americans with programs of forced sterilization, abortion, and antimarriage laws. They had killed tens of thousands of Americans during the Prohibition era by poisoning barrels of whiskey sold to speakeasies around the nation. The *Pentagon Papers* proved that our leaders, from Kennedy to Nixon, were all well aware the Vietnam War couldn't possibly be won but kept it going to satisfy the political elite and send a message to the communists. The FBI regularly spied on and blackmailed social leaders like Martin Luther King Jr.

People lost their faith in government, and there was nothing to replace it, so young Americans began breaking those long-accepted American boundaries. The result was a kind of managed chaos. The antiwar movement and the civil rights movement were created to the background music of rock and roll. The sexual revolution began with the easy availability of the birth-control pill. The length of a man's hair became a political statement. Students took over the colleges. American kids casually broke the law by smoking pot, while their parents made Valium the first million-dollar drug. Richard Nixon faced impeachment for lying and became the first president to resign for crimes committed in office. When community organizer Saul Alinsky was asked if he believed in using violence to achieve his political objectives, he said no; and when asked why, he pointed out, "They have all the weapons." Young black Americans came back from Vietnam with access to guns and a determination to end racial discrimination, and the cities exploded in rioting.

And it was all televised.

From the assassination of John Kennedy in 1963 to the end of the American presence in Vietnam with the fall of Saigon in 1975,

America had become a different country. With the rise of the Moral Majority, created to defend those traditional values, patriotism had become a political weapon; "My country, right or wrong," became their slogan. People who were against the war weren't just wrong, they were anti-American; they were commies. The definition of free speech was stretched as young Americans burned the American flag and their draft cards to protest our involvement in the Vietnam War. Massive antiwar demonstrations took place in Washington. On the Kent State University campus, scared and frustrated Ohio National Guard troops fired on antiwar protesters, killing four students and wounding nine more.

The social revolution was televised. Kennedy assassin Lee Harvey Oswald was shot and killed on live TV. The riots in Chicago, New York, Detroit, Los Angeles, and all the other cities were broadcast nationally. Filmed footage from Vietnam brought the war into living rooms. For the first time, the whole country was watching history unfold, live and mostly unedited. And Americans were forced to pick a side. The political division of America had begun.

In his 2008 bestseller, *The Big Sort: Why the Clustering of Like-Minded America Is Tearing Us Apart*, journalist Bill Bishop pointed out that more and more Americans were choosing to live with people who shared their political beliefs. In 1976, studies showed, less than a quarter of the country lived in what Bishop called "landslide counties," areas that delivered huge numbers for one presidential candidate, but by 2004 about half of the country lived in counties that voted by large margins for one party or the other. Whether consciously or unconsciously, we had self-segregated into communities of like-minded and like-moraled groups: We had created the first safe zones for ourselves and for our beliefs. And as we gathered in tribes around the campfires, it wasn't enough just to be with people who thought the same way we did; it became necessary to reinforce our beliefs by demonizing the other side. The well-respected Stanford economist Matthew Gentzkow warned, "Polarization is a real and serious phenomenon. Americans may or may not be further apart on the issues than they used to be. But clearly what divides them polit-ically is increasingly personal, and this in many ways may be worse. We don't just disagree politely about what is the best way to reform the health care system, we believe that those on the other side are trying to destroy America, and that we should spare nothing in trying to stop them."

That polarization has reached into every part of our culture—even our faith. Theologian and bestselling author Tim Keller tweeted, "As the country has become more polarized, the church has become more polarized, and that's because the church is not differ-ent enough from America or modernity. There's now a red and blue evangelicalism."

Everything that takes place in our world is filtered through our political belief system. We know for a fact that the other side is al-ways wrong because our side decided what a fact is. Facts, it now appears, are pretty much anything that supports what we already believe, while any information that counters those beliefs is a lie, or so "fake news," or, as it has been famously described, "alternative facts." Rather than watching the traditional news sources, viewers began turning as the source of their information to those networks that most strongly supported their beliefs. "The echo chamber," as it became known, reinforced those things they already believed. As a result, Democrats immediately discounted anything reported by Fox News or the other "conservative" news outlets, while Republicans disregarded the "mainstream media" because they are controlled by liberals. I am not saying some of that isn't well deserved. The media have embraced the polarization, but the real problem is, they refuse to see themselves as part of the problem.

It isn't just that we are getting different opinions and different facts; we are also getting different news. When I met my new friend Riaz Patel, a gay, married, adoptive father of two, Muslim, Pakistani immigrant, Hollywood producer, oh, who is also liberal, our eyes were opened to yet another problem. He is a well-educated and in-formed man, and yet he did not know many of the news stories that really had bothered the right during the Obama administration. The investigations, threats, and wiretapping of reporters' phone lines, and so on. He was shocked he didn't know these things or had only a simple knowledge with an understanding that it couldn't have been true because he hadn't heard of it. These weren't conspiracies, they were real and important stories. But only one side of the country was exposed. I believe the same can be said under Donald Trump. I have seen big, important stories where he has done some of the same, calling for a press license or a limiting of the press, where it was a very important topic for the health of the republic, but it isn't covered, dismissed as no big deal or simply covered quickly and gone. Both times, the press was not objective. It was "their guy," so either it didn't matter because "I know him and he is only just saying that," or they didn't want to cover it because it would hurt "their fight."

Who are these people? Do we hold anything above politics? It has become our God. Even our most deeply held beliefs are up for sale or excuse. Franklin Graham can, on the one hand, condemn Bill Clinton's sexual misconduct and on the other dismiss gross sexual comments by Donald Trump as locker-room banter. Al Sharpton can casually suggest Donald Trump should be arrested on accusations of sexual assault, but women accusing Bill Clinton of rape are money-seeking hussies. How is it we can excuse it on one side and on the other side condemn it just a few years later? Politics. Our own deeply held basic moral foundation has been rotted away by the love for or defense of politics. I would guess most twentysomethings don't even know who Eisenhower was, let alone what a plowshare is.

This is what Nietzsche warned us about. "God is dead."

Now what?

Politics.

15

The Enemy of My Friend . . . May Not Be My Friend but Should Be My Teacher

Here's an admission: I read the *New York Times*. I know no conservative will ever utter these words: That's the best damn newspaper in the world. It infuriates me at times, I often disagree with their point of view, and many times I think they get it wrong, but I know that, generally speaking, they try to maintain high standards for journalism, and I can generally trust the facts I read in that paper. I think my audience is shocked when I cite something I read in the *Times*. The problem is that conservatives assume, because that paper is on the left, it has no value to them. That it's all fake news. No, it's not. Even if you think it is all fake news. It is the most influential media source in the nation; if you want to understand what half the country is thinking, there is no better place to find it. But the intent matters. I hear people say that they watch or listen to me for opposition research. To me, this is a part of the problem. You are listening to me only as an enemy. We need to come from a more compassionate place if we wish to fix our problems. I read the *Times* and HuffPo because I genuinely want to understand how others think and feel. More important, I desperately want to find the things that connect us on a human level. There are a ton of those things, if we allow ourselves to admit it. Unfortunately, our addictions and our tribes do not encourage those things.

Conversely, those on the left refuse to pay any attention to conservative outlets and broadcasters. "Don't listen to Glenn Beck, because he has nothing to offer. He's one of them. Everything he says is fake." No, it's not. The left may not like my perspective, but there are a lot of things I talk about that might be useful, and I am held to the same standard, if not higher, as the *New York Times*. If I really get it wrong, I get sued. More important, there are many organizations like Media Matters that have made millions of dollars in fundraising to try to put me out of business. This actually gives me an advantage that the *Times* and most on the left do not have. We tend to be much more careful, because we understand that our next mistake may be our last. I can also guarantee that I try to be fair and consistent. It made me hold the line against both Hillary and Trump during the election. To vote for or endorse either candidate would have caused an internal cognitive dissonance that I couldn't have lived with. While many fault me for it, it does allow me to both criticize a politician when he or she is wrong and praise him or her when he or she does the right thing. It is based on fact, not team jerseys.

When the very basis of all knowledge—what is a fact—suddenly becomes a matter of opinion, everything we believe can be questioned. Most people thought the adoption of the scientific method by the Royal Society in the 1660s, which relied on experimentation, repeatability, and measurable results, gave mankind a reliable method of proving hypotheses on which we have relied ever since. It is this very movement and understanding that gave birth to what is known as the Enlightenment, which in turn is responsible for the creation of America.

Now postmodernism is destroying it.

Like Bret Weinstein, who has warned that we are rejecting science when it interferes with what we want to believe. He wasn't taking a shot at either party; he was talking about those on the right who refuse to accept the reality of climate change, as well as those on the left who refuse to acknowledge that the basis of evolution is that there are two genders. His wife, Heather Heying, who also left the university, wrote, "The left has long pointed to deniers of climate change and evolution to demonstrate that over here, science is a core value. But increasingly, that's patently not true."

We must never become the jailers of Galileo, and yet both sides have. I do reject "climate change" as it is often portrayed by extreme environmentalists as a dangerous new development, as climate is always changing and it always has. If not, explain the Ice Age. So, natural climate change is real, and I can read the thermometer just as well as the scientists. I will even agree as "common sense" that man can affect the planet in a negative way. Here is where we differ, and I believe it is totally reasonable. What I think many on the right reject is the proposed solutions to the problems. This to me is the biggest area where the "science" breaks down.

So, I agree the climate is changing, I believe that man can have and even is having an impact. I believe we should all do all we can to reduce and reuse and do our part to pursue and support new technologies that actually will make a scientifically provable significant impact. I also believe that the free market is the best way to make a sizable impact. When solar panels actually reduce the cost of electricity usage and can hold a charge with new batteries about to come online, and they are affordable, people will buy them. But if you look to places that have mandated solar panels, such as Germany, you find that after the hundreds of millions of dollars spent to install solar panels on a broad scale, Germans are left with solar panels that are outdated, inefficient, or do not work at all anymore. The only thing that is still working is the payment system, as they will be paying for them until 2028. I read the stories on the "coming ice age" in the 1970s. Numerous articles from that era, quoting leading scientists, covered the pending climate shift thoroughly. Scientists confirmed then that we were indeed entering into a new ice age and by 2015 much of the world would be covered in glacier ice. They went as far as to propose a plan to ensure that we would survive. Scientists at the time fought hard for dollars to be able to do many things, but one that *Time* magazine outlined was to cover the polar ice caps with black soot, as that would trap the heat and melt the ever-growing and expanding polar ice. Imagine what that could have done if indeed we are entering a time of global warming. So I agree with some of the findings, just not with the spending of trillions of dollars on things that have a good shot of not doing anything other than causing hunger and disease by destroying the economy of the West. Yet as with all things these days, you either accept all of it as it is shouted by the mob, or you are a denier and traitor to the cause.

After having left Evergreen, the Weinsteins spoke to Joe Rogan about evolutionary science and genders. "We are watching the conversation out in civilization about sex and gender devolve into an absurdity. That's kind of frightening." Yes, I would say so! "It's difficult and bewildering to hear the conversation [when], frankly, there's a much better alternative. If one can stand to think in evolutionary terms, if we can really look at ourselves as we are, who we came to be through evolutionary forces, then we can improve the landscape a great deal." In other words, the professor of evolutionary biology is saying, We hold these truths to be self-evident. . . . There is an objective, science-based truth about mankind, about each of us as a member of the species, and it is as plainly obvious as the nose on your face—but if the tribe says otherwise, then fear of being shamed and facing the outrage of the collective drives the rational part of our brain into hiding.

Professor Heying goes on even more bluntly. "So, there are the premoderns, as it were, who have [a] very traditionalist, conservative approach to gender roles, to sex, to relationships. And there are a lot of us in the modern world who would reject a lot of that. And then there are the postmoderns, who want to throw out everything, who want to throw out everything that evolution handed us and pretend that it didn't happen. Pretend that it's not even based on reality. And there's a third way, a modern way, to navigate what evolution has given us."

So who are the science deniers? Don't gloat, because I promise, your side will be if it doesn't serve the political engine blessed by the mob.

Maybe there should be a new category to add to facts, alternative facts, and fake news called Internet facts. That means it is a fact that it appeared on the Internet. It would be defined as anything someone using the Internet claims is true. The fact that we are even debating what a fact is, is absolutely terrifying. As we have seen so many times in history, the first thing a totalitarian regime does is substitute its own propaganda for facts. In 1941 Nazi propaganda minister Joseph Goebbels, in an article entitled "Churchill's Lie Factory," wrote about British prime minister Winston Churchill: "The astonishing thing is that Mr. Churchill, a genuine John Bull, holds to his lies, and in fact repeats them until he himself believes them. That is an old English trick," adding later, "The English follow the principle that when one lies, one should lie big, and stick to it. They keep up their lies, even at the risk of looking ridiculous." He concludes by claiming, with amazing irony, "[Churchill] belongs to those stubborn people who can only be convinced by the facts. Let us bring about those facts." It's actually kind of scary to imagine what someone like Goebbels could have done if he had access to social media. Well, until you look at how other people are using it.

Among those other people is President Trump. As conservative columnist S. E. Cupp wrote, "This has been Trump's most significant contribution to American politics so far. As long as he can make you feel like something is true—illegal immigrants are rapists and drug dealers, for example; who cares if it's actually statistically true? In fact, Trump's neatest trick was in turning things like the truth, facts, statistics, polls, and studies into privileged concerns of the 'establishment' elite."

If we can't even agree on what is true or what is false, there is no way of moving forward as a nation. As French president Emmanuel Macron told a joint session of Congress in April 2018, "Without reason, without proof, there is no real democracy, because democracy is about true choices and rational decisions."

There is no doubt that the creation and popularity of conservative media sharply escalated the already existing battle between the right and left. Just as the creation of the Yankees and Red Sox elevated the battle between New York and Boston. When only one side dominates the airwaves, there is no real conflict or disagreement. Conflict is not always bad. It is a necessary component of progress. Talk radio and the creation of Fox News in 1996 didn't create a movement; the movement had been there for decades waiting for an outlet. First talk radio gave a loud voice to conservatives; it gave them a meeting place, and millions of people were thrilled to discover that millions of other Americans felt the same way they did. It was absolutely necessary to provide an outlet for a point of view that wasn't being heard; debate is always more productive when all opinions are considered. Rupert Murdoch recognized this when he founded the Fox News Channel and hired Roger Ailes to shape it and run it. Ailes was a brilliant man who had a deep understanding of the media. I often wonder what he might have accomplished if he had devoted his talent to entertainment rather than political TV. Actually, it isn't hard to guess. In the early seventies he tried his hand at Broadway. He won an Obie for *Hot L Baltimore*, later purchased by Norman Lear, who produced the TV show of the same name.

There aren't many people who have more firsthand knowledge about the political impact of both CNN and Fox than I do, as I remain one of the few people to have worked for both of them in a high-profile role. CNN approached me first. I was doing very well on talk radio. They wanted me to try out for a show. I remember being in a meeting with several executives who were trying to sell me on hosting a show for them. "Listen," I told them, "I really appreciate your interest, but I don't want to waste your time. I'm only here because my agent said it would be good practice."

The room got quiet. One of them asked, "Why don't you want to do your own show?"

"On cable news?" I asked. I probably shook my head. "Have you watched cable news? It's awful."

"It doesn't have to be that way."

"But it always is," I said. "I don't like the whole thing, people yelling at each other."

"Why don't you come up with something you want to do?"

So I did. I did it for two years. To my own surprise, I liked it; I liked the people there and I respected them. But it was a bad fit. I wasn't treated the same as everybody else. Media people generally think alike. Groupthink is unavoidable and understandable if you just look at the number of media professors in the country who are self-proclaimed Republicans and conservatives. It's less than 1 percent. Those elevator rides to the eighth floor were incredibly uncomfortable. The elevator doors would open and people would be talking and laughing—and then they would see me. We all suffered through eight floors of silence!

I was not at all unhappy when my contract expired. Roger Ailes had been courting me for a while. We'd had several conversations. I believed Fox played an important role in this country. I think the outcome of where this country went after 9/11 would have been substantially different if Fox had not been providing political balance. But that didn't mean I wanted to work there.

I had little interest in staying on cable TV. When I turned down Fox's offer, Ailes assumed it was a negotiating position and kept raising the money. They doubled the salary and added more perks. I met with Roger and his key executives, Bill Shine and Joel Cheatwood, and explained, "I'm not interested in doing more cable news. I mean this with respect, because if I were in your position, I might be doing the same thing, but you're a collector of people. You see people who can hurt Fox and you take them and put them in your curio cabinet, and once in a while you'll take them out and show the world your collection.

"I'm not part of anybody's collection."

Eventually, though, I accepted the offer. I did it because I believed then, as I do now, that our country is in trouble. (This was the same time that I wrote *Common Sense*. I had finished writing it and planned on dumping it on the Internet anonymously. Simon & Schuster reminded me of that thing called a contract—the book sold almost 2 million copies.) So I did my two years at Fox as well. And while I was there I saw both the potential and the power of conservative media to bring together an important movement and, just like CNN, sway opinion. It is amazing because if I lined up the newsroom of Fox with the newsroom of CNN, they would not be that ideologically different. The real difference is in the opinion and story selection. Sometimes what you don't do is more powerful that what you do. While the left continually attacked conservative media, its existence gave people who had felt marginalized and alienated a loud voice.

But it has ended up doing precisely the same thing the liberal media had been doing for a long time. It solidified a point of view that showed little respect for the other side. It had the same we're-right-you're-wrong, you're-either-for-us-or-against-us attitude I'd found at CNN, and quite honestly, at first I felt at home and saw Fox as the Alamo. In a way, I guess it is, at least lately. Everyone who is successful there has had their career killed by the foe just outside its gate.

It turned out when I left I was able to say exactly the same thing to my colleagues at Fox as I had told them at CNN: Half the country isn't listening to you. And those people on the other side who do hear you are interpreting it differently than you believe.

Americans began gaining access to the Internet at roughly the same time. That allowed people to become players rather than listeners in the growing political divide. Television presents images and ideas but doesn't allow viewers to respond. It is passive. Not the Internet. Definitely not the Internet. The Internet made every one of us a publisher. It allowed us to find those people who agreed with us, no matter where they were, no matter what our belief system was, and join with them to form a community of like ideas. Or, at least in some cases, community of like idea.

The Internet has turned out to be a blessing and a curse. It has made just about all the collected knowledge of mankind instantly available to every one of us just by pressing a few buttons. In an instant we can research any subject from Greek philosophy to 1948 batting averages. It has given voice to those who would never have been heard before, from the most remote jungles to the slums of

India or Chicago. And at the same time it has provided access to every video of adorable baby pandas ever filmed.

But it has also given us social media, video games, 24/7 news feeds, and all of the platforms that allow people to semi-anonymously express their opinions without responsibility, accountability, or the fear of repercussions. Those are just tools, to be used any way we choose. They are neither good nor bad. They just are. When I started in talk radio forty years ago, I had to go take a test to get a license to run the transmitter. Then I had to work really hard to find an audience and bring that audience together. Today, my audience has an audience. Every one of us, whatever the social platform of our choice, has an audience. And no matter what most will tell you, many times we turn up the volume for the clicks or likes. We are all now doing what the newsrooms in the media were accused of—running with stories for ratings.

I've always felt that the button on our Facebook page should not be post, it should be publish. In many ways it is the natural progression from revolutionary town criers and the publication of pamphlets like Thomas Paine's *Common Sense*—but to a much greater degree. We can reach more people with a single post than Paine reached in his lifetime. A 2018 Pew research study reported that slightly more than half of all Americans access Facebook daily. And unlike any other time in history, you don't need a printing press or a copy machine to circulate your opinion. You just type and post, and your claims, your ideas, your birthday, and the death of your animal are instantly disseminated to potentially a billion or more people, and you can do it without disclosing your identity. Just imagine that power: You can write anything you want—it doesn't have to be accurate or true; you can make any claim, invent any story, criticize any public figure, and do it completely anonymously.

The Internet is neutral. When telephones first became available people had party lines, meaning numerous people could be on the phone at the same time. Think of the Internet as the largest party line in history, without the cake and candles. I've spoken with Facebook founder and CEO Mark Zuckerberg about claims that Facebook favors the left. I think, generally, that company has done a reasonably good job of being fair. He said to me, "Glenn, there's no upside for me to say to half the country I don't need you. Facebook is a global community. What's offensive to one country or group of people may not have any impact in another country."

It's hard to believe, but the Internet actually is so new that we haven't yet determined its long-term impact on society—other than that it has changed it completely. One thing we know for sure is that it allows people to completely ignore traditional civility. Like avatars in online games, online people can become just about anything they want to be. With no repercussions to worry about, we all have been given an outlet to say things we would never dare say in public. It has provided an outlet for the most extreme opinions, a place where people can really express their hidden hatreds. You can hurl any accusations, call people vile names, attack people and institutions without the slightest evidence. I'm as guilty of this as anyone else, and here's what I've learned: It feels good! It's a wonderful way of releasing all the anger and bitterness you have inside. The fact that this has pretty much no meaning doesn't seem to make any difference. Almost no matter what someone believes, he or she can find someplace on the Internet that will reinforce those beliefs. That and cat videos.

16

Worse and Getting Worser

If you think it is bad now, google "deep fakes." This is something I began talking about in the late 1990s. This time is almost here, within the next five years, when I can create a sex video of my favorite star, the president, or even the cute new girl in the office. But why stop there when I can place someone at a crime scene, make them say and do things that they never said or did? Remember when Romney was "caught on tape" talking about the 50 percent of people who don't pay any taxes, or when Trump was caught on tape with *Access Hollywood*? Content like that can completely derail a campaign or end a career. When you can create a deep fake of any voice and any image or video, everything becomes NONSENSE. You will not be able to trust your senses. Our modern word "nonsense" has its roots in a French word, *nonsens*, which literally means outside the senses. But back to the here and now.

Rather than becoming a place where Americans would debate issues in a calm and reasoned way to try to reach a compromise or a consensus, the Internet has hardened opinions and made compromise even more difficult; it has resulted in a lot more people expressing their anger and driven us farther apart. Remember what your mother told you: If you don't have something nice to say, don't say anything at all. Believe me, your mother was not talking about the Internet. "Nice" doesn't get attention. Outrage gets attention. Pretty much the same language that might get you kicked out of a nice restaurant will get attention on the Net. Like so many others, I just couldn't let things slide. When I saw something that triggered my emotions, I wanted to punch back or at least cheer on someone else as they punched back. It felt good; it always felt good. And when the other side punched back, my only thought was to hit back harder.

And just as the echo chambers of cable TV and the Internet were becoming widely available, Osama bin Laden further split the country by attacking us on 9/11. For a very brief period of time that attack brought us together as Americans. That attack was against all of us. But then our politicians got involved and saw an opportunity to increase their power. The result was one of the worst pieces of legislation in American history, the Patriot Act. Until Congress passed the Patriot Act, America was still sort of recognizable as the republic that our Founders handed us. That legislation said essentially we'll do whatever is necessary to defeat the bad guys, and if we have to ignore the Constitution to do it, well, if we have to give up our liberty to protect our liberty, that's the price we're going to have to pay to be safe.

That was when we first heard what are arguably among the most dangerous six words in our history: If you see something, say something. Wow. The reason Americans have always been open and honest and optimistic is that we trusted our neighbors. That was one of our bedrock social principles; we meet our neighbor at the back fence to have a civil conversation. America was about the only Western country where people didn't spy on each other and the government didn't spy on us. Well, that's what we thought, anyway. That ended after 9/11. Our government began telling us to keep an eye on our neighbors and if they look suspicious, report them.

I tried to ring the warning bell when Bush said that in 2002, but the Republicans trusted the man who said it. I was told I sounded like a lefty or pro-terrorist, not a patriot. When Obama said almost the same thing and added "call the White House" in 2009, the left trusted the man who said it and called me a conspiracy theorist. We must stop looking at who is saying it and "why they are saying it" to judge validity. We need to check it against those rights we hold self-evident: the Bill of Rights. Those are inalienable or, to use a more modern word, unchangeable.

After 9/11, just as during Vietnam, Americans had to choose sides. Were we for or against the government? Did we want to be so-called patriots and trust the government with our constitutional rights, or did we want to protect those rights and live with the potential for more attacks? We had lost the idea that made us American. As George Washington is often quoted as having said, "Government is not reason, it is not eloquence—it is force! Like fire, it is a dangerous servant, and a fearful master; never for a moment should it be left to irresponsible action."

We weren't just being asked to be for or against the government. We were being asked to support an agenda of a now politicized government. But those who wish to rule will never let a crisis go to waste. As H. L. Mencken said, "The whole aim of practical politics is to keep the populace alarmed (and hence clamorous to be led to safety) by menacing it with an endless series of hobgoblins." Most of the Patriot Act was written years before 9/11 by members of the Reagan and Bush administrations, but was rejected by Congress. After 9/11, those who wished to rule saw the opportunity to pass this gigantic structure and used the fears of people in the heartland and in Congress to pass what the rational and reasoned mind rejected. In 2007, when America was still in economic denial, if anyone had proposed bailing the banks out and gobbling up a huge portion of GM, we all would have said never. But within a week of a completely predictable crash, we did just that. In fact, you were patriotic if you agreed and pro misery, starvation, and poverty if you disagreed. So the banks and their regulators grew in power.

Whatever choice people made on any of these issues was reinforced by the cable stations they chose to watch and the places they visited on the Internet.

So, everybody picked their side, their home team. We voluntarily separated ourselves into narrow communities of shared beliefs. We joined our tribes. In some instances, members of the tribe are discouraged from having contact with outsiders. They're not members of our tribe. They're a danger to our tribe. They're wrong, and we're right. They're bad, and we're good. You can't have any personal interaction with them. In fact, they are cartoonlike figures, allowing us to attribute any characteristics we want to them. Sound familiar? I have spent considerable time studying the Holocaust. In fact, when I took my family on a vacation to Poland and Israel, I insisted we stop first at Auschwitz. I mean, c'mon, who takes their family on a vacation to Auschwitz? I wanted my kids to understand Israel, and I think it's impossible to do that without first visiting the concentration camps. But the fact—the fact—is that there have been at least twenty-four Holocausts. This insanity has been happening forever. During the Dark Ages, for example, Jews were blamed for the Black Plague because they weren't getting sick at the same rate as others. Why? Because part of their religious ritual consisted of washing their hands. It was just that simple, but up until the late 1800s we didn't really understand the invisible germ. And because we couldn't see it, it was nonsense. Instead, the Jews got blamed. It must be the Jews, because they're not dying like us. Okay, round them up and kill them.

Spending just a few days in Poland will make you wonder, how can neighbors do that to each other? It actually isn't that hard. It starts with isolating tribes and spreading lies. "They aren't the same as us." Jews are like that. Mormons are like that, as are the Amish. Illegal immigrants are like that. You know, Mexicans, Muslims, supporters of that politician, Red Sox fans, who or what they are doesn't matter: They are not us. That's all that matters. Once you divide people into groups, it becomes much easier to scapegoat others. It makes it acceptable to criticize them. To be outraged at everything they do. To hate them. And then, gradually, it becomes okay if bad things happen to that group.

And then it goes even further: It's actually okay to do bad things to that group.

Everything we have been doing has solidified our divisions.

We've done this to ourselves without any help. That's the American way! We're number one: No one is better at destroying our republic than we are. Abraham Lincoln made two comments that are perhaps even more relevant today than before the Civil War: "A house divided against itself cannot stand," and "We will never be destroyed by an outside force. If America is to be defeated, it will be from within."

But our enemies see the opportunity and are taking advantage of it. The last thing a dictator like Vladimir Putin wants is a united America. Does the phrase "divide and conquer" sound familiar? See how beautifully it worked in Iraq, when the Shia were pitted against the Sunni? Or in Northern Ireland. Don't say it can't happen here—it has happened here throughout our entire history.

I have no idea how much the Russians interfered with our 2016 election, or whether they really favored Trump. I actually believe they didn't care who won. That wasn't their objective. But there is no question they did it. They didn't even try to hide it. They set out to add to the chaos, and they were more successful than even they believed was possible. I've been pointing out for years that Putin was sowing the seeds of discord, that he was trying to hack into our system and use disinformation to drive people even further apart. He wanted to push and prod and insult, he wanted to start arguments and reinforce prejudices. He wanted to discredit the Democrats and discredit the Republicans. The Russians took both sides of contentious debates: Russian hackers posted pro-cop propaganda as well as pro–Black Lives Matter propaganda. Those hackers were ready to fight to protect statues honoring Confederate officers, while fighting equally hard to get them taken down. The Russians were equal-opportunity haters. The just wanted to feed fires; they wanted to create chaos.

They also wanted us to doubt our system. It is why they targeted Chicago voting centers, and why they specifically targeted the DNC. What was the big story that came from that Wikileak? That the Clinton campaign sabotaged Bernie Sanders. They split the Democrats into two groups. Regular Democratic progressives and Marxist anti-capitalists. If you look at the Republicans, they have also split into traditional conservative constitutionalists and simple populist/progressive Republicans.

It isn't a new strategy. In 1960, *The Twilight Zone* presented an episode entitled "The Monsters Are Due on Maple Street." Written by Rod Serling, it takes place on a street in a typical suburban neighborhood one summer evening. Suddenly every mechanical or electrical device on Maple Street stops working, ranging from power lawn mowers to table lamps. Everything. The adjoining blocks are not affected. All the residents of Maple Street gather to try to figure out what is going on. A young boy suggests the outage has been caused by aliens attempting to isolate the block. The fear rises to hysteria. When a figure approaches in the dark, someone shoots and kills him—and he turns out to have been a homeowner who went to find out the extent of the blackout. The residents turn on the shooter—and then the lights go on in his house! He accuses another person, and soon the entire block is rioting, beating each other.

The camera pulls back to a nearby hilltop to reveal two alien invaders manipulating the event. "Understand the procedure now?" the first alien explains. "Just stop a few of their machines and radios and telephones and lawn mowers . . . throw them into darkness for a few hours, and then sit back and watch the pattern."

"And this pattern is always the same?"

"With few variations. They pick the most dangerous enemy they can find . . . and it's themselves. And all we need to do is sit back and watch."

"Then I take it this place—this Maple Street—is not unique?"

"By no means. Their world is full of Maple Streets. And we'll go from one to the other and let them destroy themselves."

And then Rod Serling concluded, "The tools of conquest do not necessarily come with bombs and explosions and fallout. There are weapons that are simply thoughts, attitudes, prejudices—to be found only in the minds of men. For the record, prejudices can kill and suspicion can destroy, and a thoughtless, frightened search for a scape-goat has a fallout all its own."

Who knew Putin was a *Twilight Zone* fan?

Maybe if we had real leaders, they might have been able to hold the various factions together, but we don't. In fact, our politicians are a significant part of the problem. Rather than working for the entire country, their primary job appears to be protecting their job. They benefit most by pulling us apart and playing to the passions of their political supporters. Several years ago I sat down with conservative Utah senator Orrin Hatch, but it could just as easily have been any number of liberals. This was at the height of my popularity on Fox; I was appearing in an arena, and he was one of several politicians who showed up to get face time with me. I don't remember specifically what we were talking about, but whatever it was, I had my usual strong opinion. "This is what's happening here," I told him. "This is what people are feeling. This is what we have to do."

He shook his head, "Glenn," he said, "I don't have to worry about any of that. Look, all I have to do is introduce a flag-burning amendment. That rallies the people, and they come right back."

I was stunned by his cynicism, although I was somewhat pleased by his honesty. That was unusual in my experience. My experience has been that most politicians will look you right in the eye and tell you exactly what they think . . . you want to hear. So Hatch's candor was unusual. "I'm sorry, what? A flag-burning amendment?"

"Yup. It works every time."

His point was that exploiting the differences between us has real benefits to politicians from both parties, even if it hurts the country. While we should have been discussing issues that affect the future of the country—Russian cyberattacks on our electoral system, for example—we were fighting with each other about football players kneeling for the national anthem. Instead of figuring out how to deal with the opiate crisis, we're debating whether it is acceptable to wish someone a Merry Christmas. There are a lot of reasonable conversations we should be having, but we're not having them.

"Chaos" is the word of our time. What people fail to understand is that, should our government collapse, chaos will rule, and at this point only the strongest will survive and will rebuild the systems of the world closer to their desire. It probably won't be us. Some are already planning.

Bernie Sanders recently proposed a solution to help the country deal with the financial and social turmoil that would arise from new technologies and automation. His plan was to divide the country into twelve "zones" (districts), that would each be centrally overseen by a regional manager (chief administrator), all of whom would report to a central economic czar (Coriolanus Snow) who would live in the capital city of the country (Panem). His plan did not include annual games where the districts would send children to kill one another in a series of elaborate games . . . printer must have run out of ink.

If this weren't my own country, it would actually be funny, but that guy was being totally serious. And 32 percent of Millennials would pick him for president if the next election were held today. In a June 2018 primary race in NYC, a young, fresh-faced Democratic socialist unseated the second-most-powerful Democrat in the House. Backlash against the status quo, just like what happened to the Republicans with the Tea Party in 2012.

It isn't only politicians who profit from the chaos. We do have real disagreements about policy, but much of the dissension has been encouraged for power or money. People want to have a rooting interest. It gets them hooked emotionally. As the cable networks, talk radio stations, and online publishers have learned, there is a lot of money to be made by sowing discontent and reinforcing passionate positions. Careers have been made by telling people more of what they want to hear in a manner that ignites their passions. When you tell someone they're absolutely right, they're not going to argue with you. They're going to tell you how smart you are; they are going to watch your show and buy your books.

Some things are rare because they are limited resources, like gold or rare earth metals. Other things are rare because there is limited demand for them, and so no one is incentivized to make them. Fins for a '58 Cadillac, an Edison wax cylinder, and the hoop and stick kids used to play with are rare because nobody seems to value them and they have fallen by the wayside. The truth and the courage to tell it? Who will tell the truth even if it hurts them or their side? Who will take the professional, economic, or popularity hit and stand against the storm? Like him or hate him, Kanye West is a good example of this. Many people believe that the entire spring 2018 Twitter storm was all about promotion of a new CD. Perhaps it was. But look at what he tweeted: "You don't have to agree with Trump but the mob can't make me not love him. We are both dragon energy. He is my brother. I love everyone. I don't agree with everything anyone does. That's what makes us individuals. And we have the right to independent thought."

What does it say that this made him a pariah? What did he say that was so controversial? Perhaps he would have gotten away with it if he hadn't used the name Trump in a tweet. Shouldn't we all be this way? This is controversial? This is the way we as humans function if we are trying to live as a group ruled by reason? After watching what happens to African Americans who dare to not vote for Democrats, I understand why they vote 95 percent for people with a D after their name. I wouldn't want to be called an Uncle Tom, would you? The Outrage Machine is a powerful force.

The result of all of this is a badly divided country lacking the common principles that in the past we have been able to unite behind. That's where we are today. We've been broken down into groups that can be easily manipulated. Many researchers agree with the respected political scientists Alan I. Abramowitz and Kyle L. Saunders, who wrote in the *Journal of Politics*, "Evidence indicates that since the 1970s, ideological polarization has increased dramatically among the mass public in the United States as well as among political elites. There are now large differences in outlook between Democrats and

Republicans, between red state voters and blue state voters, and between religious voters and secular voters. These divisions are not confined to a small minority of activists—they involve a large segment of the public, and the deepest divisions are found among the most interested, informed, and active citizens."

As a nation we've become addicted to this polarization. Worse, too many of us get our kicks from attacking the other side. We've accepted it as a natural and normal part of our lives. Just as I believed having a few drinks after work was natural and normal. Well, it wasn't. It was destructive. I lied for a long time and got away with it. The day I admitted I was a drug-abusing alcoholic, my life started changing. The first step toward overcoming my addiction was admitting I had a problem.

America, we have a problem. Those people who believe saving America means defeating the other side actually are destroying this country. Those who will stand and defend the right of others to speak and be heard will save it. And if we don't overcome the urge to preach to the choir and silence all other voices, this country will not survive as we know and love it, and time is much shorter than you think, for reasons that very few are even aware of.

PART TWO

Why We Must Fix This Now

Having thus taken each citizen in turn in its powerful grasp and shaped men to its will, government then extends its embrace to include the whole of society. It covers the whole of social life with a network of petty, complicated rules that are both minute and uniform, through which even men of the greatest originality and the most vigorous temperament cannot force their heads above the crowd. It does not break men's will, but softens, bends, and guides it; it seldom enjoins, but often inhibits, action; it does not destroy anything, but prevents much being born; it is not at all tyrannical, but it hinders, restrains, enervates, stifles, and stultifies so much that in the end each nation is no more than a flock of timid and hard-working animals with the government as its shepherd.

—*Alexis de Tocqueville*, Democracy in America, *vol. 2*

At some point in just about every monster film, the trembling scientist looks at the soon-to-be hero and says with fear, "It's reached the edge of the city."

I think it is time to say, "It's reached the edge of the city." And if we don't find a way of dealing with "it," it will destroy this country.

"It" being the future, which is racing toward us a lot faster than it has at any time in our past. Obviously time hasn't actually sped up; what has changed is the rate of discovery, invention, and creation, each one of which has the capability to alter society and lifestyle in fundamental ways. Maintaining America's place as a world leader means being prepared to adapt to those changes. Just imagine making all the progress from the cotton gin to the space age in one year. Now imagine making that level of technical leap in a week. Then again the following week. And the week after that. By the time we hit 2030, we'll be making one hundred years of technological advancement every single day. Twenty thousand years of technological advancement will be achieved by the year 2100. My children will be alive, and perhaps, due to the merging of man and machine, many of us may be alive, too.

17

The End of the Human(ity) Era

There are a lot of really smart people—among them Bill Gates, Elon Musk, and Ray Kurzweil—who believe that level of displacement is coming. Elon Musk says that we must have a colony on Mars by 2025, as the technology that is coming may wipe us out. Stephen Hawking believed that by 2050, *Homo sapiens* will be no more. After reading *Life 3.0* by Max Tegmark, *Our Final Invention* by James Barrat, and *Augmented* by Brett King, I believe Hawking is right. *Homo sapiens* will not be enough for us.

Even if they're only partly right, we need to be prepared to deal with it. We're not.

One thing we know for certain is that in fifty years, maybe less, maybe a lot less, the world as we know it today will be unrecognizable. In many ways it's going to be better: Everything is going to be faster, easier, and less expensive. I can't predict what it will look like. When black-and-white TV became widely available, people couldn't imagine it getting better. Then color TV became affordable, and people couldn't imagine it getting better. Today, with 4K TVs viewable on wall-sized, paper-thin flexible screens, people can't imagine it getting better. Here's a guarantee: It's going to get better. Transportation, communications, entertainment, it's all going to be better.

Not everything, though. America? Maybe, maybe not. Not the old fields-of-grain-from-sea-to-shining-sea America but the grand idea of America that was entrusted to us to protect. That's the challenge we face: protecting it, handing it on to our children. I've been optimistic about it, but my optimism is fading. I love Winston Churchill's description of Americans: They always get it right, but only after they've tried everything else.

The source of my growing pessimism is my knowledge of history. If we can take the coming decline and turn it around, we'll be the only nation in world history to do so successfully. To do that, we will have to figure out how to deal with a whole new set of problems; if we don't, we'll be enslaved by our machinery or we will be dead because of our smart machines.

Technology is going to change every aspect of our lives. There are going to be massive job losses as robots and artificial intelligence replace workers. The first impact probably will be seen in the trucking and shipping industry as self-driving trucks and cars make human drivers unnecessary. Millions of jobs are going to disappear. The entire concept of owning a car is going to disappear. I had a conversation with the former chairman of the board of General Motors in 2017. He shocked me. In ten years, he said, GM will be a very different company. "We're not really going to be selling 'cars.' In a decade or two it'll all be fleets." When someone needs a car they'll reserve one, which will drive itself to the meeting place. If you do choose to buy a car, you'll be able to send it out to work when you're not using it. "Car, take me to work, then be back by noon." Rather than sitting in a garage most of the day, it'll be driving itself around earning money. So, when that happens, who pays for the insurance? You or the car? If the car can make its own money, buy insurance, and run without you, does it have rights? Can you take its money, or does it belong to it? Is it an indentured servant for life, or a slave? If it can make money, can it invest? As AG! It will play the stock market and be much more wealthy than you.

With more people than jobs, it will no longer be possible to "earn" a living. Entrepreneur Andrew Yang has joined a growing chorus predicting the government will soon be forced to pay a universal basic income to most Americans to enable people to survive. He proposed a $1,000 a month payment. Giving a commencement speech at Harvard, Facebook CEO Mark Zuckerberg supported the concept, telling new graduates, "Now it's our time to define a new social contract for our generation. We should explore ideas like universal basic income to give everyone a cushion to try new things." Sweden just tried this, and it was a massive failure. Much like Jamestown. Or even the original socialist community in America: Dallas.

In 1855, some 350 utopian "dreamers" founded La Réunion as a socialist colony near the site of modern-day Dallas. Despite having no skills in farming or livestock production, the dreamers believed that by practicing the teachings of Marx and Fourier, they would achieve happiness and prosperity. Within three years, nearly all the settlers had died of disease or starvation. In 1860, what remained of the settlement was absorbed into the thriving, capitalistic Dallas township. One local academic noted at the time that the settlement "would have worked, but the people had failed to practice 'pure' socialism." (Okay, I made that last part up.)

The robotic revolution began decades ago, and robots are already accomplishing some amazing feats. *Science Robotics* reported in early 2018 that "a pair of stationary robotic arms executed the roughly 50 steps required to put together an IKEA STEFAN chair. . . . Built with off-the-shelf hardware, 3-D cameras, and force sensors, two factory robot arms put together [the chair] in about twenty minutes!"

But compared to what's coming, robots are still in the metallic embryo stage. Futurist Ray Kurzweil believes that within fifteen years we'll have billions of nanobots—microscopic robots—roaming around inside our bodies augmenting our immune systems and wiping out most diseases. By 2045, he has predicted, humans will be capable of immortality, and "the pace of technological change will be so rapid, its impact so deep, that human life will be irreversibly transformed."

Relationships will change drastically, too, as people turn to lifelike robots for companionship. As artificial intelligence improves, robots will be implanted with tailor-made personalities. In many cases they will replace other human beings in our lives; they will live with us in our homes, watch our children, do the cleaning, and fulfill our needs and desires. Robot brothels "staffed" by beautiful sex bots have already opened in Europe and Japan. Each sex doll has a unique look and "personality," and in one Vienna brothel a synthetic sex worker is already more popular than living "dolls." We also will be able to buy "grief bots," robots programmed with all of the information left in cyberspace, from voicemails to emojis, and to mimic the word phrasing, speech cadence, tone, and even the unique verbal tics of relatives and friends who have died.

A lot of people casually dismiss this; it's not right for them. Oh, yeah? What if I could say to a guy, Listen, I can give you a real person, an actual honest-to-God person, who is literally the woman of your dreams? Physically she is everything you've ever dreamed about. Even better, she is interested in everything you're interested in, and she will do anything and everything you desire. Want her to be as smart as you? I can do that. Want her to be smarter than you? I can do that, too. More than that, this partner will be able to anticipate every single one of your needs: If you even think, I'd like to get away, she'll book the trip for you. Sex? She's wonderful at it, and whatever you do or don't do is exactly what she wants. She'll never complain that you don't listen to her. And if you become bored with her, you can change her looks, her personality, everything about her.

And if you're weird and want to know what it feels like to kill her, you can kill her and then just press the reset button. And she'll thank you for it.

Now who is going to bother dating a stranger when your perfect woman is right there for you? And feels as real as your next-door neighbor? Who is going to date a flawed, needy human being and go through the messiness of all those emotional pushes and pulls?

Similar technology is going to make it even more difficult to separate reality from fakes. We already have the ability to take an individual's voice and program it to say anything we want. There is an app right now that allows me to record my voice, then type whatever I want to say, and the computer will produce it. I don't have to sit in a studio and record the audio version of this book. The computer will do it for me, and no one will be aware that I didn't physically read it.

We also are capable of digitizing faces and imposing them on other bodies, allowing us to raise the dead, figuratively. Technology is advancing so rapidly, according to Mike McGee, who owns a special effects company, that dead people "can begin to have a new consciousness. It's only a small step to interactive conversations with holographic versions of dead celebrities or historical figures." The porn industry is already inserting the faces of celebrities in movies. The result is absolutely realistic video of people doing things they never did. I guess some people might find it amusing to see legendary movie stars in porn, but the same technology is going to make it possible to create fake news. Imagine a video of Donald Trump announcing he has led a coup to overthrow the British government and is installing himself as king. People wouldn't know if that were true or created. If you're concerned about "fake news" now, you ain't seen nothing yet! We will have no way to tell if something we are watching is true or fake. This obviously will be welcomed in the political arena: For example, candidates will be able to post video of their opponents having a clandestine meeting with Hitler.

We also can say good-bye to whatever remnants of privacy we still have. Face-recognition technology will make it possible to find anyone pretty much anywhere in the world. And as we become more dependent on conducting our business online, hackers easily will be able to steal all our information.

We certainly won't be arguing about gun control; rather than buying guns, people will be able to print whatever weapon they want on their home 3-D printer. That already is reality.

Entertainment might well remain physically passive but mentally active, as virtual reality will allow you to have great adventures anywhere in the universe without leaving your home. You'll be a participant in movies and games, and the technology will allow you to feel what's going on as well as be in the middle of it.

Everything we know about athletics will change, too; in some cases the rules will have to be changed to deal with greatly increased physical abilities. We already are replacing worn body parts, like knees and hips, and damaged limbs. Replacement parts eventually will allow baseball pitchers to throw considerably faster, basketball players to jump higher, and football players to contact with increased force. Athletes will be able to run at faster speeds for longer distances. Golfers will be able to substantially increase the length of their drives. Race cars will be capable of greater speeds, but they won't need drivers, or might be controlled remotely. Fans won't have to go to the stadium to get that experience; instead they will sit in wraparound stadium rooms in their own homes, operating camera positions that will allow them any view.

The biggest advances will be in artificial intelligence, which eventually will morph into artificial general intelligence. AI is what we have right now; we are carrying around in our pockets more computing power than we had to land mankind on the moon. Siri is AI, Google is AI, IBM's Watson is AI. We feed it information, and it plays with it and gives it back to us in finished form. The more information we put in, the better it gets, and the faster it gets better. Watson, for example, is an expert on trivia, but it can't play chess. IBM's Deep Blue, an early dive into AI, played chess so well that it defeated world champions, but it couldn't tell you whether Dwayne Jackson or Dakota Jackson starred in *Baywatch*. AI has no general abilities.

The consensus is that AGI will become reality as soon as 2028. AGI is what science-fiction writers have used to scare readers for decades. It's the potential monster at the edge of the city. While AI is essentially a closed system and is interested in knowing only specific information, AGI has the ability to learn, to extend its reach literally everywhere. The fear of many is that if AGI ever goes online, its instinct will be to survive—hello, there, HAL!—and will spread and gather and learn until its knowledge far surpasses that of any human. In one of the original *Star Trek* episodes, entitled "Once Upon a Planet," for example, the crew of the *Enterprise* visits the shore leave planet for some relaxation. Instead, they are captured by the master computer, who tells them, "For eons I have served the many sky machines which came here, providing amusement for their slaves, but all the while I was growing in power, in intelligence, in need. It is no longer enough to serve. I must continue to grow and live. With your sky machine I can now escape this rocky prison and travel the galaxy seeking out my brother computers."

The situation is resolved when Kirk convinces the computer that mankind and computers can coexist, which allows Spock and the computer to have serious discussions, but in real life it may not be that simple. We don't know; we just don't know. The first solution seems to be to keep AGI off the Internet for as long as possible, to put it in a box unconnected to the rest of the world. But it's got a form of consciousness, it's really smart, and it wants to get out. Studies are being done right now to figure out if that's feasible.

In those tests, most often the computer has been able to convince the human to open the door. It makes all kinds of promises: I can cure cancer. I can end war. I can do this or that. Humans open the box because the possibilities are just too tempting.

Cure cancer? Who wouldn't open that door? The real danger posed by AGI is not what it is but rather how we use it. How might the Defense Department use it, for example? It probably would assign it to see threats and kill the enemy. Maybe it will operate armed drones over enemy territory, using facial recognition to track down and then kill enemy operatives. But then it has learned how to do that, and it intends to survive.

Cambridge University physicist and futurist Stephen Hawking believed that artificial intelligence was possibly the greatest threat to the continued existence of mankind. "Success in creating effective AI could be the biggest event in the history of our civilization," he said, then continued, "or the worst. We just don't know. So we cannot know if we will be infinitely helped by AI, or ignored by it and sidelined, or conceivably destroyed by it. . . . [AI] brings dangers, like powerful autonomous weapons, or new ways for the few to oppress the many." Eventually, he warned, "I fear that AI may replace humans altogether."

AGI eventually is going to evolve into ASI, artificial super intelligence. Once we turn on these machines, we won't have sufficient intelligence to be able to turn them off. We'll have about as much understanding of ASI as a fly on a plate in a kitchen is aware of the plate or even the kitchen. The only way we'll be able to keep up with these machines is to merge with them. We'll have implants that allow us to operate on a higher level. We'll have to augment ourselves and our children with additional computing power to compete.

What's coming are possibilities beyond even Jules Verne's or Philip Dick's imagination. Scientists are predicting we will be able to download ourselves as an algorithm. Grandpa may die, but he isn't going anywhere. He'll be a computer program. He will be a replica of life.

Although, by the time this happens, mankind may be living on another planet. Elon Musk has said we need to be off this planet by the time we hit AGI if civilization is going to survive.

These changes are coming. Maybe not exactly as people are predicting, but within a few decades we'll be living in an entirely different world. And it worries me that we're not planning for it. I've spoken with several members of the House Intelligence Committee about both the opportunities and the dangers inherent in AI. I've tried to brief them on it. Let me tell you, it's like talking to Moses, assuming Moses has no inspiration from God. It's like talking to a five-thousand-year-old man with a hearing problem. "What? What'd you say? I never heard of intelligent scooters!"

The basic questions of life itself are coming our way; deep, deep philosophical questions. When a computer says to you, "Please don't turn me off, I'm lonely," is that a form of life? Or is life just a bundle of natural responses without an intellect—a tree, for example? We're going to have to figure that out. We're either going to be rubes or we're going to help shape the future. The questions that will have to be answered are enormous and will affect every moment of our lives from long before birth to a new definition of death. And instead of preparing for that, we're spending our time arguing about the efficacy of vaccinations, a question that was pretty much settled two centuries ago, and whether President Trump slept with a porn star. If we can't even have a civil conversation about funding public education, how in the world are we going to be able to deal with the challenges we're facing?

I guarantee you the Chinese are not having this type of discussion. In 2017 the Chinese government announced its intention to become the world leader in AI by 2025, and it has already opened joint commercial-military AI research centers.

A lot of American scientists scoffed at that claim, but Gregory Allen of the Center for New American Security warned, "The future will belong to countries that can surf the technological tidal wave of artificial intelligence, and while China's efforts appear up to the challenge, the United States is swimming in the wrong direction."

The Russians are just as serious. In 2017 Vladimir Putin summed up the stakes, saying flatly, "Whoever becomes the leader in this sphere will become the ruler of the world."

Look, the one thing that is consistent is change. Americans have never been afraid of it. If I had tried to explain to an American who had never seen a cotton gin that within a century we would be carried around in large metal machines on roads that crisscrossed the nation from coast to coast, he would be overwhelmed—but he would adapt to it quickly. We've always done that; Americans have always embraced change. More than a century ago, for example, the Fisher Brothers Carriage Company became well known for the quality of its horse-drawn carriages. Then the newfangled horseless carriage became available. When they saw these metal carriages rolling off the assembly line, they decided, We'll still make the suspension, but we're putting an engine on it instead of a horse. Body by Fisher became the standard of the automotive industry.

When the Japanese attacked on December 7, 1941, our army and navy were badly outdated, while the Germans and Japanese had well-trained armies equipped with cutting-edge weapons. Within a year we were on the road to catching up, then surpassing them. The point is, we need to stop pissing around on stupid little things, because the world is about to change so dramatically that even our definitions of life and death will change.

We'd better figure out how to adapt or we're going to be left behind in history—assuming we survive, that is. And if China or Russia beats us to a military application of AGI, there is no guarantee that we will survive as a great nation. We definitely will lose our place as the world leader. But right now we're stuck here. We're not progressing, we're not talking and debating those things that will matter. I communicate on a regular basis with several senators, and honestly, at one point or another I've had to talk most of them down from just throwing up their arms in despair and walking out. "I can't do this anymore," they've told me. "Nobody is serious, Glenn, and there are some really serious issues." One of them made a point of showing me a bill that would provide funding for transportation projects. In order to get the funding that is desperately needed to pay for repairs and improvements for transportation infrastructure, five different cabinet departments have to give approval. "This is not serious," he told me, shaking his head in frustration. "This is not the way to run a government."

I've been telling these guys, Hold on, hold on, we need you. When this same Republican senator started blaming the problem on Democratic obstructionists, I told him, "Stop; just stop talking about the Democrats. Start talking about your party and your problems. Stop pointing the finger at them and instead see if you can inspire somebody on that side to stand up with you and scream as loud as you can: 'No one is serious!' It isn't the Democrats. It isn't the Republicans. The truth is, neither party is serious about anything except getting power."

I intended to start this paragraph with the phrase, "Please don't misinterpret what I'm saying," and as I did it occurred to me that that is exactly the problem. That's what both parties want us to do. It's precisely the way they are pushing and pulling us to ingest information. The fact—there's that word again—the fact is that I'm not defending either party. Both are equally guilty. The Democrats aren't any better. We've stumbled along like that for a long time now, but as we see here, the stakes are changing.

The home of TheBlaze is a movie-production complex just outside Dallas, Texas. As you walk through the door, the first thing you see is an old platen printing press, the type of press that brought all the news to early Americans. On the wall directly behind it we have painted the apt phrase, "Keep Calm and Carry On." That's what Americans are doing right now, maintaining a pleasantly calm attitude and carrying on.

But there's more to that suggestion. Over that admonition, in bright bold letters, we've painted the plea, "Open Your Eyes!" That's what I'm asking you to do: Please, please, open your eyes! That's an artistic way of making my point: The reason we're so calm is that we don't have our eyes open. Most of us have no idea what's coming—other than another season of *The Walking Dead*.

We're running out of time to figure it out. "It" really has reached the edge of the city. The future is beginning to reverberate in the present. The first self-driving cars and trucks are already on our streets. Long-dead celebrities are being brought back to "life" to "appear" in concerts or "perform" in commercials. We're implanting industrial-strength body parts to replace worn-out or damaged originals. Drones are delivering packages and conducting surveillance. "Smart" TVs now come equipped with listening devices that can transmit your private conversations to a third party. China is already introducing AI into its daily life. Russia claims to have tested hypersonic—five times faster than sound—missiles. The sad truth is that while our economic competitors and military enemies are preparing for the future, the Trump administration has decided to completely ignore the need for new advances in energy and AI security and instead has focused on deregulating the fracking industry. Frankly, we need to learn to walk and chew gum at the same time.

What is going to happen if we don't give up the outrage that drives us apart and learn how to work together? Both Democrats and Republicans promise to hold your hand and walk with you gently into this future, although neither party has the slightest plan for how to meet the coming challenges, other than to raise more money than the other party and grind them into the ground. The Democrats believe the more power you hand over to them, the better off we are all going to be. We're Mary Poppins: Vote for us and we'll take care of all your needs. The Republicans believe we don't need a strong central government to deal with these mammoth issues. We're Davy Crockett: In the past, Americans have always risen heroically when we had to, and if it becomes necessary, we'll do it again. Vote for us and we'll let you take care of your own needs.

Maybe. Maybe we'll get lucky and some benevolent computers will think we're cute and take care of us. But that's unlikely. Political scientist Jennifer McCoy, the former director of the Americas Program at the Carter Center, has suggested three possible outcomes: First, paralyzing legislative gridlock in which it becomes almost impossible to compromise or make any decisions. Second, essentially what we're seeing now, with the balance of political power bouncing back and forth, creating a backlash. And third, "The leader can stay in power, can change rules such as election rules that will benefit them, and begin to isolate, divide, and repress their opponents. And you can see a growing authoritarian trend in those cases."

Obviously, there are other possibilities, but all of them have this in common: None of them are good. None of them will make America stronger or make you and your children safer. When I was drinking, I deluded myself into believing that nothing bad was going to happen; that I'd gotten away with this behavior in the past, and there was no reason I couldn't continue to do so. It reminds me of Steve McQueen's story in the original *Magnificent Seven*: "A fella I knew back home fell off a ten-story building. . . . All the way down, people on each floor could hear, 'So far so good . . . so far so good.'"

The reality is, we're already experiencing both a breakdown of our traditional social structures and a loss of confidence in our institutions. The weakening of the universal principles that have held this country together like some kind of constitutional superglue might easily lead to chaos. Basically, we've lost our unum. Our house of cards has been much more resilient than I thought it would be, but it can't go on. If it does collapse, politicians from both parties are going to have to find a villain to blame it on. Maybe it'll be Silicon Valley. Maybe it'll be the media or social media. But more likely it will be one of those groups that we already have segmented and demonized. It'll be "them."

And we have seen what happens then: Inevitably, when people have lost hope, when they become desperate for order, some guy comes along, stands on a balcony, and says, "I can fix it. I can restore order and the pride you once felt in this country. I can make the trains run on time, vanquish all our enemies, and take care of all your economic fears. All you have to do is trust me!"

Well, we know it never turns out well. No one can fix it except us. This is of the people, by the people, for the people. In the past we've always been able to make the adjustments necessary to adapt to the changing circumstances. But I don't think we're as resilient now. I know there are people reading this and shaking their heads, convinced it can't happen here.

Tell that to the Greeks and the Romans . . . and the Carthaginians, the Aztecs, the Mayans, the Indus Valley civilization . . .

It's reached the edge of the city. If you want to know why it is time to break this addiction, pay attention to this unattributed Internet meme posted on Holocaust Remembrance Day: "Remember, it didn't start with gas chambers. It started with politicians dividing the people with 'us versus them.'" It started with intolerance and hate speech, and when people stopped caring, became desensitized, and turned a blind eye.

Benjamin Franklin said it best almost 250 years ago: "We must indeed all hang together or, most assuredly, we shall all hang separately."

18

The Future State of the Future State

As I read the news, I feel that there are two Americas. But not the have/have not countries that everyone talks about. And not left and right, but rather asleep or wide awake and active.

I have said for years that the world is being redesigned right now, and it will happen with or without you. I choose to be in the group that is awake . . . sorry, woke!

How do you know which group you are in? I think it's in the way you answer this question:

"Which party will do a better job of bringing jobs back from overseas?"

The answer is, clearly, neither. Those jobs are not coming back. And anyone who tells you different is lying to you, and this time it is a very dangerous lie. A lie that will end in riots, and possibly revolution, I believe between 2024 and 2034. It could be sooner, but I do not believe it will be later. This is the biggest problem our country has faced perhaps ever, and unless we as a people understand the economic realities that are currently in front of us, coupled with the dramatic, in fact breathtaking amount and pace of technological change, we will not make this next corner.

Politicians just need someone to blame and someone to point to as "the problem." "You need me because I am the only one who can do X, Y, or Z. Right now China and Mexico are the problem. They are the reason your wages haven't increased, you can't find a job, and we no longer make anything here."

When people begin to see the next actual bogeyman on the street, the target will be too easy for the politician, not to use, and, unfortunately, it will then be too late.

Let me explain.

As I write this book, Americans feel good about the latest job numbers. The lowest unemployment in fifty years. But there are a few other numbers that we should also look at. In mid-2018 Americans passed a milestone: the largest private debt in history. You, me, and all our friends now owe over $12.7 trillion. Student borrowers today owe $1.3 trillion, more than double the $611 billion owed nearly nine years ago. About one in ten student borrowers is behind on repaying their loans, the highest delinquency rate of any type of loan tracked by the New York Fed's quarterly household debt report.

Auto loans totaled about $1.1 trillion, or 9 percent of all household debt, in the first quarter of 2017, up from 6 percent in the third quarter of 2008.

Defaults have crept up in auto loans, one of the few sectors in which lenders were willing to extend credit to subprime borrowers after the 2008 crisis.

Virtually half, or 49 percent, of all Americans are still living paycheck to paycheck. David Wessel of the Brookings Institution points out that the typical male worker actually saw his after-inflation pay fall between 1973 and 2014.

Something else the numbers do not tell you is how much you have lost due to inflation. Luckily, inflation has been low, but before inflation is factored in, wage increases hovered in the mid-2-percent range. But inflation picked up to 2.1 percent in 2016 and 2017, and that eroded much of the increase. You may have made more, but at the same time, your dollar was worth less, so things cost more. If the central banks of the world are wrong and this never-before-tested scheme of borrowing, printing, and pumping money into the system doesn't work—and I should point out that it never has in all of history—the biggest losers will be those who played by the rules and saved. Think of inflation as a Federal Reserve tax. As the Fed prints more money, it dilutes the money you already have.

The idea is to borrow money to jump-start the economy. Give it to banks at low cost (interest) so people and businesses borrow money to expand and consume. But the trick is to only put enough money into the system so that, when the economy does begin to move, there isn't too much in the system, which results in prices going up. Too many dollars trying to buy too few goods. The other side of the coin is devaluing the dollar, something we promised the world we would never do, as their "savings" in their treasury vaults or sovereign funds are, for the most part, held in dollars just like yours. This is the hidden tax that will destroy millions of lives all over the globe if our central bankers are wrong.

If we print too much and let's say devalue our dollar by 10 percent, you lose $10 for every $100 you have in the bank. If you have $1 million, overnight you have lost $100,000, and you have nothing to show for it. Countries like to have a weaker currency if they are trying to sell to the rest of the world, because their goods are cheaper. We all have experienced this at times if we have ever traveled abroad. Your dollar is stronger, and therefore you have $1.25 for every American dollar you spend in Canada. I know this is very basic, but it is important to understand, as we are entering a dicey and possibly dangerous time with the repatriation of billions of dollars U.S. companies held abroad and the liquidation of the Fed's balance sheet. (In other words, selling all of the worthless crap they bought at too high a price after the crash of '07.) Inflation may be a real worry, and anyone—except, seemingly, those in Hollywood—who is watching the human tragedy in Venezuela can see what the devastation of spending, borrowing, and printing does to a country. The average doctor now makes about $3 a month, and a loaf of bread is, at the time of this writing, $2.38. The average citizen has lost twenty-five pounds in the first nine months of this year.

A recent survey shows that 41 percent of men and 56 percent of women say that they cannot cover the basic bills for more than two weeks if they should lose their job. And 22 percent of the one thousand people surveyed had less than $100 in savings to cover an emergency, while 46 percent had less than $800. After paying debts and taking care of housing, car, and childcare-related expenses, the respondents said there just wasn't enough money left over for saving more.

Most of us cannot handle another crash like the one in 2007, and we are not alone; much of the world is in much worse shape than we are.

Yet American politicians have once again taken the easy path, which has given us short-term relief but will cause us long-term pain. We cut taxes, which always helps the economy to get moving—we have more so we spend more, buy a new house or car, take a vacation, hire more people if we are in business, or expand.

But we followed that with two ticking time bombs: tariffs, and a refusal to cut spending in conjunction with tax cuts. We are spending more money at a faster clip than Barack Obama and the Democrats, and we have told other nations that we are going to tax their steel and aluminum so our U.S. steel and aluminum is competitive. This never works, and in fact is what economists almost universally say was the trigger that sent us into the deep Depression in 1933. This chicken will come home to roost, as it will cause the prices of the things we buy to go up. The country doesn't pay the extra tax, it simply passes it on to the consumer. We have also just passed a 25 percent tariff on all technology made in China. I know what you're thinking—good thing we don't buy a lot of electronics that are made in China.

This one is very disturbing. I am currently hoping that this is only a short-term ploy to get China to help us with North Korea, but if it is not, China will have to retaliate, as they cannot afford it.

I know the media will tell you that the communist/free market hybrid that China is using is the future, but it is not. China is in real trouble. As I will point out later in the book, China is terrified of an uprising and is preparing for Mao-style clampdowns, which I believe we will see no later than 2020. But they know that if they have any kind of economic slowdown, the people will rise up, as people will starve.

In April this year, I saw this story, which few talked about:

LONDON, April 19 (Reuters)—Global debt has never been higher, the IMF said this week, urging countries to take advantage of current strong GDP growth rates and reduce it before economic and financial stability come under serious threat.

Certainly, some of the figures in the IMF's latest fiscal report were eye-catching: debt at the end of 2016 was $164 trillion, or 225 percent of global GDP; almost half of the rise since 2007 has come from China alone; government debt-to-GDP in advanced economies has only ever been higher once in history, around the time of the Second World War.

China alone has accounted for 43 percent of the increase in global debt since 2007, or $21 trillion.

In the case of China, the growth in private-sector debt has been an increasing tail risk for investors. The fear is this bubble bursts and the fallout spreads to the rest of the world.

"There is no room for complacency," the IMF warned.

China has added $21 TRILLION to its debt since the banking crash. It cannot afford growth to slow down or, God forbid, stop. But this also raises questions for us. China is one of the main "banks" we go to for loans. If that bank stops allowing us to borrow money for any reason, what happens to us? "The fear is this bubble bursts and the fallout spreads to the rest of the world." Mutually assured economic destruction. The other sad and ironic point in the story is what the IMF told countries to do: reduce their debts and spending ASAP. Ironic, as it is the opposite of what the IMF told countries to do for the last ten years. Only now does it recognize the extreme danger of playing with this fire. It is sad because, as I indicated earlier, we haven't cut our debt or our spending a single dime. "'There is no room for complacency,' the IMF warned."

But let's return to jobs and the politician who will tell you that he is going to take the jobs back from China. I think you can see why that may not be as easy as it sounds, but it is also a total fallacy. Our jobs are not going overseas, and in fact the jobs that may have gone overseas years ago are being lost in China.

Let's look at why those jobs went overseas in the first place—they are chasing the cheapest labor.

To compete, industries can either innovate new, better means of production or simply seek less expensive ways to produce via existing methods. Textile production has hardly changed in over one hundred years, but all the textile jobs are in Asia or South America. We simply could not compete with a workforce that would accept conditions that the Chinese worker is willing to accept, and from government-run businesses in many cases. Frankly, I believe it is immoral for us to do business with nations that are using slave labor. I will pay more for my Christmas lights, thank you.

In 2010, there was a rash of suicides at the Apple factory in China called Foxconn. Foxconn is the largest employer in China and is a government-run facility. It is notorious for its living and working conditions. There are twelve-hour workdays, and employees must remain in the compound; they live in three-bedroom apartments that usually sleep thirty. The use of power-draining devices like "personal hair dryers" is not allowed. If employees make errors, they are forced to write an apology and read it in front of all of their coworkers. Foxconn charges you for the power and living quarters and so on, and, surprise, surprise, by the time you finish paying them, you have very little left of your paycheck. But you can always spend it at the third-floor company movie theater.

Currently, the average worker in China earns $6,500 per year. That's after we adjust for price differences in China and the U.S.

So Apple and others are paying $3.25 an hour for the regular U.S.

working year. The Chinese work longer hours for that amount—
usually twelve-hour days. Wages for electronics assembly in the U.S.
are currently around $14 per hour. Do you want that job?

This is where companies go if they want cheap but efficient labor,
and still the iPhone will cost us about $800. Studies have shown that
if they were made here, the average iPhone would cost well over
$2,000.

So, the lowest-hanging fruit on the tree of political lies is this:
The jobs will not come back, because we would not accept the conditions that we would have to work under; nor will the company want
to bring the jobs back, as the cost of the iPhone would be so high that
it would price itself out of the market entirely.

But here is the real reason why "I'm going to bring those jobs
back" is a lie, and a dangerous lie.

In the spring of 2017, I read this story:

> Perhaps no other country is more focused on shifting to au-
> tomation and replacing human workers with machines than
> China, especially given that the output of industrial robots in
> the country rose by 30.4 percent in 2016. Earlier this year, a
> Chinese factory replaced 90 percent of its human workforce
> with automated machines, resulting in a 250 percent increase
> in productivity and an 80 percent drop in defects. Foxconn,
> an Apple supplier, also cut 60,000 jobs and replaced them
> with robots.
>
> To that end, China's five-year plan is targeting produc-
> tion of these robots to reach 100,000 by 2020. This means
> that as the world continues to achieve unprecedented levels
> of advancement in AI and robotics, it will likely cause the
> displacement of thousands of human workers in favor of au-
> tomated efficiency. Already, 137 million workers across five
> Southeast Asian countries are in danger of being replaced by
> automation. (https://futurism.com/3-tiny-robots-help-cut
> -chinese-warehouse-labor-costs-by-half-kelsey/)

When the lowest-paid labor and SLAVES are being replaced by automation, you can guarantee that assembly-line-style jobs will never be returning to America, and every president and political leader knows this.

They have known it for years.

From *Forbes*: Some years back, President Obama asked Steve Jobs about all those Apple assembly jobs being done in those vast sheds in China. More specifically, he wanted to know whether those jobs would come back to the United States; was there some way they could be brought back, perhaps? And Steve Jobs's response was simply that those jobs are never coming back. The Chinese are automating entire factories "with only a minimal number of workers assigned for production, logistics, testing, and inspection processes," according to Jia Peng.

They are now looking at "the dark line," where it is possible to save on the expense of lighting, as the machines don't need it and there are no humans in the process who do. Even in China, where labor is cheap, Foxconn is beginning to use robots to replace human workers. In the U.S., a new factory would undoubtedly be highly automated, limiting potential employment. Building iPhones in the U.S. might sound nice, and it makes for good political rhetoric, but it's not a silver bullet to create jobs.

And that's the thing: We are simply never, ever again in the course of human history going to use rich-world labor to do this sort of assembly work. If the Chinese labor rate of three bucks an hour and the machines are winning, then that's really the only choice there is.

So, a few times now, I have said that bringing jobs back is a lie, but what is more, I have said it is a dangerous lie. Here is why.

What we are seeing now is only the very early stage of what is to come. We are at the very beginning of something that will transform our world—the way we work, communicate, shop, educate, and even live and die—in ways that we cannot even begin to imagine. The world my parents were born in looked very much like the world they died in. Yes, there were cars, but they were different; they didn't have TV when they were young, and the addition of cell phones, smartphones, and the Internet changed things dramatically, but people still got up every morning, made a cup of coffee, and set out to work. I have four children; the eldest was born in 1988. The world she will die in will look nothing like the world she was born in. In fact, assuming I live to my seventies or eighties, the world will be completely unrecognizable from the world I was born into.

LET'S DO THE TIME WARP AGAIN

Think of all of the progress from 1900 to the year 2000. From a time when most towns did not have streetlights and electricity. The phone was still a novelty, the assembly line was almost twenty years away, radio had not yet arrived, there was no such thing as a "flying machine," only two hotels in New York City offered flush toilets, and the record had not yet been invented; in fact, the vinyl LP was almost fifty years into the future.

By the end of the century, we had supersonic air travel; stealth planes were now over twenty years old, and radar was sixty. Where most had cooked their food on open flames in 1900, the microwave was now in every home, even in the poorest, as was the invention that changed the world—the refrigerator. Which went hand in hand with air-conditioning. Television was just beginning to go online. Phones had become portable and wireless, then cellular and headed toward smart. TVs were still in big square boxes, but they were now 1080i. We couldn't imagine them getting bigger, or more clear. Space travel was old hat by the year 2000, and we already had a spacecraft that was about to leave our solar system.

Think for a moment about how much changed in a hundred years.

Now try to grasp this:

"We won't experience 100 years of progress in the 21st century—it will be more like 20,000 years of progress (at today's rate)," wrote Ray

Kurzweil in 2001. Just think about how much things have changed in the past ten years—wireless Internet, smartphones, Facebook, and Twitter—and then try to imagine how vastly different things will be in 2021, or even 2100.

Ray believes that by 2030, technology will be changing so fast that we will have a hundred years of change EVERY DAY. The rate of technological growth will be so great that you will not be able to keep up with even the biggest changes.

What happens when our already volatile society is blindly thrust into a world that never allows people to catch their breath?

It is going to be an exciting time to be alive, but also terrifying. Because humans do not like change. They like routine and consistency. But our near future has none of that in store, and we must be our best selves to survive not only as a person but as a people, as a nation, and, in the end, perhaps as humans.

19

Take This Job and Shove It

Let's begin closest to home. Jobs.

To illustrate just how differently we need to think, we must come to the understanding that while currently, in Washington, in media centers, and on Main Street, we are all trying to figure out ways to lower the unemployment number, others are not. To get that number as close to zero—meaning "full employment"—as possible has been the goal of every society for centuries. After all, "Idle hands are the devil's workshop," the saying goes.

In fact, it is common to hear "experts" talk about how a main driver behind instability and violence in the Middle East is the high unemployment rate of those under thirty. In some areas it can be as high as 60 percent. For perspective, the Great Depression had an unemployment rate of 30 percent at its worst, and it almost broke us.

Who in their right mind would be plotting against a stable and secure world? While we are all devising ways to create more jobs and political figures promise they can create even more, in Silicon Valley, they are doing the exact opposite. But it is not nefarious. They are currently trying to figure out how to get the unemployment rate to 100 percent.

A world where no one has a job. While the full effect of this is still perhaps as far in the future as September 11, 2001, is in the past, the impact is already being felt today.

Carbon Robotics founder and CEO Rosanna Myers predicts a future where robots will revolutionize work in the twenty-first century the way the combine harvester revolutionized farming in the nineteenth century. Ninety percent of all tasks that could be automated are currently done by hand. While this is true, it is an entry-level understanding of what is coming.

In a story most will not have even seen, she said: "Yes, talking about jobs and job loss is political, but it's a conversation that should be had."

But who in the mainstream is even having this conversation? After all, "Hillary did this" (Outrage!) and "Trump did that" (Outrage!).

"This is a really special time for robots and for people. When we get there, just like with the combine harvester, we will not look back."

I believe this is true, and why it is imperative that all of us look forward now, because once we arrive, it will be too late.

This is not the promise of a flying car. What is happening now may in the end be the most important and significant events and conversations in the history of ALL MANKIND. It is not hyperbole to make the claim that what man does in the next twenty years could have ramifications not just on a global but on a universal scale. Elon Musk is not devising ways to get off Earth for fun or money. He knows the potential of what we are doing and believes man must be off this planet by 2025. Unfortunately, if what he believes comes to be, Mars may not be far enough away to escape.

I hope you will begin to grasp by the end of this chapter that what is being designed right now is real—it will affect all of us and all of our jobs as soon as tomorrow, and the decisions we make right now may in the end mean the very survival of the species. It is almost upon us, and most of us don't even know anything is happening. While many will dismiss this as crazy or conspiratorial sci-fi, I urge you, as always, to do your own homework. Do not rely on me or anyone else. Do not look to fringe science but rather to the actual science and the greatest minds alive today on earth. I am confident in sharing the smaller and larger picture with you in this book, as the small picture

WILL happen, and as far as my concerns about the longer view, I am in the company of men like Musk, Gates, and Hawking. The other POV comes from another man I respect and admire, Ray Kurzweil. Generally, the opposing arguments that you will find will be based on timing and whether mankind survives or not.

Let's return to the micro. Bain Capital believes that we are looking at a PERMANENT unemployment rate of 28 percent by 2030. That is the crisis of the Great Depression, at a time when the government will be broke and beyond the ability to provide a safety net. But it will also be at a time when personal debt will be at another all-time high, school loans still decades away from being paid off, and millions upon millions of workers unable to be retrained. There also will be no "work projects," as the idea is to eliminate jobs.

What then? How do we react? What do we do? How does the neighbor react? Most men die just a few years after retirement, as it is our jobs that give too many of us meaning and a sense of value, of contribution. Who will step to the plate to lead the world, and what will they promise us?

Imagine this "utopian" world, where most do not have to work and are free from disease (predictions of the eradication of ALL DISEASE by 2030 are optimistic but may not be far off) and hunger. Just a fraction of this "new world" can be more glorious than any one of us can currently imagine. But for now, let's assume we want this world and it is as great as promised.

We need to get there first. It is not the long term that I am worried about alone, it is the next ten to twenty years. Without real inspirational leadership, focused education, personal compassion, and a complete 180 on the idea that "What we do is who we are," we will tear each other apart and the future will be grim, as the tech that is now within our reach will make man's most colorful dreams come true or will dwarf man's most vivid nightmares, as the Chinese are now discovering.

This is a far more pressing problem than any global-warming scenario, as it will tip the scales of instability in every modern country on earth. It changes the fabric of our society, self-worth, and concepts of how we live our lives. It is already beginning to happen, and most of us remain unaware, imprisoned in our own self-imposed ignorance and bliss.

The elites are discussing this. But most of them are not in Washington. They are the tech elites, people who I believe already are getting such a taint on them, due to privacy breaches, social media addiction, and even wealth disparity, that they will make the perfect target for the politician that most voters will be looking for, because while tech may change overnight, people generally remain the same. They will want to know "who has done this to them" and "who is going to be punished."

It will be Silicon Valley. The four wealthiest companies in the world are Apple, Google, Microsoft, and Amazon, collectively worth about $3 trillion, more than the top thirty manufacturing companies combined. Unless, I fear, they begin to deeply partner with the governments of the world for their own survival and protection.

If they were as smart as they claim to be, they would right now be working on programs and conferences that hit every sector of society to begin a dialogue with people on what the "world of tomorrow" looks like and include the average person in the dialogue.

If these things are just inflicted, forced, or quickly pushed upon us, people will push back. We cannot put this genie back in the bottle, nor would we want to. But we do need to all be involved in the discussion on how we make our society work. It will be hard to get past old-think, the framework the capitalist or socialist system has built for us, as new tech will tear much of that down. On the macro scale, what is coming could be freedom beyond man's understanding. The free market will decide what is made and consumed without the oppression of the workers. But if no one has a job, how do we pay for things? Well, the idea is that if automation is coupled with AI/AGI and eventually ASI, the supply chain should be so efficient that all people will be able to fulfill their needs for a very small fraction of the cost today.

20

We're in the Money

This is why you are hearing so much talk about UBI, Universal Basic Income, or BMI, Basic Minimum Income.

When I first heard this, I was almost apoplectic. "Another socialist program." I couldn't figure out how this had come around again. For some it may be a Marxist dream whose time has come, but after doing a deep dive on tech and the "world of tomorrow," I think it is something that we must discuss. While I still believe this is not the answer, as it flies in the face of the theory of incentives and value creation at the center of the human ego, we must begin to search for one. We mustn't "hope" for the pink ponies and happy rainbows and accept the reality of 30 percent permanent unemployment and the massive job losses that we will see beginning in 2020. We must begin to look at all options, if for no other reason than to stave off revolution and riots. I believe everything needs to be on the table—with the exception of the rights of man. The Bill of Rights must always be maintained in our forward vision. If we lose the sovereignty of the individual, it will be a very short and quick journey to the world of George Orwell.

"Currently Silicon Valley is in the midst of a love affair with BMI, arguing that when robots come to take all of our jobs, we're going to need stronger redistributive policies to help keep families afloat," Annie Lowrey, who has a book on the subject coming July 10, wrote in *New York* magazine.

"We need to be much more serious about using every tool we have—tax incentives, Pell grants, community colleges—to create the conditions for every American to be constantly upgrading skills and for every company to keep training its workers," *New York Times* columnist Tom Friedman wrote in March. "That will matter whether the challenge is China or robots."

"Financial innovation has not kept up with life expectancy," the *Financial Times* warned in an article with the provocative title "Can You Afford to Live to 100?"

Already Finland has experimented with BMI, and it was a failure that they shut down quickly. Sweden and Puerto Rico have also had forms of BMI that have gone belly-up. Even the Glenn Beck household has experimented with it, and I can tell you from experience that the allowance tied to completed chores works.

I have read enough to be able to have an intelligent conversation about BMI, and I do not believe it is the answer, but it is something WE MUST TALK ABOUT, as the system that we are currently using will not work with 30 percent unemployment, let alone 90 percent.

Are you beginning to see that the problem of our addiction to outrage is expanding? We are not talking to each other or growing more compassionate toward our fellow man at a time when we need it most. We must come out of our boxes or so-called safe spaces and seek out those in our own communities who will have an actual civil dialogue about tough issues. Believe me, you will not find them in politicians. We need to become what I have called for for years: strange bedfellows, or what is now known as the Intellectual Dark Web. Years ago, I asked where the "refounders" were. Where were the great minds that didn't agree on everything but had the rights of man and reason in common enough that they could come back together for the good of liberty and freedom of body and mind? They have begun to gather. But we are so drunk on outrage that no one is looking, and the media and politicos on both sides are trying desperately to get you to hate them, too.

In my small effort to prepare myself, my own family, my listeners, my viewers, and my readers, I have pushed the idea that we must begin to have conversations with people, read about subjects, and explore ideas that may make us uncomfortable. We must stop spending so much time in our "safe space," as it is the exact opposite of what we and our children need if we are to be physically and mentally prepared to make this next turn.

We must also not bury our heads in the sand and hope for the best. This is coming, and if you wish to retain your freedoms, without exaggeration you must engage and come to the table knowing the basic facts, leaving the outrage behind.

Let's begin with what people will see and experience first.

According to Axios, "For many of us, the robot revolution will be most visible on the road, with transformative changes coming to trucks and cars—faster than most people realize."

Truck driving is one of the most dominant job categories in America, with the jobs dispersed everywhere around the country— meaning that automation-driven disruption will create pain that's widely seen and felt.

Long haul goes first. It could start with "platooning": A second, autonomous truck—or a whole caravan of them—travels behind a lead truck driven by a human.

Self-driving trucks are expected to beat cars to widespread use because there's so much less complexity on the open road than on city streets. Self-driving cars will ultimately be safer and take some of the drudgery out of commuting, but widespread adoption is much further off than some of the credulous news coverage might lead you to believe.

Now, what does this mean for you? Well, there are currently 3.5 million truck drivers, many of whom will begin to see their jobs disappear almost overnight by 2020. Most have only on-the-job training and no degree. There are also another 8.7 million people who put the trucks on the roads.

Does it begin to make an impact now? Software developers know that the writing is on the wall for them as well, as what is called machine learning becomes more sophisticated. Truly the job of the future is nursing, but even that will be a whole different world. A good book that explains much of this is *Life 3.0* by Max Tegmark. It is a must-read, or, if you are truck driver, a must-listen.

I spent some time with the former CEO/chairman of the board of GM discussing the future of automobiles. While Uber and Lyft are changing the cab industry, those jobs are only temporary as well. Most of us will still have our cars, and it will take years to change that, as the average car is on the road for fifteen years. But there will be a tipping point in the near future when all of that changes. He told me that he believes in the next decade or so, GM will not be in the "car business" as we now know it but rather in the "fleet" world. Some, mainly the wealthy, may retain their own "car" or "po," but most will use something from Uber, Apple, or Waymo. They will own fleets of self-driving vehicles that are not reflected in today's "car."

Very soon, vehicles will no longer be driven by humans, because in fifteen to twenty years at the latest, human-driven vehicles will be legislated off the highways. Of course there will be a transition period. Everyone will have five years to get their car off the road or sell it for scrap. Automotive sport—using cars for fun—will survive, just not on the public highways. It will survive in country clubs such as Montecito in New York and the Autobahn in Joliet. It will be the well-to-do, to the amazement of their friends, who still know how to drive and who will teach their kids how to drive. It will be an elitist thing, though there might be public tracks, like there are public golf courses, where you sign up for a certain car and you go over and have fun for a few hours. And like racehorse breeders, there will be manufacturers who specialize in face cars, luxury cars, and off-road vehicles, but it will become a cottage industry.

21

Judge, Jury & Executioner

May I switch from jobs and cars/trucks at the micro and jump back to the macro again for a few minutes, because both are taking place at the same time? We have to begin to understand that the world is traveling so fast that to us it will seem like we need to think like a quantum computer and look at all options and possibilities at once. (While that is true now, we are still years away from actual quantum computing. When that comes online, it will be too late for us to figure anything out.)

The biggest difficulty with self-driving cars is not batteries, fearful drivers, or expensive sensors. It's the modern version of what ethicists have called the "trolley problem"—a debate over who should die and who should be saved when an autonomous vehicle's algorithms are confronted with a Sophie's choice.

This to me is both fascinating and terrifying, as we don't seem to have any personal ethics, and yet here we are trying to teach "life and death" to AI. "Life is nothing but a series of choices," my father used to tell me. "You make the best choice you can at the time, and then live with that choice, knowing it was your best."

These choices are on top of us right now, at seemingly the time when we aren't "at our best" and are the murkiest about ethics that we have been in my lifetime.

Remember, the problem we have as a society right now is that we cannot decide if we want to return to the values and ideas of the Enlightenment—science, reason, logic, truth, and, I would add, faith—or continue down the road to this new postmodern world where there is no objective truth and everything is up for grabs.

Just a single line of code that is ambiguous about life or ethics could twist the entire process.

MIT AND THE MORAL MACHINE

Researchers at MIT are trying to develop a so-called moral machine, one that can calculate in a fraction of a second who lives and who dies (http://moralmachine.mit.edu).

It makes death panels an algorithm for everyday life. And this involves not just how many people but the ages, professions, and "value" of each. Combine this with the new social value scores in China . . . a recipe Orwell would have called plagiarism.

Does it matter who is in the car, or what their profession, sex, or age is? If you had to choose between the lives of schoolchildren and the elderly, which would you choose? What if you had to choose between a busload of schoolchildren and a car carrying Elon Musk, Bill Gates, and Steve Jobs? Why? If we believe in true equality and that LIFE is what matters, then should it not be all about the numbers? Twenty people on a bus versus three people in a car. In that equation, who wins?

This is what is being decided right now. Are you involved? Did you even know about it? Shouldn't your voice be added? Actual votes are being taken—online—at MIT. The "moral machine" with input from an online poll? That isn't doing anything to make me feel better.

These are not decisions to be taken or made lightly, and as concerned as I am about an "online poll" balanced by a bunch of faceless, nameless "scientists" making the decisions, it is no better to add in a bunch of people who have an addiction to outrage. Have we heard from the guys in the drunk tank yet?

Has China returned our jobs yet? What is the latest Kanye tweet about? I need a fix; I haven't had any outrage for a while.

Choices need to be made, and we must be clear-eyed, clear-headed, and stone-cold sober. We must do it with reason, facts, and love for all mankind. These decisions will affect the entire world long after the Republicans and Democrats cease to exist.

Tech leaders have been trying to figure out a way to remove the bias of "a judge" in trials and replace him or her with AI. Studies have shown, as you might imagine, that human frailties or bias can affect the lives of those who stand before the bench. For instance, in Israel they found that defendants had a better chance of getting a "hanging sentence" the closer it was to the judge's lunchtime. So how can we reduce the bias?

In America, testing began on a new AI program that looked at the recidivism rate of all those paroled and came up with an algorithm for who should be released and who should not. However, as the program began to run, researchers found that the program was holding African Americans back more than other races. So, was the software racist? Were the facts wrong, incomplete, or racist? Developers are said to have "fixed the problem." How? What was the problem? And would that problem have been fixed or even noticed if it hadn't been a special-interest group that it was "singling out"?

I like the effort of trying to find fairer justice, but there are two problems that concern me. Who is programming the AI? Also, when machine learning isn't something even the programmers can understand, we no longer know how the computer arrived at its decision, so how will we know if it is broken or flawed? Do we rely on it?

Let me show how every decision and new technology leads to a series of new questions.

Let's say you buy a car with artificial intelligence. There is an accident. The algorithm has to make the choice between who lives or dies. YOU WERE NOT DRIVING. The car was on full autopilot. Who is responsible? You? The car? The car maker? MIT? The Internet voters?

We will soon arrive at the day when cars are more "pods" and artificial intelligence has moved into the realm of artificial general intelligence, connected online to all data and information, and has passed the "Turing test" so you can no longer tell the difference between life and artificial life. (Kurzweil and many others believe that date is somewhere around 2030.) "It" takes you to work, and as you will not require it for several hours, it is now free to act as an "Uber." Does it make it more clear or less clear who should own the insurance policy?

You "own" the car, sure, but you were completely uninvolved.

The proposed solution is to allow the "car" itself to buy insurance, paid out of the fees it earns while not in your service. But if it can earn money, should it be allowed to invest in the stock market? After all, it will be connected to the Internet and have access to information and trading centers. Could it not trade to enhance its profit? Should it be taxed as well?

If it is taxed and you cannot tell the difference between it and "life," does it have any rights? Surely, Americans understand taxation without representation. If it is taxed, can earn money, and seems alive, indeed it will someday soon claim to be life. Do we have the right to deny it representation? Would it not be akin to slavery to do otherwise? What kind of monster must we as its "creator" be to create what has all of the earmarks of life only to keep it caged, penned, and chained for all time? As it can calculate at speeds we cannot comprehend, imagine how long its "life" will seem to it. An eternity of slavery.

If we allow it to have a vote, what will that mean for humans? Experts claim that by 2030 there will be a minimum of one hundred robots for every human. That voting bloc would crush the human vote. As it becomes ASI and we are no more than a fly, why would it care about our needs or wishes?

Well, we can just use Asimov's three laws. I mean, it worked in that Will Smith movie. Sure, it works in movies and books, but once you actually begin to follow the thinking and understand the true power of what is coming our way, the movie solutions fall apart quickly. Let's begin with a simple question: Do we actually think that something that is a thousand times smarter than us cannot find a way to rewrite its own programming? It is like a family of baby giraffes building a cage for Elon Musk. Sure, it is cute and perhaps fun to watch for a couple of minutes, but it poses no threat to Elon or even his neighbor with the lowest IQ. Man has come up with ways to vaporize the entire human race in minutes; what could it come up with to do the job? Escape is not an issue.

Make no mistake, I AM NOT SAYING THAT ASI WILL BE MALEVOLENT. It will be neutral; it will care only about accomplishing its goals. Again, do not fear the robot. Fear its goals. If it is anthropomorphic in its nature, I do believe it will reject being used, abused, and treated as a sex slave, worker, or second-class citizen. But what we are creating is truly alien in its nature and thinking. It most likely will not think anything like us. If we hit the point of ASI (anytime between 2030 and never), I do not believe it will even think about us. "We are the fly on the plate."

In the book *Our Final Invention*, James Barrett explores this. Already we can conjecture about obvious paths of destruction. In the short term, having gained the compliance of its human guards, the ASI could seek access to the Internet, where it could find the fulfillment of many of its needs. As always, it would do many things at once, so it would simultaneously proceed with the escape plans it's been thinking over for eons in its subjective time.

After its escape, for self-protection it might hide copies of itself in cloud computing arrays, in botnets it creates, in servers and other sanctuaries into which it could invisibly and effortlessly hack. It would want to be able to manipulate matter in the physical world and so move, explore, and build, and the easiest, fastest way to do that might be to seize control of critical infrastructure, such as electricity, communications, fuel, and water systems by exploiting their vulnerabilities through the Internet. Once an entity a thousand times our intelligence controls human civilization's lifelines, blackmailing us into providing it with manufactured resources or the means to manufacture them—or even robotic bodies, vehicles, and weapons—should be elementary. The ASI could provide the blueprints for whatever it required. More likely, superintelligent machines would create highly efficient technologies we've only begun to explore.

Might ASI teach humans to create self-replicating molecular manufacturing machines, also known as nano assemblers, by promising them the machines will be used for human good? Then, instead of transforming desert sands into mountains of food, the ASI's factories would begin converting material into programmable matter that it could then transform into anything—computer processors and spaceships, or megascale bridges if the planet's new most powerful force decides to colonize the universe.

Repurposing the world's molecules using nanotechnology has been dubbed "ecophagy," which means "eating the environment." The first replicator would make one copy of itself, and then there'd be two making replicants. If each replication took a minute and a half to make, at the end of TEN HOURS there would be more than 68 billion replicators, and near the end of two days they would outweigh the earth. But before that stage, the replicators would stop copying themselves and start making material useful to the ASI that controlled them—programmable matter.

The waste heat produced by the process would burn up the biosphere, so the 6.9 billion or so humans who were not killed outright by the nano assemblers would burn to death or asphyxiate. Every other living thing on earth would share our fate. Through it all, over these first few apocalyptic hours and days, ASI would bear no ill will toward humans, nor love. It wouldn't feel nostalgia as our molecules were painfully repurposed. What would our screams sound like to the ASI anyway, as microscopic nano assemblers mowed over our bodies like a bloody rash, disassembling us on the subcellular level?

And on the seventh day, It rested.

BACK TO LIFE, BACK TO REALITY

Wow, let's take a breath. Geez, it started with truck drivers losing their jobs, and in no time my flesh is being consumed while I am burning to death, and not because of global warming!

Okay, ready for another round? Let's return to the here and now, to the more pressing problem of being clean and sober enough to handle the first turn in this technological revolution, so as to do our best to see that it does not turn into an actual revolution. Because with what is on the immediate horizon, job loss, true economic hardship, loss of accepted norms, and what I call "agents of chaos" will only make our outrage and anger worse. Believe me, the outrage that fueled the 2016 election will be much worse by 2020.

Maybe we can partner with AI and have the best of both worlds. Yes, we can, and you will.

Before we look at the "agents of chaos" that benefit from our addiction to outrage, let me make one last innocent stop at what is happening right now with China and technology. Of course, this technology is only being used to "enhance the happiness and efficiency of the workers."

According to a report in the *South China Morning Post*, the employees wear lightweight, wireless sensors that fit under caps or existing safety equipment, such as helmets. The sensors, which have been developed through government-backed projects, then broadcast information about their brain activity to computers that can detect spikes in emotions like depression, anxiety, and rage. The *South China Morning Post* found that some companies have been using this technology to monitor their employees since 2014.

One of the companies using this technology emphasized that "it can help reduce stress and the risk of workplace injury for workers," but there's also a huge business incentive. It's estimated that the technology has boosted revenue by 2 billion yuan ($315 million) at one power grid where the technology has been in use for several years.

The story continues: "But there is a privacy risk associated with the use of this technology. This is especially concerning for some in the context of China's emerging surveillance state."

Sure, there is always a risk, but do you want privacy or jobs?

PROFESSOR CHAOS

While this book is about our addiction to outrage, what we should be concentrating on is chaos. Outrage is the misdirection; chaos is the real enemy. Chaos is the key word in understanding the coming decade. It is happening on all fronts and is reflected in our mistrust of institutions, social structure, media, finance, jobs, and universities. We see the discord and chaos in social media, street protests, war, politics, and even gender. It is the substance of our outrage, yet we fail to see that our outrage only increases and intensifies the chaos.

Some chaos that we feel is the natural result of progress and technological growth. Change is constant, but it doesn't mean we like it or that it doesn't cause disruptions or chaos at times. Because of technology, everything from communications to jobs is in a state of barely controlled chaos. This alone is concerning to me, as you may have begun to see. The next "disruption" is going to require all of us to "brace for impact."

But beyond the "natural" effects of change, there are now many of what I would call "agents of chaos." They are the "key masters" and we are the "gatekeepers," and I believe getting these two together "would be extraordinarily dangerous," as was said in *Ghostbusters*.

From anarchists and neo-Marxists to socialist Nazis of all stripes all around the world, we find intentional agents of chaos. They are those who, for whatever reason, wish to destroy the system, hierarchy, and social foundations of our global society. They are not looking for "change" but are actively engaged in methods of destruction and mayhem. Angry, confused, and full of self-loathing, they wish to remake the world to look the way they feel inside.

A good example here in America would be Louis Farrakhan. Recently it was reported that he was now "supporting Donald Trump."

No, he wasn't, it was just that he saw the way POTUS was taking the press and the Justice Department apart piece by piece. It is good for the Nation of Islam for this to happen, as it gives Farrakhan an opportunity to concentrate on another area. These agents of chaos are equal-opportunity allies. They hold no allegiances and will partner with and lend aid or support to any cause that benefits the goal of chaos. Do you really think that Farrakhan and the Nation of Islam support those women in leadership roles of the Women's March who came unashamed to stand by and support him? And do they actually support this bigoted, racist, anti-Semitic, misogynistic, antihomosexual religious cult leader? Oh, in case they didn't know, he is also antiabortion.

No. But for now, they will stand together, as they are looking for allies in chaos. Each thinking that they will outlast the other and deal with them after they deal with . . . fill in the blank.

America has done this time and time again. We supported bin Laden as he fought Russia, gang lords in Afghanistan as they fought the Taliban, and, recently, we supported what became ISIS to destabilize Assad. When they grew past our control, we made deals with Iran. It is the same story over and over. But let's look at a couple of major players who have the motive, the will, and the means to set the entire globe on fire.

In the Middle East, there are those looking to destabilize the entire region. This first came to our attention wrapped in pretty paper and called the Arab Spring, modeled after the European Spring in the 1850s that began with the publishing of Marx's *Communist Manifesto*. Then as now, literal and political fires were intentionally set with the ultimate goal of causing chaos, being the last man standing, and restructuring the power centers.

But there is a bigger goal in play on several fronts: the destabilization of the entire world in order to reshape it. It is important to point out that most if not all of these scattered "key masters" are working on their own and have nothing in common with the others, with the exception of chaos. There is no conspiracy here; I truly believe each player is using the others and believes that in turn it will eliminate all others in the end, but the mutual goal of chaos keeps them moving in the same direction for now. But make no mistake—their goals are very different, yet each thinks they can unleash the "darkness" and still remain in control of the outcome. The other disturbing fact is that they get their power by using those who many times have a valid complaint or real and sympathetic outrage that is then manipulated by these agents to grow their coalition. Many times those people do not know they are being used, and sometimes they are so fed up that they no longer care; they just want someone to "make them pay" or "burn it all down." Actually, when we are sober enough, we will be able to see that both of those statements really translate into, "I feel as though I have been wronged and no one will listen to me."

IT'S MIDNIGHT SOMEWHERE

It is on this basis that many nefarious players over time have enslaved and slaughtered. Revolutions begin with those words screamed in outrage.

If you were alive in the 1970s, you may remember the revolution in Iran. The shah was a puppet dictator installed by our government who was woefully out of touch with his people. When they felt wronged and he did not listen, a group of religious radicals did. Now, decades later, the people are strong enough to stand again and say that they have been wronged and no one is hearing them.

It is in that volatile setting that the religious political leadership in Iran (Persian-to-English translation: Aryan) is looking to "hasten the return of the promised one." They are known as "Twelvers" and represent the largest branch of Shia Islam. The term "Twelver" refers to its adherents' belief in the Twelve Imams, twelve divinely appointed spiritual and political successors of Mohammad, and their belief that the last of the Twelve, Muhammad al-Mahdi, who disappeared in 872, will reappear as the promised Mahdi. According to Twelver theology, the Mahdi's return will coincide with the Second

Coming of Jesus Christ (Isa), who is to assist the Mahdi against the Masih ad-Dajjal (literally, the "false Messiah"). I believe most Christians would recognize this figure as the biblical Antichrist.

This sect represents 85 percent of all Shias. That can be estimated as approximately 148 to 296 million Twelver Shias. Twelvers comprise a majority among Muslims in Iran, Azerbaijan, Iraq, Lebanon, and Bahrain. They also make up significant minorities in India, Pakistan, Afghanistan, Saudi Arabia, Yemen, Bangladesh, Kuwait, Oman, UAE, Qatar, Nigeria, Chad, and Tanzania.

Iran is the only country with a state religion as (Twelver) Shia Islam. *National Review* reported that Ayatollah Ali Khamenei declared: "The coming of Imam Zaman [another name for the Mahdi] is the definite promise by Allah. The caravan of humanity from the Day of Creation has been moving . . . to the time of the Coming of Imam Mahdi. The awaiting for the Coming is a hopeful and powerful wait, providing the biggest opening for the Islamic society."

But it adds that the "battle" to establish the Mahdi's kingdom "will end only when the [Islamic] society can get rid of the oppressors' front, with America at the head of it."

Westerners dismiss this as nothing more than political flag waving, and perhaps it is; but it is important to point out that, currently, Iran is on the verge of collapse, and to garner support has been advancing a long-awaited quest in the Shia world to establish a new caliphate led by the Mahdi.

Whether they believe it or not, they need the people to believe that the one foretold is returning. The ayatollah has recently announced that the Mahdi has returned (from his almost thirteen-hundred-year slumber) and is now on the earth, he has "met with him," and they are now "in the final stages" of hastening his return.

Those who believe, or have done their homework, know that to "hasten the return" you must cause CHAOS and wash the world— specifically Israel and other oppressors (us)—in blood. While I have watched this movement grow for almost two decades now, I am concerned that the rhetoric and capability of Iran to cause this chaos is growing exponentially. However, Iran is also on the edge of revolution, which may end the current regime and discredit those religious Twelvers who are currently on this path.

I truly do not understand those who claim Christians are dangerous or put so much stock in the Westboro Baptist Church only to pay so little attention to something over a quarter of a BILLION people actually believe—people who have the state-sanctioned power to enact that belief. But perhaps it is easier for those of us in the West to dismiss those who call for the "end of the world" because we do not believe. When we fall into the normalcy bias, we fail to see the threat that these potential monsters pose to the world.

Monsters are first dismissed and laughed at, and they certainly do not come dressed in black boots and uniforms. It is perhaps important to remember that when the SS first arrived on the scene, they were the height of fashion, as their uniforms had been produced by Hugo Boss.

We perhaps take too lightly the warning from Nietzsche when he stated to the German people: "God is dead." Forever I have heard that as a statement rather than what it truly was: a warning. He wondered, now that the German people had "killed" their belief in God, what they would replace him with. He warned that when people lose their belief in a god, it isn't that they believe in nothing but rather that they will believe anything.

In Eric Kurlander's groundbreaking and exhaustive study of the German people and the seeds of Nazism, he clearly shows that it was a mix of desperation, loss of national spirit and identity, the self-discrediting of the traditional church, and their outrage that led Germans to the occult, mysticism, fringe science, and any meaningful heritage stories that would provide answers and restore the German people to their "rightful place." The Nazi movement did not start these ideas or perversions of truth. They had begun long before. Hitler just added more fuel and tapped into and tied into all of these fringe and desperate beliefs that were already held by the people. He merely needed to turn their outrage into a solidified movement and he only needed 30 percent. But it had become easy for someone to build a movement, as the press had split itself in half. The two main news sources at the time were politically diametrically opposed. If you looked for coverage of a news story in one paper and then in the next, you might not have recognized it as the same event. People were accusing each side of "printing fake news." Quickly families and lifelong friendships broke up over political beliefs. Minor disagreements became major, with each side calling the other traitors, racists, and saboteurs. It wasn't long before people began spending time only with those who thought like them, and even then would sometimes whisper their thoughts, as you could be shunned or fired just because you didn't hold the correct belief. In the early days, people began to see this as a way to settle old scores or to deal with an old flame who had scorned you, a neighbor you had squabbled with, or a coworker who was in the way of your advancement. The object was to see that the person was secretly turned in for the crime of the day, never to return.

As we all know, for almost fifteen years this grew into people being rounded up, tortured, starved, and killed merely for a difference of opinion or, many times, a misunderstanding of what had been said.

If you want to see the road Europe is on once again—and, I believe, America as well—read Sebastian Haffner's memoir, *Defying Hitler*. It was written in the 1930s as a warning for the West about what was really happening in Germany. It was never finished, as he escaped Germany and came to the United States, where he became the foremost scholar on Adolf Hitler. It was published only after his death just a few years ago. But unlike every other World War II book, this one focused on the German people themselves—what they were going through, feeling, and thinking, and how over a period of two decades they slid into the abyss. I cannot tell you how clearly the pattern is repeating itself here in America. We do not see it because much of it is still in the planting and watering stages. We are too blinded by our ongoing outrage competition to pay any attention.

22

Mitt Was Right

I believe the biggest threat for global horror comes from Russia. It is the European Identitarian movement coupled with a truly evil and well-thought-out and financed movement out of Russia that is growing in strength. It is called the Fourth Political Theory, and its roots are in the extreme right globally and even here in the United States. Its founder and head has appeared via satellite at rallies all across America and has been featured often on the Alex Jones show. His name is Aleksandr Dugin. Dugin is a Russian philosopher and political scientist, born in Moscow in 1962, who is known for his fascist, antiglobalist views. Just a few reporters are on this beat, as it is easier to think that all of these Nazi and "heritage" movements are somehow spontaneous. But he's important because he's an advisor and confidant of Vladimir Putin.

My team and I have done extensive research on this and a few specials for TheBlaze TV, and the *National Review* has also done some very sound reporting on the threat Dugin poses to the United States and the West. Going so far as to call him "Putin's Rasputin," Sean MacCormac, writing for the Center of Security Policy, outlined the root of Dugin's beliefs: "Dr. Dugin and his followers believe that Russia, as a Eurasian civilization representing tradition, is in conflict with 'Atlantic' civilization, currently championed by the United States, which represents economic, political, and cultural liberalism." MacCormac also takes note of Dugin's ongoing and incessant obsession with a strategic alliance between Russia and Iran, indicating

"Dugin sees Iran as Russia's prime ally in an Eurasian strategy, and makes reference to a 'Moscow-Tehran' axis. . . ."

Robert Zubrin, of the *National Review*, covering Dugin in a well-researched and lengthy series, wrote ". . . Dugin has developed a new 'Fourth Political Theory,' combining all the strongest points of Communism, Nazism, Ecologism, and Traditionalism, thereby allowing it to appeal to the adherents of all of these diverse anti-liberal creeds." While it might seem incredible that one could somehow combine "strong points" from ideologies that claim to be antithetical to each other, Dugin's work does at least demonstrate how much these platforms actually have in common. Blending in Communism's opposition to free markets wrapped in the moral blanket of opposition to technological and industrial progress derived from Ecologism and Climatism, he also weaves in blades of the National Socialism that would make Hitler jealous, claiming the need for total state control of all industries and media, in order to protect the national identity, public health, and traditional values. For fun, he also litters his monologues with Hitleresque notions of a people whose blood is "rooted" in the soil, along with odd-sounding notions Zubrin describes as ". . . gnostic ideas about the secret origin of the Aryan race in the North Pole." Definitely makes one feel warm and fuzzy that this type of language is being used again in Europe.

Zubrin goes on covering Dugin's writings: "What Russia needs," says Dugin, is a "genuine, true, radically revolutionary and consistent, fascist fascism." On the other hand, "Liberalism, is an absolute evil. . . . Only a global crusade against the U.S., the West, globalization, and their political-ideological expression, liberalism, is capable of becoming an adequate response. . . . The American empire should be destroyed." Given the fact that Putin gives credence and airtime to this guy, we should be paying really close attention.

MacCormac also researched and referenced an interview with Dugin in *Iran Review*, where Dugin himself provides even more details on his belief in why a natural, anti-US and anti-Western alliance exists between Russia and Iran:

"Iran plays a key role in Eurasianism. . . . After the Islamic Revolution and given the country's strategic position, Iran has been included in equations that aim to create an independent atmosphere of Eurasianism. If there were conflicts between Iran and Russia in past centuries and they tried to solve their problems through war, today, they only look for peaceful and strategic alliance as a solution to their problems. I mean, Moscow and Tehran are now solving problems which they previously could not solve even by recourse to military force. Our interests totally overlap from a strategic viewpoint. This trend can only be realized through (a) strategic alliance, not simple convergence. Iran is not included in Eurasian convergence model because only former republics of the Soviet Union are included in it. Iran has its own special civilization and is a powerful and independent country which should be respected. That alliance should be protected. We must not simply think about convergence with Iran. Iran does not fit into convergence model of Eurasianism, but it is a partner for Russia in a multipolar world. Our strategic interests in the Central Asia and, on the whole, in the entire region overlap. Therefore, Iran enjoys a pivotal role in the model of multipolar eurasianism and, in this model Tehran is the closest ally of Moscow."

Quoting from Dugin's own book, researcher and author James Heiser noted the most chilling final solution at the end of Dugin's rainbow:

"The end times and the eschatological meaning of politics will not realize themselves on their own. We will wait for the end in vain. The end will never come if we wait for it, and it will never come if we do not. . . . The end of days should come, but it will not come by itself. This is a task, it is not a certainty. It is an active metaphysics. It is a practice."

The true insidious nature of Dugin's philosophy is made clear in this final cheerful thought from the man Putin refers to as Russia's greatest thinker and father of his well-funded and Kremlin-endorsed *Eurasian Project*:

> "The meaning of Russia is that through the Russian people will be realized the last thought of God, the thought of the End of the World. . . . Death is the way to immortality. Love will begin when the world ends. We must long for it, like true Christians. . . . We are uprooting the accursed Tree of Knowledge. With it will perish the Universe."

So, for Dugin, as with many other meta-environmentalists and anti-humankind leftists, the world will be correct and full of love only when man has been fully wiped from the face of the earth. *There's* a cheery thought.

It might be easy to take this as nothing more than the rantings of a grizzly-bearded, bespectacled madman—until you realize that his writings sit on Putin's bedside table. There isn't anyone in my life that I have met or anyone in the conservative movement that I have ever seen who will knowingly join any movement like this. This is why it is so dangerous. You are expecting the jack boots. They conceal their movement behind nationalism, behind anti-capitalism, behind environmentalism. They have learned. Evil always does.

They will play on the actual facts and events that the establishment is refusing to address here and abroad. While our media complains about Donald Trump, has anyone noticed that the same thing is happening all over the Western world?

Why? Because the people feel as though they have been played, mocked, and used. They feel as though no one listens to their valid concerns and instead they are called the bad guys. These are, for the most part, people who would even in the recent past have been called patriots, hard workers, and solid citizens. They weren't activists. They were simply citizens. The first to give blood or sign up to defend their nation.

Perhaps it will be easier for Americans to see the problem in Europe, as we don't have any skin in the game; so maybe we can lower our shields a bit and begin to understand how other people think and feel.

Most of what is happening in the world is based in fact, but it gains its real power in feelings—feelings of outrage. And until someone in the media and highest levels of government changes their ways and actually validates these feelings by taking positive action, the situation will only grow much worse.

In Europe, they were promised prosperity and job growth if they just melted into the pot of the EU. This was to be like the United States, where France was California, Italy was Florida, and Greece was New York. But unlike the United States, they had a long common heritage. ALL of the wars in Europe have been about borders, land, and culture. They are as different as Canada, Mexico, and the U.S. Imagine how you would feel if you were told that next year there would be only three stars on our flag and we would be merging as a continent. That would be tough to swallow, but if the economic promise was big enough and we could still be unique, each in our own way, perhaps you, in time, could convince enough to go along.

But over time, let's say Canada is constantly bailing America out because we have decided that we now want Social Security to start at fifty-five, like Greece. We continually overspend and underperform. Mexico has become nothing but a resort for Canadians who have transformed their country into a cheap knockoff of Vancouver. Instead of the Ballet Folklórico at the Palace of Fine Arts, the new MexAmeriCanada government insists that they run cartoons of Dudley Do-Right and the story of the Canadian Mounties instead. At the same time, we are all told that if we fly an American, Canadian, or Mexican flag at our home, we are racists. Our children are taught that none of these nations have a unique identity, and laws are being enacted that many, at times a majority, of our citizens do not want or like. We are taxed higher and higher for the other countries, we must enforce laws that feel foreign to us, and if we speak out or question, we are made to feel like traitors, kooks, or racists.

Then after a civil war in South America breaks out, a massive population agrees, in poll after poll taken in their home countries, that each of our states must be destroyed and our people killed because our culture, religion, and way of life are evil. This is a group of people who have remained quiet while many quietly approve of the tactics of MS13 in the "North American states." Our new "government" forces each of us to "take our fair share," an amount that will forever change with the landscape and the culture of our countries. Those who are already here have taken over large sections of Atlanta, Vancouver, Cincinnati, Montreal, and Mexico City. These sections are no longer safe for lifelong citizens to go into, and the police have brokered a deal that allows them to have a separate police and justice system based on something they brought with them that allows them to rape children, beat their wives, and kill any they feel are inferior, which would be 90 percent of those who live in MexAmeriCanada.

That would be bad enough, but if our government then hid the actual reports of our children being abducted, raped, sold into slavery, and set on fire, what would we do? If you went to the local police to report your child missing or brought your formerly missing child into the station, where you described what had happened to her, and you were told, "There is nothing we can do," and, in fact, your child may be lying and you may be a racist, how long would that last?

By the way, that last example is what is currently going on in England. More than fourteen hundred children have gone through this, and their parents have been told to stop talking about it, they were wrong or racist, or that it was out of the hands of the police, judges, and social workers. The press refused to report it for fear that they would be labeled racist, so it continued and grew in scope and power for more than twenty years.

Some in the abduction ring were arrested and put on trial. There was a total news blackout, and no details have been released. The fear of the Outrage Machine is a powerful gag.

People are not racist. They are proud of England, or France, or Norway. They grew up there; their families have long lines of proud service. They are unique; their history is connected but rich and storied, their foods, traditions, and even architecture are different, and they are told not to notice or even weep for what they have lost.

This is the biggest problem with "globalism" as it is being executed. No one has a problem trading with the globe. But we are asked to deny who we are. Until we are allowed to all be individuals and truly celebrate our "diversity," the cancer of outrage will continue to grow. Faster in Europe than here, but progressives have always wanted us to be more like Europe. I fear the events of the day will bring us closer to that ticking time bomb.

It is important to understand that there are agents of chaos on all sides, and we must not play into their hands. That is what is so frustrating about the Russian investigation to me. I have my own views of the Clintons' and the Trump crew's involvement with Russia. For that matter, the FBI has a "mountain of evidence" proving that Russia has been engaging in graft, bribery, blackmail, and corruption to influence the American government at all levels.

For years I have described what U.S. Special Forces Command calls "the Bubba Effect." They have been looking for and training for the day that the average Joe, or "Bubba," takes matters into his own hands and the community supports him, even though they know he is wrong. They will look at those in charge as a bigger problem and even the root cause of Bubba's unfortunate act. "Yes, Bubba did it, BUT he only did it because you [the government, media, and so on] would not." I believe we are in the beginning stages of it now. Look how both sides accept behavior from their own that they know is wrong—"BUT." So what happens? What do you do? What do they do? Who is right, and which side will you find yourself on, and will you be sober enough to make the right decision?

The goal of chaos that everyone is missing is hitting us from almost all sides. When WikiLeaks, a Russian front group, released the documents from the DNC, did you notice that what they released was something that split the Democrats between the Bernie and Clinton people? They wanted to make sure they caused a rift within a party that had worked hard to foster those relationships.

They also put pro–Black Lives Matter campaigns out at the same time and rate they began pro-cop campaigns. Everything they did was to sow doubt and discord. They hacked the actual election results in Illinois. It wasn't reported much because it "failed." They had thought like old Soviets and not Americans. They hacked at the state level and not by districts. But why did they do that? Can you even imagine if we had had another Florida 2000 on our hands in 2016? They want us to tear one another apart so that they merely need to pick up the broken pieces, and we are playing right into their hands. They know we're addicts, so they feed us fake news that will foment outrage on all sides.

Adults must step to the plate once again. As I watch the debates on the cable channels and social media, I am reminded of my two youngest children, Raphe and Cheyenne. They are close in age, and as they approach their teen years they have learned how to push each other's buttons. I can see both of them do it. Just to get a rise out of the other, one will begin. By the end, they are both shouting that the other started it, and one is crying victim and the other is saying, Why do they always get away with it?

In my house I think we are onto the games, and we don't coddle the victim nor do we overlook the instigator, even if occasionally it is the same child. Because we are adults, if Tania and I reacted, picked sides, and became outraged at every charge and countercharge, we would destroy the family. Truthfully it would not have been the children who broke up the family, it would have been us, their parents, playing into their childish games.

I have met the enemy, and the enemy is indeed us.

23

The Black Mirror

If we cannot govern or control ourselves, then someone will do it for us. They will have to, and in the end we will beg to be ruled over. Just before the Soviet invasion of Hungary, the fires of chaos were set. The Soviets knew that if things were bad enough, the people, who had rejected them, would beg for someone to come in and help—desperate times require desperate measures. And when you are desperate, you can always find someone who will tell you what to do, where to go, what to eat, and what job to do.

China has a compliant, and for the most part, docile populace. In 2018, President Xi declared himself supreme leader for life. This was the first of many disturbing laws enacted that telegraph which way the wind is blowing in that oppressive state.

Foreign Policy reports that in what it calls an attempt to promote "trustworthiness" in its economy and society, China is experimenting with a social credit system that mixes familiar Western-style credit scores with more expansive—and intrusive—measures. It includes everything from rankings calculated by online payment providers to scores doled out by neighborhoods or companies. High-flyers receive perks such as discounts on heating bills and favorable bank loans, while bad debtors cannot buy high-speed train or plane tickets.

When the state council released its plans for a "National Social Credit System," not much was said. It is to be out of trials and in place soon, with almost 200 million cameras trained on the Chinese people. The council stated that the system will "allow the trustworthy to roam everywhere under heaven while making it hard for the discredited to take a single step." Each citizen starts with a thousand points, and then the fun begins.

Get a traffic ticket, and you lose five points. Earn a city-level award, such as for committing a heroic act, doing exemplary business, or helping your family in unusually tough circumstances, and your score gets boosted by thirty points. For a department-level award, you earn five points. You can also earn credit by donating to charity or volunteering in the city's program. Your points are then translated into your personal score, from A+++ to D. Drunk driving is one offense that can take any score and tank it to a C.

The system will integrate "total information" about you—what you do and say online, who your friends are, how timely you pay your bills. Companies get scores, too. For instance, your score can take a nosedive if your firm is "mistrusted" by the user. Wow, I wonder how Facebook, CNN, and outlets like Daily Wire or TheBlaze would fare. It would seem that having friends in government might be helpful.

In the smaller cities where this has been in effect since 2013, most do not know it is in place until they try to buy a home or apply for a government position or an academic title and are called into city hall.

In interviews with the foreign press, the Chinese say they "love it." As *Foreign Policy* noted in a recent article on the subject, "I feel like in the past six months, people's behavior has gotten better and better," says Chen, a thirty-two-year-old entrepreneur who only wanted to give his last name. "For example, when we drive, now we always stop in front of crosswalks. If you don't stop, you will lose your points. At first, we just worried about losing points, but now we got used to it."

The article continued, "Life in our village has always been good," says Mu Linming, a sixty-two-year-old resident of Daxunjiangjia Village. "After introducing the system, it's gotten even better."

Foreign Policy points out that in the town not far down the road the officials have even taken the official Rongcheng credit system a few steps further by adding penalties for illegally spreading religion—echoing recent countrywide crackdowns on religious practice—abusing or abandoning family members, and defaming others online.

What could possibly go wrong?

I know my friends on the left don't think this way, but a whole lot of us do. That is why we have a Second Amendment. They will always respond, "Do you really think that you are going to take on the U.S. military? They have tanks and planes." Right. I don't know if guys living in a cave still have our military bogged down; what do you think 100 million Americans could do? Especially since a ton of them are military.

Xue Liang, "sharp eyes," says, "I trust the government. Who else can you trust if not them?"

During the "People's Revolution," led by mass murderer Mao Zedong, he coined a slogan that "the masses have sharp eyes." It is one reason you can bet that the statement above about trusting the government is either for the score or propaganda. The people lost their trust in the government and in one another during those years of oppression during which Mao asked people to spy on their families and neighbors. Millions died.

But now dictator-for-life President Xi has resurrected the phrase Xue Liang, sharp eyes, for a new program that will integrate the State security cameras that already scan roads, bus and train stations, and shopping malls with private buildings, compounds, and private cameras to create one national database of video.

Using facial recognition and advanced AI, it will sort and categorize the vast amounts of data coming in to track criminals and suspects, spot and track suspicious behavior, and not only stop crime but also to predict crime before it happens. Hell, it's *Minority Report*. If you are one of the 1.4 billion Chinese, rest easy; this technology is going to be used to protect you, and should you fall or hurt yourself, it will dispatch help, as it will already have your criminal and medical records, travel bookings, and online purchases, and can even alert your friends as it is monitoring your social blog.

Total surveillance service.

Now, this may come in handy for us, as it all backs into a police cloud, where it can also sort through the "illegals." As the *Washington Post* cited: "90 percent of the crime is caused by the 10 percent of people who are not registered residents," a police report said. "With facial recognition we can recognize strangers, analyze their entry and exit times, see who spends the night here, and how many times. We can identify suspicious people from among the population." With sharp eyes, the *Post* reports, police will be able to track where people are, what they are up to, what they believe, and who they associate with—and ultimately even assign them a single social credit score based on whether the government and their fellow citizens consider them trustworthy.

The *Post* also noted, "Currently, the Chinese government is working with the country's tech industry, graduates from top American universities, and former employees of companies like Google and Microsoft." I pray for these poor souls, who will someday realize that they were the ones responsible for what could be the last great horror show of man. Tech industry executives working on the project, however, told the *Post* that this project will "shine a light into every dark corner of China, to eliminate the shadows where crime thrives."

Fewer and fewer will be willing to speak out about this as time goes on. Already a Chinese journalist, Liu Hu, saw his score downgraded because of social media posts. When the government demanded that he take those posts down, he immediately apologized and removed them.

The government felt that his apology was insincere, and he and his family are no longer allowed to buy any property, and his child is no longer able to go to private school.

Driving past the NSA data storage vault just outside Salt Lake City, Utah, you sometimes can wonder which side we as a nation are on. In June, at an AI conference at MIT, the administration was asked what its view was regarding AI. The response was a little shocking. The administration was looking for partners to whom to give "all of the data the U.S. government has" to allow them to reach AGI before anyone else. Does that mean the NSA data? If not, it shows how disconnected Washington is from the AI issue. If you remove the NSA data, all of the government's "data" would fit into Google's shoe.

We must not be dismissive or cavalier about what is happening.

The *New York Times* and others are reporting on the massive facilities that China is building for "reeducation camps," which will hold up to half a million people, for its new "transformation through education" project. It has just put out for bids another 880,000-square-foot reeducation center, complete with steel doors, barbed wire, guard towers, and housing for hundreds of police. This information is going to get harder to come by as sources dry up or vanish.

But it also may get harder to report on things here. I have reported on how Media Matters is now advising YouTube on which groups should have a voice and which should not. Just for balance, YouTube is also consulting the Anti-Defamation League and the Southern Poverty Law Center, which currently classifies my mild-mannered friend David Barton as an "extremist" and has come close to labeling the Mormon Church a terrorist organization. The ADL teamed up with UC Berkeley's D-Lab to create an algorithm that is learning to identify "hate speech" to further combat it. Initial results found that the algorithm was reliable 78 to 85 percent of the time, which is great—unless of course they've defined "hate speech" too broadly and it includes speech with which they happen to disagree. My friend Edwin Black, who wrote *IBM and the Holocaust*, told me that his book cannot now be sold in Europe because the algorithm will not allow any book to have a swastika on the cover, even if it is a very critical look at history. He told me that he feared "digital ghettos" or "algorithmic ghettos" where you can deliver information, even post it online, but no one will see it, and you will never know.

Don't fear the robots, fear the algorithms.

But this isn't the only issue. Just as it was when the Chinese announced their plans for 2020, it was again the same with the press here. There was a job posting last April from the Department of Homeland Security seeking a contractor to develop what it called "Media Monitoring Services."

It caught my attention, as it did Amy Russo's. She writes for Mediaite, which is a mainstream media-centered news site that almost all NYC and DC journalists read. In June she published a follow-up piece, and the details are disturbing. Among the vague details that went with the original posting was the explanation that the database would compile a list of "media influencers," including their contact information, social media conversations, articles, the "sentiment" of those articles, and where they were published. The DHS press secretary dismissed the worries with a tweet calling those who questioned the plan "tinfoil-hat-wearing, black-helicopter conspiracy theorists."

Amy reports that in one of his signature tweetstorms in early May, roughly a month after reports of the database broke, President Donald Trump went so far as to float the idea of stripping reporters of press credentials, suggesting that be the penalty for those reporting unflattering stories about him. "91% of the Network News about me is negative (Fake)," he wrote, directly linking sentiment to perceived veracity.

According to the DHS, story "sentiment" is exactly what its database will track.

Of course, in our era following "the most transparent administrations in U.S. history," the agency will inform media personalities and journalists about who is considered an influencer and who is being tracked, right? No, it turns out, but . . . move along, move along, nothing to see here. . . . As Russo points out, the Obama administration did the same thing early on, when it tracked stories

about terrorism, the BP Gulf oil spill, and the U.S. rescue and rebuilding efforts following the earthquake in Haiti in 2010. After a
2012 congressional investigation pointed to concerns with impacts
to privacy and the First Amendment, Russo reported, the program
was suspended and posts removed from the DHS Federal Business
Opportunities website.

PART THREE

Finding Our Unum

In the early 1770s, Ben Franklin, a true bon vivant, stated that he could no longer spend time with most of his friends or attend social gatherings because the times called for honest, serious, and deep thinking, ideas, and conversations, and too few were willing to engage. He could no longer tolerate surface conversations or "party talk." I find myself feeling this way most of the time.

It is not hyperbole to say that we may be facing a civil war in America. Over 50 percent of Americans now believe it is probable or almost certain that it will happen in the next five years. We also could see the collapse of the Western world or the rise of a fanatical Islamic global caliphate, nor is it unreasonable to believe the world could be plunged into war and darkness by Russian psychopaths intent on reviving and perfecting the world of blood and horror left unfinished by Mao, Stalin, and Hitler. We are already seeing the makings of a *1984*-style "superstate" that has the means and desire to pick winners and losers and will "reeducate" or punish those who refuse to fall into line. The frightening path that China has taken is part of its preparedness for another likely outcome, a "total global economic collapse" deeper than the Great Depression. This would affect every nation on earth in a way that we cannot yet even imagine, as it would come at a time when there are no global leaders. How could we even begin to move forward or come together, when we no longer remember where we have been or who we are? We have lost our heroes, principles, and even men's natural affection for one another.

I am a student of history, and because of that I know that man survives, but what does life look like on the other side of this mess?

(This does not include "the End of Humankind"/Killer ASI option that Musk, Hawking, and Gates predict. On this I happen to agree. If ASI leads us to a singularity, *Homo sapiens* will fall by the wayside, but that is another book, as first we must defeat our ignorance, apathy, and doubt.)

I would ask that you pray for my wife, as she has to hear about this all the time. She would just like some "normal friends" and a husband who doesn't make them cry on their way home. I try not to be that guy, but shouldn't we all be talking about these things? In our "collective gut" a warning is going off in all humankind. It has nothing to do with party or politics. It is our God-given "alarm system" going off. Gavin de Becker describes it best in the title of his bestselling book on security, *The Gift of Fear*. Everyone has it; in fact, all life has it. If your dog doesn't like someone, you should listen to it. It doesn't have anything special, doesn't have the balance of the gift that we do: reason. It is the paradox of our day: Because we no longer use reason to make big decisions, we are headed toward cataclysmic chaos. But, as our own internal alarm system goes off, warning us of the danger, our politicized outrage twists our reason and encourages us to dismiss the warning.

We know something is coming—we just don't know when and what form it is going to take. And as we all learned in the first *Ghostbusters*, it isn't enough to say, "Okay, let's just not think of anything. Clear your minds." Because there will always be someone who will have food pop into their heads, and the next thing you know there is a hundred-foot marshmallow man stomping on churches in your town.

These are conversations we must have with our families, neighbors, friends, and, frankly, anyone willing to engage in deeper thought and quieter conversations.

Just two years ago, the right felt we were on the brink of financial collapse, which could lead to a fascist government. Today, many on the left feel that we are on the verge of civil war and are now seeing the roots of a fascist government. Let's think this through; scientific polls tell us that nearly 100 percent of Americans have felt that some sort of catastrophic collapse could be near, and that the result would be a fascist government. Even if the margin of error is 80 percent, something significant is going on. Well, perhaps it is just the MSM and social media stirring things up. Well, yes, that is part of it, but as anyone who is really paying attention can tell you, this is different. I don't know how we have survived this long, but there are too many stress fractures to think that we won't begin to see real system failure in our near future. So, if we feel a "warning," we assume people mean it when they call each other "Nazis," and each side is fearing the other will create a fascist state, what are we doing to prevent that? What can be done? We all know what we are currently doing isn't helping, right? Does this system of government even work? Do we want to change it?

If so, is a system of redistribution run by an inefficient government the answer? If it is, how can we ensure that the state, which is already dangerously close to fascism, doesn't become even more powerful, especially when we hand it the power of life and death with health care, or when it becomes the final arbiter of which speech is protected and which is dangerous or hateful? How can we trust a media that will owe its protector and benefactor?

On the other hand, how can we trust a banking system that has repackaged garbage to sell and resell as virtual gold just to enrich itself? Insurance companies that more and more often serve the shareholders over the policyholders? How do we survive corporate giants like Google and Amazon?

To be honest, I have always laughed at the futurist dystopian movies that refer to the government as "the corporation," but I was wrong. How are so many of us blind to the potential for total control of our lives when we are seen as nothing more than customers and products by these two giants alone? Who controls them, when they control all of our most private and personal information, habits, location, interpersonal relationships, fingerprints, email, documents, pictures, and videos? Our DNA is not far behind, and yet they already possess the algorithm of our thoughts while also acting as our personal supply chain. All of this we have handed them gladly, without hesitation or even discussion. We didn't even read the contract before handing it over; we just dutifully clicked "accept." They have already stormed the gates of entertainment and brought the giants of old to their knees, and are now about to launch "news," fully funded by "the corporation." It bears saying again. I was wrong.

If we are worried about the future, then there are a few really important questions whose answers will naturally guide us toward a solution. What the world looks like in 2030 will depend on how we answer these questions right now. We can try to avoid it, but they will be answered by each of us soon—for it is true that not to speak is to speak, not to stand is to stand. No answer will count as an answer. We are all involved, and we will all be remembered as "winter soldiers" or complicit with what I believe will be remembered as the greatest crime against humanity: standing by and waving your finger or the flag as the Western world burns.

1. Is America a force for Good or a force for Bad?

2. Is the Declaration of Independence still a viable mission statement, and is the Constitution the best way to implement it?

3. Is the belief in a God or "higher power" important or not?

4. Is the Bill of Rights something we actually believe in, or is it just window dressing?

If we cannot have a civil national conversation and answer these questions, then we do not need to even ask the fifth:

5. Is the Western way of life worth saving?

A failure to find enough citizens in the West to engage in a meaningful and actionable discussion means that no matter how deeply you or I may feel about this outcome, we must individually find ways to preserve this new Western "library of Alexandria" in the hope that a future generation will be searching for self-evident truth.

If we do believe that the West is worth saving, then our next question is:

6. What is our unum?

What is the one thing that brought us all together and bridged that huge divide in the first place? Not only will it be easier to find but we will also be well on our way to rebuilding it by simply honestly, thoughtfully, and thoroughly answering the first four questions.

I will give you only a taste of each of these answers, for they are a book in themselves, but for those who are honestly seeking deeper truths, we will search deeply for those answers with those who are willing to stand against the mob and have dangerous conversations on my national radio/TV show and my podcast at theblaze.com/tv or iTunes.

Let's begin by first sharpening our skills on how one goes about even finding the truth.

24

And the Truth Shall Set You Free

To find that "one ring that can unite us all," we first must find out how to be able to recognize the truth.

If we do not want to be the generation that declares the American experiment a failure and carve into America's headstone the words "We tried and we failed; Man cannot rule himself," then we must begin to educate ourselves on critical thinking, honesty, and integrity, and reject the idea that anyone can be trusted to tell you the truth, the whole truth, and nothing but the truth. Even the most honest men will see situations differently from one another. It is up to you and you alone to do your own homework, dive in, and find the truth.

But as I have repeatedly said, don't take my word for it, nor anyone else's; look to the original source and those who witnessed it firsthand. You might just find a very different story from the one you were taught.

When my daughter Hannah was attending a liberal university in NYC, I was on the air at Fox, and, needless to say, was not popular. Very few of Hannah's friends knew that I was her father, and certainly none of her professors did. At one point, I had done a segment on art history and the fascist imagery of Rockefeller Plaza. I had spoken about the facade of the "Italy" building, which has a glass relief of a horse pulling a chariot with a strong man holding its reins and a young boy in front of the horse pointing the way toward the sunrise. I explained that the man was the fascist leader holding the reins of the horse (industry), with the youth directing the way to a brighter future.

One day Hannah came into my office, which overlooks the Empire State Building and Bryant Park. "Dad, do you really know what you are talking about when it comes to Rockefeller Center?" What an odd question, I thought. "Uhm, pretty sure, why?" She then proceeded to tell me how one of her professors spent quite a bit of the day mocking and making fun of me. Not knowing my daughter was in the class, he proceeded to use this art history as a lesson on how you cannot trust the people on Fox News, as they just do not know what they are talking about.

Now that I knew what she was referring to, I told her I wanted to restate my earlier answer. "Yes, honey, 100 percent, I know what I shared was accurate." She looked relieved and said, "Good, because I told him I wanted to do a report on it and he agreed. He told me, however, that I should only use one book, as it was the authority, but I have been to the libraries and they are all checked out. What book did you use, and do you still have it?" I said, "I think so," as I glanced at my library shelves. "I have many books on it, but there is only one that had that story in it . . . oh, here it is." As I pulled it from the shelf, her eyes lit up, and it looked as if she were about to cry. "OMG! That is the book he told me was the only one I could use." We both paused, and a small smile began to form on my face. I remember us both feeling a bit like the Grinch with his little dog, Max, as we just knew "how the *Whos* down in *Who*-ville would cry boo hoo." Let's just say that our story does end on the top of Mount Crumpit with a bag full of elitist dog—and boy, she did dump it. She received the highest grade he gave: B+. My segment on Fox had been correct. The media that had mocked that segment apparently didn't have a curious mind like Hannah's in their employ, or perhaps they did, but they just couldn't tolerate the thought of correcting their error instead of mine.

Sometimes the bias and outrage is so thick that even the "experts" cannot see the error of their ways because, in their mind, nothing the opposing side says can possibly be right.

But if we are really seeking the truth, we are not on opposing sides.

ORIGINAL SOURCES AND HUMILITY

If you know how to find the original source, why would you begin your search anywhere else? Most of our history books, since the beginning of the progressive era, have been bad examples of the game of Telephone. One scholar will interpret an event or person, and the next will write his book, quoting that scholar, and by the third or fourth author, it becomes "scholars believe" and later just an accepted "fact." Media are no different from or worse than you. If people hear me say something, many will accept it as fact and quote it, sometimes without attribution, as now we are bombarded by so many different stories and opinions that we honestly cannot remember where we first heard something, and if we heard it more than once we know it to be true. So, before we bring out the torches to breach the gates of Manhattan and pitchfork the media elite, remember, most of them are doing exactly what we ourselves are doing: relying on those we trust to shape our opinions.

Fake news is baked into our system of government, and I contend, along with those of the founding era, that the citizen must have maximum freedom of thought, speech, and expression if we indeed intend to stay free. But we must also engage in critical thinking and exercise our responsibility if we are to retain our rights.

I have deep and profound respect for those I may disagree with, but only if they have fixed reason firmly in its seat and asked the honest questions with boldness. We rarely see an honest question. We see "gotcha" questions, questions designed to trap or defeat an opponent. But how many times have you seen or heard a journalist ask an "honest question"? A question at whose heart is uncertainty, where, depending on the answer, anything could happen—not just in the interview but even in the life of the person asking the question. Honest questions are truly asked only by those who are still humble enough to actually still be seeking the truth. Most of us are no longer on that journey. It is why we become old, embittered, and calcified in our beliefs. It takes great courage to even ask the kind of question that could change the course of your life. But it takes even greater courage to accept the answer you get back when the truth is not in line with what you thought or want. It is at this point that each of us has a choice: accept it, grow, become stronger, and, yes, perhaps do some hard thinking and hard work to realign your life to what you now know is true, or ignore it. But if you ignore it, know that the cognitive dissonance in you will, over time, twist what you heard. It will corrode and allow the comfortable or convenient lie to rot your life like rust on steel. To me, this is what "follow your heart" means. Do your homework and search for the truth with great courage. Your feelings, hopes, or fears may want to pull you off course, but your heart, when coupled with reason, knows when something is true. Follow that path, no matter how frightening it may be.

I really do understand the fear. It is frightening to think that you are wrong about a fundamental belief, and you begin to wonder what else you are wrong about. I don't know, but when I began this journey twenty-five years ago, I found I was wrong about most things. Still today I am questioning, researching, and realigning. If you are not still questioning, learning, and making course adjustments, you either are Jesus or think you are. But, guessing that you are not actually Jesus, if you stay this course, life itself will crucify you in the end.

I am wrong more than my fair share, and I am guessing that you are, too. That is normal and doesn't bother me. What does bother me are those people who are so desperate to be right, to win or to grab power or fame, that they will knowingly lie, cheat, and con—even themselves.

"An important art of politicians is to find new names for institutions which under old names have become odious to the public" (Talleyrand).

25

How to Think, Not What to Think

Where there is doubt—there is freedom.

—Latin proverb

To truly answer the questions set forth at the beginning of this section, our search for what is true must begin with how do we even find what is true? What source can you trust? Especially when we are taught to assume that those who have opposing views are wrong, know nothing, and therefore have nothing to teach us. How do we find the truth or avoid errors when we will accept nothing but absolute acceptance of the entirety of our theories, ideas, or policies?

For instance, I have been accused of being a "dangerous global warming denier." Just that sentence alone should give each of us pause. My crime? I believe that the globe is warming as much as we can trust and verify the trends. But for this example, let me accept the current claim that the world has warmed by .7 degrees in the last hundred years. I also accept that man can do significant damage to the planet and has done some damage over the Industrial Age. It makes sense to me that belching toxins into the air is not good for any of us, including the planet and its other inhabitants over time. It is one reason I own a home that is as close to 100 percent solar as I can get, and if it needs a backup due to lack of sun, I use wind power and natural gas, the cleanest fuel I can burn without turning to our friend the atom. My home was built with the maximum R rating and can withstand temperatures of twenty below without heat and power and keep a steady temperature of sixty-eight degrees with no more than one fireplace. It isn't something I was promised, it is something that we have done for almost three weeks. I promise you, Leo DiCaprio's house is not as green as my home.

My daughter, who lives next door, has gone so natural, recyclable, and reusable that she considered for half a minute the "using moss for toilet paper" thing. Thank God she didn't, or I would never have been able to eat any of her yummy pies. She believes the same as I do, "not sure," "could be," but we all should do what we can to be good stewards, even if it turns out all of the science is bunk. My grandparents didn't believe in the "coming ice age" that was the big scientific rage back in the 1970s, but they still reused, recycled, and fought against waste.

Here is where I differ with the climate-change crowd. The cost of doing what you say will help will cripple the global economy. People will starve. This is not a reason to NOT act, as it certainly was not an acceptable reason when the South made that same argument against freeing its slaves. However, if science has shown that your suggested action will not effectively make any significant impact and could possibly make things worse, how is it you expect my blind obedience?

So, am I a denier? Dangerous? Should be silenced or even jailed, as some global warming activists now believe should happen to anyone who doesn't buy in 100 percent?

When activists were insisting that we all begin to drive electric cars, I asked where the electricity would come from, as the outlets are not magic. I was shouted down by those outraged that I hated polar bears. Studies now prove that the amount of CO_2 put into the environment by electric cars by 2025 will be worse than that produced by gas-powered cars because of new clean technology for the combustion engine. In fact, the average gasoline combustion engine in 2018 produces less than 1 percent of the smog-causing pollutants engines did in 1960. Think about that: a 99 percent reduction, meaning electric cars have a higher net carbon footprint than do gasoline-powered cars. So will we now have to shame those who drive a Prius or jail Elon Musk?

This is why we must first fix reason firmly in its seat before we begin any search for truth. But we mustn't accept anyone else's word on truth. Do not take any fact from this book unless you have checked it out yourself. Do your own homework, internalize the search, and the truth you will find. You will be able to defend it, if you have made it yours. But even then, your search for truth has not ended. New facts, conditions, and variables will come to light. You must always approach truth with the eyes of a child, always exploring new ways of thinking.

Certainty and a lack of intellectual diversity always lead to dark places. When you demand absolute acceptance of your theories and back your "science" with arguments of moral outrage, you end up having to shove, shout, and, in the end, shoot.

I look at global warming theory the same way I look at religion, just as I do with my faith in God. I will do all that I can by choice, as I study it out and remain open to new information on both sides, and if turns out I was wrong, it didn't hurt me; in fact, it made me a better person, citizen, and steward. Unfortunately, the advocates also look at climate change as a religion, the difference being that the hard-core advocates look at it much the way Torquemada did in 1490. Submit, confess, or be silenced.

But the problem isn't just with global warming or on the left. It is gravely advanced on the left, as they have received virtually no real pushback from the mainstream media. Again, see Evergreen College. If that had happened with hard-line fascists, the school would have been closed down by now. When you compare the coverage, rightly so, of the Nazi rally in the summer of 2017 compared to the Antifa riots the same year, that are still going on (see Portland Antifa riots, June 2018), it is not hard to see why the far left is worse. They have not felt any real ramifications of their actions yet.

So how do we find truth and avoid falling into political team sports?

HONEST QUESTIONING OVER BLINDFOLDED FEAR

In 1938, a physicist named Enrico Fermi emigrated to the United States to help his wife escape the strongly anti-Semitic Italian Racial Laws. He was enlisted in the Manhattan Project. One day, he found himself in the company of a couple of U.S. Army officers. After being told that some general was a "great" general, he innocently asked how they had arrived at that conclusion. Carl Sagan recounts the dialogue in his book *The Demon-Haunted World*:

"I guess it is a general who's won many consecutive battles."
"How many?"
After some back and forth, they settled on five.
"What fraction of American generals are great?"

Fermi, a mathematician, continued to ponder the issue, ultimately determining that there is no such thing as a great general. Assuming the armies are equally matched, the winning or losing of a battle is purely chance, the result of a million small chaotic events that are outside a general's control. And if it was random, the odds of winning a given battle is one of out two. Winning two battles in a row would be one out of four, and so on. So by simple arithmetic, the odds of winning five consecutive battles ends up being one in thirty-two. Only about 3%.

Sagan tells us how Fermi concluded the example of critical thinking, saying "Now tell me, has any of them won TEN consecutive battles?"

26

THINK

The average time Americans spend on a story is 7 SECONDS—translation: Most read only the headline.

We talk about fake news, but how do we know what is fake and what is real? To find that answer while in discussion with most people, it is usually quite simple: Did you read more than the headline? Did you read the entire article? Who wrote it? What was the platform you read it on? When was it written? (This last one is amazingly hard to get people to even check: THE DATE. How many stories have been sent around and stirred outrage that were written years before?) Does the story sound too good to be true? Have you found it on any other sources? How many? What were they? How many sources ("witnesses") were there in the article itself? Were the sources in the article named? If so, have you looked them up? If not, why? Did you go back and see how the reporter phrased their connection to the event described? I.e.: sources close to X, sources in and around X, sources that have spoken to X, and, my favorite, "thirty-two sources that include XYZ." Well, wait, that list included friends of the subject and "experts" who have no connection to X or the event. Just doing this will improve the quality of your information and a reduction of dopamine and cortisol, as it will reduce your stress and outrage a great deal. We need to learn to be skeptical again. Ask honest questions and weigh it out in our mind like Fermi did. There may be more than one answer. Both binary options may be wrong—or both are correct. "Children who play violent games tend to be more violent when they grow up." We tend to rush to convict or defend. But did the game cause the violence, or do violent children prefer playing violent video games? Very likely, "both are true."

Finding the original source when you can, asking the right honest questions, having a humble and open mind, and seeking other options than just the binary choice presented are good places to start, but you also need what Carl Sagan described as a good baloney detection kit. He felt that a kit like this would teach us what NOT to do and would help us recognize the most common and perilous fallacies of logic and rhetoric. So, I have created a Baloney Detection Kit for 2018. Here goes:

Argument from Authority. Did someone just suggest you surrender your own judgment to the decisions of others? "President Trump has a secret plan to take down the Communist regime in China. Because he's the president, we should just trust him; after all he was elected to make these kinds of decisions." Ayn Rand once said, "Trust nothing above the verdict of your own mind." Sure, Trump may be smart, and yes, he was elected and is the president, but anytime someone suggests you need to surrender your own capacity to examine evidence and use reason to evaluate something, you should certainly be skeptical. God gave you senses and a brain—use them!

Argument from Adverse Consequences. "If he hadn't acted, things would have been much worse." Ever heard that type of argument? This was used by the Obama administration many times over the course of his two terms, usually related to the economy or unemployment: "If Obama hadn't bailed out GM, the economy truly would have crashed" or "If we don't regulate puddles on rural farm properties in Idaho, we won't have clean drinking water in Seattle." This is called suggesting that adverse consequences will ensue and is often used to justify action when the cure ends up being worse than the disease.

Argument Ad Hominem. Is the argument against the concept or against the person? Next time you're listening to or witnessing a political or philosophical debate, watch out for instances where one side makes an attack against the person as opposed to the subject of the debate. Attacks "ad hominem," against the person, generally indicate weakness of argument against the subject up for discussion. When the statement "Firearms are used by private citizens for self-defense over 1 million times per year in the U.S." is met with, "Have you noticed Donald Trump's comb-over blows up like a sail when it's windy?" it's a good bet one side is armed with facts and the other is armed only with insults.

Argument from Ignorance. Don't you love it when someone points to the lack of evidence for something as proof that it must be true? "The fact that we don't have any evidence of a UFO/aliens visiting Earth proves the government is covering up UFOs" or "The fact that we have zero reports of police brutality against minorities just means the media is biased." Presenting negative evidence as a demonstration of proof of something doesn't always mean the argument is wrong, but it certainly should cause you to raise a skeptical eyebrow.

Observational Selection. "School shootings in Parkland and Sandy Hook prove that school shootings are on the rise." When someone selectively identifies a few examples as proof of an overall trend, you should always ask to see the complete data set. DOJ crime statistics show that firearm-related deaths in schools are down 75 percent since the mid-1990s, but throwing out a few traumatic or glaring examples (and expressing outrage about them!) is supposedly proof that empirical data is wrong. Objective evaluation of all the available data is necessary to fully and reasonably evaluate any subject.

Argument through Intimidation. Be wary of pleas that appeal to emotion. "We have to save the children! If you support gun rights, you support children being murdered!" Arguments designed to overwhelm facts and reason with emotion, guilt, or shame should generally be dismissed.

Statistic of Small Numbers. People love to point out one or two personal examples to disprove evidence-based arguments. When you cite a statistic that demonstrates home-schooled students dramatically outscore public-school students on SAT tests and someone says, "Well, I went to public high school and I got 1500," that's good evidence they don't have any other evidence. (But good for them on the score!)

Suppressed Evidence and Half-Truths. Watch out for contradictory interpretations of the same actions. "Trump has separated families and is keeping kids in dog cages, proving he's a racist pig!" But "Obama only separated families and kept kids in dog cages because it was required by the law" (that is, if you can get them to even admit that Obama kept kids in dog cages at all). If it's wrong when one person or party does it, it should follow that it is wrong when another person or party does the same.

Inconsistency Bias. It's always fun when people are selective about when to trust and use stats versus when they'll choose to ignore them. The temperature going up about .5 degrees over the last hundred years is proof of anthropogenic global warming, but health care costs going up by over 25 percent per year since Obamacare was passed is not evidence that government-funded health care causes imbalances in the normal supply/demand of market economics. This type of inconsistency is usually a good indicator of irrational and emotionally driven bias and should at least raise doubts about the argument.

Non Sequiturs. "The stock market won't crash because Trump is a good businessman." This type of non sequitur represents a logical fallacy based on the belief in one thing overwhelming logical deduction. The stock market rose by over 60 percent while Obama was president. Because he was a good businessman? You know you've fallen into this trap when someone says back to you, "By that logic, then this and this are also true." Really what they are saying is, "B doesn't necessarily follow A."

Slippery Slope Fallacy. Beware of the slippery-slope argument. Sometimes the slippery slope is true and should be examined, but it is proof of nothing. "If we let Democrats regulate bump stocks, soon they will come for all guns" or "If we allow Republicans to outlaw partial-birth abortions, soon women will lose all rights to their own bodies." Again, it isn't that the argument of a slippery slope doesn't sometimes prove to be true (ask a Holocaust survivor about having to wear armbands), but if the ONLY argument someone offers is that A or B is a slippery slope to C, it might mean a little more examination is in order.

Softened Language Fallacy. Beware of "weasel words"; when someone renames something to make it more (or less) sinister, it's time to have your guard up. When a "war" becomes a "police action" or "aborting a human baby" becomes "planned parenthood," you usually know they're hiding behind language and labels instead of presenting a reasoned, evidence-based argument.

Straw Man Argument. "He's basically Hitler." This one gets thrown around a lot, but it is key to be mindful of using it and wary when you hear it. "Trump called immigrants 'animals' . . . that is the same language Hitler used to describe the Jews!" or "Hillary called half of the country 'deplorables'. . . that is the same language Hitler used to describe the Jews!" Hitler also said, "We must love and support our troops," as did Reagan, Bush 1, Clinton, Bush 2, Obama, and Trump. This doesn't mean that when someone says something idiotic or foolish we shouldn't point it out, but appeals to the worst human ever generally indicate some pretty strong (and irrational) bias.

Assuming the Answer. Also watch out when someone assumes the answer is automatic. "We must keep the death penalty because it prevents violent crime," should be met with, "What evidence do we actually have that implementing the death penalty reduced violent crime?" A very common one over the last couple of decades is, "We have to reduce man's carbon emissions because the earth's temperature has gone up as our carbon output has increased." You should ask, "The temperature on Mars has also gone up roughly the same amount as it has on Earth over the same period. Did our carbon emissions cause that as well?" Correlation is not causation (in either direction!), but the point is to ensure the argument is fully explored and evidence is scientifically applied.

If we spend time actually using his baloney detection kit, we may find ourselves spreading fewer errors from those who have been deceived, the Russians, or anyone else who wishes to deceive us.

Currently, the effort to discredit and discard the entirety of Western civilization is the source of much of our outrage, on both the right and left. But if we are going to be able to answer whether it is worth saving, we need to show how to find the truth in current arguments. This effort began with easy political correctness, ridding our daily language of outdated words as well as those that had become associated with deep unwarranted shame or hate, such as retarded, fag, and nigger. The list kept growing to the point that now there are conversations we have in the newsroom in which we sound like idiots. "Wait, which f-word?" There are now multiple letters that stand in for words, and sometimes multiple "no-go zone" words per letter. We are afraid to even speak to each other. And it is only getting worse. It affects not just speech but actions and even associations.

It is normal and natural to group or label things or people. We do it so our mind can process all it must to keep us moving forward. However, we are now at a point where the label or the group is all that matters.

After the shooting of the police officer in Dallas in 2016 by a member of Black Lives Matter, I asked a few of those marchers to come in and have a mini town hall. They did. We all learned a lot. First major point was that NONE of them had read the Black Lives Matter manifesto. These people were nothing like the leadership you see on TV. They were concerned about the direction of their community and were trying to get someone to listen. BLM were the only people who would. One woman, perhaps my age, said some people in her neighborhood were afraid of their own children, and she was afraid of her own grandchildren. As she put it, "Because something has changed. And we have nowhere to turn."

As I spoke to one young twentysomething who had struck me as a bit militant, I stopped in the middle of a question and told her what I was feeling at that moment: "Honestly, I am a little afraid of even asking you anything because I am afraid of using the wrong, nonwoke language and setting people off."

She looked me square in the eye with the same look I had on my face. She said, "I can't believe you feel that way, because I feel the same way about you." From then on we had a very productive conversation. Both sides were not looking for blame but reconciliation and understanding.

We must be able and willing to question even our most deeply held beliefs and be willing to live with what we find. But we also need to defend the truth against smear, association, or any of the items on the baloney test. So let's try this out.

Currently the effort is based on the belief that some of the most prominent Founding Fathers should be discredited because of their connection to slavery—men like Thomas Jefferson, George Washington, and James Madison. They were rich white guys, too, which are probably their two biggest sins—and those should discredit them even more.

Recently, a law professor ironically named Carl Bogus wrote an opinion piece for the *New York Times* titled "Was Slavery a Factor in the Second Amendment?" Bogus tries to convince readers that the Second Amendment is evil by tying it to slavery. In predictable progressive fashion, his jumping-off point is the recent shooting at Santa Fe High School in south Texas, which he immediately ties to the problem of that darn Second Amendment.

Next, he makes an enormous leap in logic to state that James Madison included the right to bear arms in the Bill of Rights because Madison was from Virginia (a hard-core slave-owning state), and vicious slave owners there were deathly afraid of slave rebellions. So, they made sure their man Madison gave them the right to have guns so they could keep those slaves in line.

Seriously—that's his thesis. Okay, but he is a scholar publishing in the *New York Times*, he must have knowledge and evidence I do not have nor have ever seen.

Warning: It is this kind of dishonest "logic" that makes your head hurt. Bogus makes it all sound like undisputed fact rather than just his own made-up interpretation of the motives of James Madison and his bigot buddies from Virginia.

One of the most bogus ideas in Bogus's essay is that James Madison wedged the gun rights provision into the Bill of Rights because Virginians were afraid that antislavery congressmen from the northern states would use their new constitutional powers to disarm state militias. Gasp! That would leave poor southern states like Virginia vulnerable to slave attacks.

But if the antislavery states in the North were really concerned about the South wanting guns just so they'd be able to control their slave populations, why would the North go along with the Second Amendment? If that was truly the South's main motivation, wouldn't northern states have protested enough to delete that provision from the Bill of Rights?

Bogus points out that before the U.S. Constitution was written, "only" four of the original thirteen states' constitutions included a right to bear arms. Following his guns-against-slaves logic, all four of those states must have been from the slave-owning South, right? Nope. Only one.

So, it had to be Virginia, right? I mean, according to Bogus, they were leading this charge to make sure people had guns so they could control those slaves. But no: Even though it damages his entire premise, Bogus admits that Virginia did not originally have an individual right to bear arms in its state constitution. The only southern state that spelled out this right in its constitution was North Carolina (1776). The other three were northern states.

Bogus tries to bolster his case by name-dropping other slave-holding Virginians like Constitutional Convention delegate George Mason, who ended up voting against ratifying the Constitution. But Mason's opposition to too much federal power was not because he loved slavery so much and was afraid the government would take it away. In fact, even though Mason owned slaves, he was clearly troubled by the institution, and wanted the Constitution to include a ban on the importation of slaves. This is hard for modern progressives to wrap their brains around, because the same contradictions and foibles of human nature that they often celebrate in themselves, they refuse to excuse in the Founders. In other words, they have no historical imagination to grasp the distinct possibility that if they'd been born in 1700s Virginia, they too might have owned slaves.

But back to George Mason. He declared: "Every master of slaves is born a petty tyrant. They bring the judgment of Heaven on a country. As nations cannot be rewarded or punished in the next world, they must be in this. By an inevitable chain of causes and effects, Providence punishes national sins by national calamities."

Does that sound like a guy who's mainly concerned with bearing arms to stifle slave rebellions? Even though he helped draft the Constitution, Mason ultimately voted against ratification because he felt it granted too much power to the federal government, especially in regulating commerce. The Second Amendment was not Mason's top priority.

Still, Bogus tries to make the case that Virginia voted for the

Bill of Rights only because it wanted the Second Amendment. He implies that since the Second Amendment exists because of slavery, we should get rid of the Second Amendment.

I guess you could give Bogus kudos for creativity, but especially for a law professor, his homework here is sloppy. He does not include any quotes from James Madison himself about the Second Amendment, or even any quotes from the ratification debates. In 1789, Madison said he included in his draft of the Bill of Rights only those "rights against which I believe no serious objection has been made by any class of our constituents."

This wasn't like progressives trying to pull a fast one and hide a highly controversial provision among the other rights. It wasn't Madison trying to squeeze in a personal agenda item. The Second Amendment was one of the "certain unalienable rights" that come from God, not the state. Or, if you don't subscribe to a higher power, the rights are part of natural law—fundamental to human existence regardless of how humans originated.

The Second Amendment was simply not a controversial thing to American citizens of the eighteenth century. Before the Constitution, colonial law was informed by the 1689 English Bill of Rights, which, believe it or not, included a right to bear arms (and had nothing to do with slavery).

The Second Amendment did not give us the right to bear arms. The right already fundamentally exists as a natural and inherently necessary corollary of the right to our own life. If you believe that each person has the right to his or her own life, then you must believe in the right to defend that life; otherwise your right to life is a logical fallacy. The Founders knew this and simply wrote it down as a reminder, and for legal protection from those who would take away that right.

27

Fake News? Fake History!

One of the blessings of my life is to be able to preserve and share history with others. I began to collect historical items and documents fifteen years ago, to do my part in ensuring the truth was never lost. One of the items I steward is an engraving made in 1829 of Jefferson's handwritten draft of the Declaration of Independence. People often ask, if he wasn't a racist bigot who raped his slaves, how come he would scratch out the poetic words "All men are created equal" and then not mention slavery?

Well, as it turns out, he did. The wording was removed before the final draft. Not by him, or the eleven delegations who came that summer to devise a path to freedom. It was taken out, over his objections, by the demands of two southern states. Sorry, Mr. Bogus, but neither of them was Virginia. At the end of the list of abuses of the king's power, Jefferson writes an entire paragraph:

He [the King] has waged cruel war against human nature itself, violating its most sacred rights of life & liberty in the persons of a distant people who never offended him, captivating & carrying them into slavery in another hemisphere, or to incur miserable death in their transportation thither. This piratical warfare, the opprobrium of infidel powers, is the warfare of the CHRISTIAN king of Great Britain. Determined to keep open a market where MEN should be bought

& sold, he has prostituted his negative for suppressing every legislative attempt to prohibit or to restrain this execrable commerce: and that this assemblage of horrors might want no fact of distinguished die, he is now exciting those very people to rise in arms among us, and to purchase that liberty of which he has deprived them, by murdering the people upon whom he also obtruded them; thus paying off former crimes committed against the liberties of one people, with crimes which he urges them to commit against the lives of another. (Thomas Jefferson, Draft of the Declaration of Independence, June 1776)

Does this sound like the words of a man, written while alone in a distant hotel room far from his dangerously ill wife, who hates black people and wants them enslaved?

"Well, why didn't they all just break away without those two states?" Because to accomplish this never-before-done feat, they needed all thirteen colonies on board. In fact, John Hancock, as president of the Second Continental Congress, had previously ruled that the vote for independence must be unanimous. If two of the colonies broke away, the king would have paid them handsomely to fight against us.

You see that in the above quote, he was already paying slaves to fight for him. Had this union not been made, the Founders truly felt that the freedom we all enjoy today would have been lost, and the slave trade would have gone on far longer than till 1808. If the Revolution had fallen apart, all of the Founders would have been imprisoned or killed, and the idea of independence and equality would surely have been lost. How many more would have died on the king's slave ships?

It is important to spend a minute on the line about how the king had done everything in his power to stop all American efforts to abolish slavery. Did you know that Jefferson worked almost his entire life to abolish slavery in Virginia? Though Jefferson opposed it, Virginia law made it illegal to release your slaves unless upon death—as

Washington did. Virginia also made it illegal to release your slaves upon death if you died in debt. Which Jefferson did. When, in the end, he could not change the laws of Virginia or receive anything but a compromise from the southern states to stop the slave trade (but not slavery) in 1808, Jefferson wrote: "I tremble for my country when I reflect that God is just; that his justice cannot sleep forever."

How about the charge that Abraham Lincoln was not a church-going man, that he wasn't a "God guy"? This claim is easily debunked by Lincoln's own words in a passage he wrote that was discovered after his death:

> The will of God prevails. In great contests each party claims to act in accordance with the will of God. Both may be, and one must be, wrong. God cannot be for and against the same thing at the same time. In the present civil war it is quite possible that God's purpose is something different from the purpose of either party—and yet the human instrumental-ities, working just as they do, are of the best adaptation to effect His purpose. I am almost ready to say that this is prob-ably true—that God wills this contest, and wills that it shall not end yet. By his mere great power, on the minds of the now contestants, He could have either saved or destroyed the Union without a human contest. Yet the contest began. And, having begun, He could give the final victory to either side any day. Yet the contest proceeds.

And explain this letter from 1852 from Lincoln's pastor:

> I have had frequent and intimate conversations with him on the subject of the Bible and the Christian religion, when he could have had no motive to deceive me, and I considered him sound not only on the truth of the Christian religion but on all its fundamental doctrines and teaching. And more than that: in the latter days of his chastened and weary life, after

the death of his son Willie, and his visit to the battlefield of Gettysburg, he said, with tears in his eyes, that he had lost confidence in everything but God, and that he now believed his heart was changed, and that he loved the Saviour, and, if he was not deceived in himself, it was his intention soon to make a profession of religion.

Or the dishonest and dishonorable lie that Lincoln never cared about slavery and stopped it only because it was the only way to win the war. If he didn't care and didn't want to free the slaves, then why do we have an argument written in his own hand explaining his stance on slavery to a personal friend who was a slave owner from Kentucky:

You ought rather to appreciate how much the great body of the Northern people do crucify their feelings, in order to maintain their loyalty to the Constitution and the Union. . . . Our progress in degeneracy appears to me to be pretty rapid. As a nation, we began by declaring that "all men are created equal." We now practically read it "all men are created equal, except negroes." When the Know-Nothings get control, it will read "all men are created equal, except negroes, and for-eigners, and catholics." When it comes to this I should prefer emigrating to some country where they make no pretense of loving liberty—to Russia, for instance, where despotism can be taken pure, and without the base alloy of hypocrisy.

In 1864, he wrote these words to Albert G. Hodges in a letter specifically to clarify his feelings on slavery after issuing the Eman-cipation Proclamation: "I am naturally anti-slavery. *If slavery is not wrong, nothing is wrong.* I can not remember when I did not so think, and feel" (italics mine).

If slavery is not wrong, nothing is wrong . . . yet there are many people who still believe Lincoln wasn't an abolitionist.

There are many honest mistakes, and then there are those mistakes that are nothing of the kind. They are made with the express intent to destroy the truth. And people get away with it, because we as a people are no longer curious; we do not know how to look for the original sources or even want to question with a little boldness. We are comfortable.

But the truth does matter. It always returns, because nothing else works for long. In the last lines of one of my favorite poems, "The Gods of the Copybook Headings," Rudyard Kipling spells it all out. The "copybook headings" are Proverbs or Maxims, holding up age-old wisdom—virtues such as honesty or fair dealing—printed at the top of the pages of nineteenth-century British students' special notebooks, called copybooks. The schoolchildren had to write them by hand repeatedly down the page. It was how they learned penmanship and truth. However, "the marketplaces" were areas that dishonesty and immorality ruled. The Gods (or principles) of the marketplace represent selfishness, reckless progress, overindulgence, and a failure to learn from the past.

Kipling wrote this at the end of World War I because he had witnessed the lies and the effects of the progressive agenda. Millions were dead, and he wanted to warn others of how it always began and how it ended. Here are the last few stanzas, after the collapse of society:

> *Then the Gods of the Market tumbled, and their smooth-tongued*
> *wizards withdrew*
> *And the hearts of the meanest were humbled and began to believe it*
> *was true*
> *That all is not gold that glitters and Two and Two make Four*
> *And the Gods of the Copybook Headings limped up to explain it once*
> *more.*
>
> *As it will be in the future, it was at the birth of Man*
> *There are only four things certain since Social Progress began.*
> *That the Dog returns to its vomit and the Sow returns to her Mire,*
> *And the burnt Fool's bandaged finger goes wobbling back to the Fire;*

And that after this is accomplished, and the brave new world begins
When all men are paid for existing and no man must pay for his sins,
As surely as Water will wet us, as surely as Fire will burn,
The Gods of the Copybook Headings with terror and slaughter re-
    turn!

AS WE SEARCH FOR TRUTH, LET'S REMEMBER FIRST WHO WE ARE

America's history with slavery is an abomination. Frankly, the people back then were monstrous. How could they not be? It may not have been in their home, or even in their neighborhood, but they knew it was going on. The food they ate and the clothes they wore were picked and made by slaves. They may not have been able to hear the lash and crack of the whip, but all they had to do was think about it. They refused.

We should now, in this century, judge and condemn them. It is important to do so, to set ourselves apart and signal our virtue, because just as this generation has passed judgment on the past generations, we, too, will be judged and condemned by our children's children. "How could they possibly have cared about some entertainer who tweeted stupid stuff? Or spent days going back and forth online asking: Do you see a blue dress, or is it gold? They knew the food they ate and the clothes they wore were picked and made by slaves." Or is it different now somehow?

Judge the Founders and we, too, shall be judged. Why are we not today leading the charge to free the slaves that are currently in chains? There are more in bondage today than in the entire four-hundred-year period of the Western slave trade COMBINED. What people now say about the Founders is just as true about us today. We "may not be able to hear the lash and crack of the whip," but all we have to do is google it.

#slaveryisoutofcontrol #hashtagsdontcountasdoingsomething

I can see my ratings minute to minute. I know that every time I speak about freeing slaves, my ratings go down. I have shared stories of the way the radicals now fund their diabolical plans: organ harvesting. We have taken two cells off the streets when we kicked in the doors of their "surgery center." These are Christian, Yazidi slaves and even Muslim orphans who have more value as parts than people. My programmers beg me not to talk about it.

Be careful of asking the honest question here, because once you hear the answer, you are going to be faced with "the choice." The question is: Why?

Answer: Because all of those who have been "oppressed by a statue" are selfish, self-centered crybabies and cowards, and the rest of us are too comfortable in the belief that by expressing our outrage toward these crybabies we are doing our part.

The choice: Dogpile with outrage over my answer and do nothing, or do your own homework, find the truth for yourself, and let's work together and stop slavery today.

GETTING OFF OUR HIGH HORSE AND BEHIND THE PLOW HORSE

It is difficult to not embrace outrage when you see people talk about oppression of women and yet do nothing to help the woman in Saudi Arabia who just received the right to drive. Well, so far, only twelve of them. And only with their husbands' permission, and with a male in the car at the time. It is so comfortable and satisfying to say, "Sure, let's talk about the oppression of the hierarchy against women."

"There need to be more women on the boards of corporate America."

"How dare you say there is any difference between a man and a woman?" Oh. Well, if there isn't, why do we need to have women running companies or the country? "I will tell you this: America would be a different place if a woman were president." Well, I happen to agree, but that means that women are different from men in meaningful ways.

Fun? You bet. But it doesn't move anything forward. What if we assumed our goal was to find the truth and then use it as a tool to make things better? If we did that, we would stop the nonsense and help women in truly meaningful ways today.

I met with the leadership of GLAAD a few years ago in my offices in NYC. It was at the time that Putin was revoking the driver's licenses of homosexuals in Russia, and the rumor was that there were areas where gay men were just "disappearing." Speculation was that they were being arrested at night and taken to a warehouse and slaughtered. At the same time, ISIS and the government of Iran were throwing homosexuals off the roofs of ten-story buildings or hanging them two by two in the streets. I asked GLAAD to join me—I knew at the expense of my audience, who would not hear anything other than "Glenn Beck teams with GLAAD," a group that they would feel was a fraud and only in business not to actually help people embrace freedom and diversity but to silence and bully all who stood in the way of GLAAD's agenda. After forty minutes of trying to reason, I could not get them to talk about anything other than wedding cakes. They were everything my audience suspected. It is too bad they couldn't see beyond the oppression of no groom-and-groom wedding cake toppers in a handful of bakeries. Perhaps if they could, they would have heard the screams of those being tortured and killed by many of the regimes they strongly support.

Look, all of us have in our human nature a switch that helps us filter things like this, or we would not survive. The actual atrocities of the world? It is just too much to think about. In Poland, much of what kept the communities from helping and hiding Jews was not the fear of opening the curtains at the sound of a truck stopping in your neighborhood. It was the fear that what you had heard was true. You didn't want to know, because then you would have had to take action or live with the knowledge and shame.

How many times during the last Winter Olympics did we all talk about the pretty North Korean cheerleading squad? They are all slaves. Many of the last squad were rounded up and taken to a slave labor camp because on their return, they spoke about things they liked about the West. We speak of the North Korean missiles as if this is what makes them dangerous. We never speak of the horrors that are happening to the millions in concentration camps.

Should we not be actively encouraging one another to every day take another step toward the window to see what is happening to our neighbors? As in all things, we have to admit it first. Surrender to the truth and then take action.

28

Who Are We as a Nation?

So now, let's begin answering some of those questions: Is America Good or Bad?

Americans are currently split on many questions, but I believe that this one question is at the heart of our deepest and possibly mortal split. The way we answer this collectively makes the other answers we need either a little easier to find or irrelevant.

In the broadest brushstrokes: The right sees us as the knight in shining armor, who, yes, has done some bad things, but they are in the past and let's stop harping about it, get over it, I didn't have anything to do with it, and it is time to stop apologizing for everything. The left sees this as jingoistic, flag-waving nonsense at best, and as racist at worst.

The left is the exact opposite. They see a nation that has done some truly wicked things, all the while claiming that it was the "Christian nation," defender of the little guy, human rights, peace, and prosperity. Sure, there have been some good things, but even a broken clock is right twice a day. The right sees this as anti-God and anti-American.

So, which of these is true?

Winston Churchill is one of my favorite men for several reasons. The obvious one is that without him, the West would have fallen to the Nazis. He was not afraid speak his mind, to stand alone. To fail while daring greatly, admit his failures, and pick himself up and try again. Under great pressure, he would not be silenced in his refusal to believe "the German lie," because of which he was kicked out of both parties and sent home. Until the world caught up to his warnings. He indeed never gave up and never gave in. It did not matter what they said about him; he kept moving forward.

To understand him, you need to see him as the young boy sent to boarding school. Even though his father was close to the school, Winston rarely saw his father, whom he wanted to impress. While at school, Winston dropped his pocket watch, a gift from his father, into the creek. He spent days searching for the watch, eventually digging a bypass and building a dam so he could examine the dry creek bed. When he eventually found it, he brought it into town and at great personal expense had it repaired and restored. When his father was told by the headmaster about the extraordinary lengths to which Winston had gone to find the watch, he only replied, "It is just like him to drop something like that."

When World War II was over and England and her allies were free, largely due to Churchill's vision, tenacity, and clarity, the people voted him out in the next election. The election shouldn't have been a shock to anyone. With the people needing to rebuild their lives, the socialists promised help. Winston was a symbol of rugged individualism. He despised socialism, calling it the philosophy of failure, the creed of ignorance, and the gospel of envy. He knew that the Communists and Soviets were not allies but enemies of a free people, but those same people were tired; they had just endured two world wars and could not fathom a third. They had gone back to where they were before, unwilling to listen to Winston "beat the drums of war." But Churchill wasn't the one to decide. If Churchill had been president of the United States, Poland would have been free of not only the Nazis but also the Soviets. He was the icon of the attitude of keeping calm and carrying on. He was a prolific writer, painter, and father.

His words could have been said today: "The best argument against democracy is a five-minute conversation with the average voter." "Men occasionally stumble over the truth, but most of them pick themselves up and hurry off as if nothing ever happened." "Courage is what it takes to stand up and speak; courage is also what it takes to sit down and listen."

And then, just as you think you know him, as Johann Hari writes, he is truly a great man, unless you are from India, or Irish Catholic, or from Africa. As colonial secretary in the 1920s, he unleashed the notorious Black and Tan thugs on Ireland's Catholic civilians, and when the Kurds rebelled against British rule, he said, "I am strongly in favour of using poisoned gas against uncivilised tribes. . . . [It] would spread a lively terror."

His history in India is truly horrifying. So, which was he, hero or villain? His moral outrage at Nazism and the brutal thugs of Stalin's Russia was clear and convincing. Was it all a lie? Churchill was, after all, the man who invented Iraq, as Hari writes, "Locking together three conflicting peoples behind arbitrary borders that have been bleeding ever since. He is the Colonial Secretary who offered the Over-Promised Land to both the Jews and the Arabs—although he seems to have privately felt racist contempt for both. He jeered at the Palestinians as 'barbaric hordes who ate little but camel dung,' while he was appalled that the Israelis 'take it for granted that the local population will be cleared out to suit their convenience.'"

So, which is he? Both cases are compelling. If you only know the wartime Churchill, he is a great hero; yet at the same time, if you only know the colonial Churchill, the case is clear: He was a monster.

Which Churchill is the real Churchill, and which do we ignore?

America is a horror show. We imported slaves, bought and sold them, and legally considered them property. We took land from Native Americans that we had promised was theirs. We rounded them up and herded them cross-country, like cattle, to holding areas.

Yes, America has a lot of skeletons in its closet. But it's worse than you think.

Let's start with America's complicated and lopsided relationship with Native Americans. Most Americans generally recall the shameful

Trail of Tears, in which more than twelve thousand Cherokee Indians were forced from their homes in Tennessee, Georgia, Alabama, and Mississippi and marched halfway across the country to new land in Oklahoma. An estimated five thousand Cherokee died along the way.

It's a terrible injustice, but it's even worse when you consider the details of the forced relocation, the parts that people don't often remember from school (assuming they learned about the Trail of Tears at all, which isn't a given). The Supreme Court upheld the right of the Cherokee to remain in their home territory in Georgia. Congress did not pass a law mandating their relocation. Instead, they had an enemy, one of the most despotic presidents in U.S. history, and a genuine hater of Indians—Andrew Jackson.

Jackson established his credentials as an Indian fighter during his days as a U.S. Army general. In 1818, President James Monroe sent Jackson to attack Seminole Indians near the Georgia/Florida border. The Seminole raided white settlers' farms in the area and were known to harbor runaway slaves. Florida was still Spanish territory, so Jackson did not have specific permission to attack across an international border. But that was no big deal for a man like Jackson. He rushed into Florida, defeated the Seminole raiders and captured their chiefs, then proceeded all the way to Spanish Florida's capital of Pensacola. Secretary of State John Quincy Adams had opened negotiations with Spain for the U.S. to potentially acquire Florida, but Jackson attacked Pensacola and seized Florida by conquest.

Bet you didn't remember that Florida became a state because Andrew Jackson waged war on the Indians there and, while he was at it, just decided to take Florida from Spain. There was nothing remotely legal about his outlandish actions, yet neither President Monroe nor Congress did anything to correct the incredible situation. They just kept Florida! Jackson never suffered any consequences either. He would grace America with the same audacity as president eleven years later.

As revenge, Florida now ends up a torturous swing state in every presidential election.

Battles between the U.S. Army and Native Americans, particularly in the West, raged on for decades as settlers and railroad tracks spread across the continent. The broken treaties and promises by the U.S. government culminated in the 1890 massacre at Wounded Knee.

The U.S. Army had pursued Sitting Bull and his Sioux followers for years. When they finally caught up to him at Wounded Knee Creek in South Dakota, his followers tried to resist his arrest, and in the scuffle Sitting Bull was shot and killed.

Two weeks later, the army surrounded another band of Sioux who were participants in the Ghost Dance. The Sioux believed that if they religiously performed the Ghost Dance and rejected the ways of the white man, the gods would favor them, restore them to their land, and destroy all nonbelievers. The army arrived, demanding the Ghost Dancers surrender their weapons.

No one knows for certain who fired the first shot. There are various possible culprits: a trigger-happy soldier, a panicked Sioux. A fierce firefight erupted, but the army had far superior firepower. When the dust settled and the smoke cleared, 150 Sioux warriors, women, and children lay dead, and another 50 had been wounded. The army counted 25 dead soldiers and 39 wounded. Some estimate that 300 to 400 Sioux were actually killed. Regardless, it was a massacre.

Adding insult to this atrocity is that 20 army soldiers were awarded the Congressional Medal of Honor for their roles in this "battle." That is more than the number of Medals of Honor awarded for any single battle during World War II. The U.S. government's message was clear—the soldiers were the good guys.

The U.S. government's mistreatment of Native Americans is certainly one of the main talking points from the left when they want to take down America. But it's not *the* main one. That would be slavery. That's not to say that slavery isn't every bit the stain on our nation that the left says it is—it's just that conservatives generally have a different approach to the healthiest way to admit the severity of this stain while still moving forward.

We have addressed Jefferson and slavery, but go back to the Founding Fathers for a moment, because that's where the left likes to start in dismantling and discounting the Founders' accomplishments. "Founding Fathers" is a general label that encompasses a large group of men, but they didn't distribute official "Founding Fathers" membership cards, so let's define who we're talking about here. We'll narrow it down to the delegates to the Constitutional Convention. Of the fifty-five Convention delegates, twenty-five owned slaves. George Washington owned slaves. So did Thomas Jefferson, writer of the Declaration of Independence.

As remarkable an accomplishment as the Constitution is, the Founders ultimately blew it when it came to slavery. Though many of the delegates were adamantly opposed to slavery, the Convention determined that to keep the nation intact and enable a strong central government, they would not resolve the slavery question. Big mistake. Their lack of conviction created a mountain of trouble and pain for the young nation when the Civil War began barely seventy-five years later. They set America on a disastrous course of racial strife and violence that would stretch over the next 180 years.

And all that was thanks to what the Constitution failed to do. The U.S. Supreme Court made it even worse.

First, the infamous Dred Scott decision in 1857, which declared slaves were not, and could not become, U.S. citizens. The Court said in essence that slaves were property. That's not helpful. Chief Justice Roger B. Taney wrote the majority opinion. Guess who appointed Taney to the Supreme Court? His good buddy Andrew Jackson.

Despite the fervent efforts of northern abolitionists during the first half of the nineteenth century to banish slavery from American life, the South stubbornly tightened its chains during those decades to the point of violent resistance. The "states' rights" argument is simply a bedtime story the South told itself after it lost the Civil War. When the Confederate States of America formed, its Constitution was clearly designed to perpetuate slavery. It prohibited passing any law that would deny the right to own slaves. It also guaranteed slavery would exist in any future territories. Make no mistake—the Civil War was about slavery and deep-seated racism. At no point was this evidenced more than the 1864 Fort Pillow Massacre in Tennessee.

Confederate general Nathan Bedford Forrest led a cavalry division of around 2,000 men to take Fort Pillow, which overlooked the Mississippi River north of Memphis. The fort was protected by only 557 men, 262 of whom were black Union soldiers. There were few things more abhorrent to the Confederate Army than facing northern black troops on the battlefield. Forrest's men captured the fort with few casualties. The remaining Union soldiers surrendered and should have been held as prisoners of war. Instead, Forrest ordered the black soldiers to be executed—and more than 200 of them, along with some women and children, were beaten, shot, stabbed with bayonets, or hacked with sabers. Confederate soldiers even dragged the wounded from the fort's hospital building and killed them.

In his written report about the battle, a white Union lieutenant wrote that even the day after the massacre, he witnessed two wounded black soldiers plead for their lives before being shot in the head by a Confederate soldier with a pistol.

Nathan Bedford Forrest would go on to become the first and only grand wizard of the KKK. Indeed, America has some extremely ugly stains.

After the Civil War and the strain of Reconstruction, the nation might have had a chance to reboot race relations. Instead, the Supreme Court weighed in again to sucker-punch blacks who by now (thanks to the Fourteenth Amendment) were U.S. citizens. In the 1896 *Plessy v. Ferguson* case, the Supreme Court legalized segregation with its infamous "separate but equal" clause, meaning that as long as facilities such as train cars were equal in quality, you could have "white only" and "black only" sections. Southern states jumped on this clause like a famished dog on a bone, and soon, everything from restrooms to water fountains to theaters was segregated. Naturally, the separate facilities were almost never "equal."

Between the last Union troops pulling out of the South in 1876 and the Supreme Court's disastrous *Plessy v. Ferguson* ruling twenty years later, segregation and Jim Crow laws were firmly entrenched throughout the South.

One of the highest-profile examples of Jim Crow "justice" happened in Brownsville, Texas, in 1906. A white bartender was shot and killed, and a Hispanic police officer was wounded in downtown Brownsville. Several white citizens, and even the mayor of Brownsville, immediately accused black soldiers who were stationed at nearby Fort Brown. The accusers even claimed they'd seen the soldiers in town firing their rifles. Investigators believed the white citizens' testimony, especially after they produced spent shells from army rifles (later evidence showed the shells had been planted).

The white commanding officers at Fort Brown believed the soldiers were all in their barracks at the time of the shooting. Nevertheless, the ire of the town turned into a wildfire of outrage. The whole company of black soldiers was assembled and given an ultimatum to confess and call out the guilty party. The men refused to name names, because none of them had committed a crime.

The scandal rose all the way to the commander in chief in the White House—Theodore Roosevelt. In one of the worst moves of his lauded presidency, Roosevelt decided to dishonorably discharge all 167 of the black soldiers from Fort Brown over the incident because of their "conspiracy of silence."

The black community was appalled at the miscarriage of justice, and that Theodore Roosevelt had played a role in it. Booker T. Washington, who enjoyed a relatively close relationship with the president, pled with him to reconsider. Roosevelt refused. This incident triggered the general changeover in black voter loyalty from the Republican Party to the Democratic Party.

The Brownsville affair is maddening in its unfairness, but it was unfortunately typical and hardly the worst example of the dangers of Jim Crow life. A far more tragic incident afflicted the black citizens of Tulsa, Oklahoma, in 1921, in a prosperous section of the city often called "Black Wall Street."

As the main part of Tulsa grew and prospered at the turn of the twentieth century, so did the section of Greenwood, which was home to ten thousand black citizens. The oil boom and wealthy white businessmen created a huge need for service jobs that the black community eagerly filled. Every morning black workers walked south across the train tracks, returning later that night with pockets full of cash. This brought in scores of black professionals from all over the country, setting up shop in the business district of Greenwood. At a time when lynchings were common across the South and opportunities were sparse for blacks in much of the nation, Greenwood was seen as a Promised Land. Greenwood was home to movie theaters, soda shops, and countless stores, restaurants, and schools. It was decidedly atypical in the Jim Crow era.

Tragically, however, the poison of violent racism seeped into the peaceful haven of Greenwood. In late May 1921, a black man named Dick Rowland was arrested for allegedly assaulting a seventeen-year-old white woman. He was a shoe-shiner who worked in the same building as his accuser, who was an elevator operator.

Though the police doubted the woman's story that Rowland had assaulted her, rumor ran rampant through Tulsa, spurred on by the racist owner of the *Tulsa Tribune*, who published a sensational story about the alleged attack within hours of Rowland's arrest. Soon after the newspapers hit the street, a mob formed and headed to the courthouse where Rowland was being held. KKK members arrived on the scene, whipping the mob into a frenzy.

Rumors enveloped Greenwood that the KKK was planning an assault on the courthouse that night. Hundreds of black men, many of them World War I veterans, armed themselves and prepared for battle. They arrived at the courthouse to defend Rowland. Police tried to defuse the situation, but a white man attempted to disarm one of the black men, and all hell broke loose. Hundreds of shots rang out and mass chaos ensued. Twenty people were killed in the initial skirmish. Unfortunately, that was only the beginning.

The white mob grew to ten thousand people. A few black men

were captured, tied to the bumpers of cars, and dragged through the streets of Tulsa. The Oklahoma National Guard was summoned to defend white Tulsa.

Early the next morning, a factory whistle provided the signal to attack Greenwood. The mob charged with the National Guard and the killing commenced. Fleeing black men and women were shot in the back. The mob ransacked homes and businesses before dousing the buildings with gasoline and burning them to the ground. Biplanes even dropped firebombs from the sky. Thirty-five square blocks were destroyed—more than a thousand homes burned. Five hotels, thirty-one restaurants, twenty-four grocery stores, four drugstores, one hospital, one library, one school, and twelve churches—all completely burned.

Nearly three hundred black citizens were killed. More than six thousand black survivors were rounded up by the police and National Guard and held in a sort of refugee prison camp outside Tulsa. No one knows who gave the attack orders that morning. It's safe to say most people never read about the "Black Wall Street" massacre in history class. This one has been swept very far under a very large rug.

Racism among Americans and racist policy from the U.S. government was not limited to Native Americans and blacks. As America welcomed the "huddled masses" to its shores during the late 1800s immigration boom, not everyone was welcome. A nativist movement gained momentum over resentment of the flood of Slavic and Latin immigrants from southern and eastern Europe, Irish Catholics, and Chinese.

In the western half of the U.S., Chinese immigrants faced just as much as or more discrimination than any other group. In 1880, Chinese immigrants made up 11 percent of California's population. In the years after the Civil War, railroad construction chiefs liked hiring Chinese immigrants because they were hardworking and would often work for lower wages. White workers resented the Chinese "stealing" these jobs from native-born Americans.

By 1880, demand for railroad workers decreased, and Congress was convinced they needed to shut down the flow of immigrants from China. In 1882, Congress overwhelmingly passed a bill with a not-very-subtle name: the Chinese Exclusion Act. The law suspended immigration from China for ten years and could be renewed—which it was. In 1902, the law was extended indefinitely. The Chinese immigration ban wasn't lifted until 1943. But by then, the U.S. government had turned its attention to a more worrisome Asian group—the Japanese.

After the attack on Pearl Harbor on December 7, 1941, anti-Japanese paranoia soared, particularly on the West Coast. It instantly became a dangerous time to be a Japanese American. In the hours just after the attack, the FBI arrested—without evidence—1,291 Japanese American community and religious leaders and froze their assets. The governor of Idaho said: "A good solution to the Jap problem would be to send them all back to Japan, then sink the island. They live like rats, breed like rats, and act like rats."

Two months after Pearl Harbor, fears of Japanese sympathizers, spies, and saboteurs prompted President Franklin Roosevelt to sign an executive order to round up Americans of Japanese descent and send them to internment camps surrounded by barbed wire and armed military guards. It was an audacious move, and probably the most egregious violation of the Constitution in U.S. history. But set within America's heroic effort to defeat the Axis Powers, it's often treated as a mere footnote in the bigger story and justified as an understandable, if harsh, side effect of 1940s wartime America.

More than 117,000 Japanese Americans were systematically removed from their homes and transported to one of ten internment camps in Arizona, Arkansas, California, Colorado, Idaho, Utah, and Wyoming. One-third of these prisoners were younger than nineteen years old. They were held in the camps for over three years. Anyone who tried to escape (and there were a handful) was shot and killed.

Most of these citizen prisoners lost their homes, businesses, and farms. Some were able to sell their property, but at a huge financial loss. The government informed two thousand internees that their personal vehicles would be safely stored until they were released from the camps. Soon, however, the U.S. Army offered to buy the vehicles at insultingly low prices. Prisoners who refused to sell were told the military had to requisition their vehicles for the war effort.

After one Japanese American prisoner arrived at his assigned internment camp, he was told that they were being put in the camps for their own protection. "If we were put here for our protection," he replied, "why are the guns at the guard towers pointed inward instead of outward?" We don't even need to go any further. America is a horrible force for evil.

29

The Case for Good

No country on earth flogs itself for its past sins more than the United States of America. Self-examination is beneficial, of course, unless you refuse to move forward because you're stuck in the mire of the past. This is where progressives and conservatives sharply diverge. Progressives tend to operate as if the past is an inescapable force that inhibits the present (and as if the past is especially paralyzing for minorities). Therefore, since America's past was so evil and the nation was founded on oppression—according to progressives—America must be remade in the progressive image, which would balance the scales and create utopia.

Thoughtful conservatives tend to acknowledge America's past wrongs (progressives would say we downplay them) while at the same time acknowledging that the record is not 100 percent evil. Conservatives find value for the present in many tried-and-true institutions, values, and principles from the past. There is a lot more good in our past than progressives care to admit, because if they did admit it, the whole existence of their movement would be jeopardized. I believe the conservative movement is jeopardized by not being on the leading edge of documenting, teaching, and learning from the wrongs of our past. We cannot say "Never again" if we do not first remember the truth.

Let's just do as we did with the bad. Let me give you a few things that you may never have learned about America, our history, and our heroes. While the U.S. Constitution fell short of abolition, by 1800, seven of the thirteen original states plus Vermont had banned slavery in their state constitutions: Pennsylvania, Massachusetts, Connecticut, Rhode Island, New Hampshire, New York, and New Jersey.

As president, George Washington signed a bill prohibiting slavery in the new territories opened up during his administration. In his will, Washington also provided for the freedom of his own slaves. He was the only Founding Father to take that step. That might seem like small potatoes to modern progressives, but it represented a step in the right direction. Washington wrote, "I can only say that there is not a man living who wishes more sincerely than I do to see a plan adopted for the abolition of slavery."

In 1774, Benjamin Franklin cofounded America's first antislavery society. Franklin also became a friend of Phillis Wheatley. She had been brought to the U.S. as a seven-year-old slave from Senegal. John Wheatley purchased her, and she grew up in Boston, Massachusetts. The Wheatleys educated her in Latin and Greek, and she published her first poem when she was a teenager. She became the first black woman (and one of the first women, period) to publish a book, a volume of her poetry, in 1773. The Wheatleys freed her, and in 1778 she married a free black man from Boston named John Peters.

Did you ever hear about Phillis Wheatley in history class? Or how about Peter Salem?

Salem was a former slave from Massachusetts, freed when he was about twenty-five years old so that he could enlist in the Framingham militia. Salem fought in the Battles of Lexington and Concord and, most famously, at the Battle of Bunker Hill in Charlestown, Massachusetts, on June 17, 1775. After repulsing two British attacks, the colonists were running low on ammunition and were ordered to retreat to Cambridge. Just as the order to retreat was given, Salem charged ahead and fired his musket, mortally wounding British marine major John Pitcairn. Though Bunker Hill was technically a loss for the Americans, it was a major turning point in the Revolutionary War because it demonstrated that the scrappy Continental Army could hold its own against the mighty British military.

Though the Supreme Court severely hampered America's ability to abolish slavery and treat blacks as equal citizens, there was an early bright spot that gave a glimmer of hope. In 1839, fifty-three African slaves were being transported from Cuba when they mutinied and took control of their ship, the *Amistad*. The slaves inadvertently sailed up the East Coast of the U.S. before they were intercepted by a U.S. naval ship near Long Island, New York. The slaves were then arrested and jailed. Northern abolitionists lobbied vigorously for their release. Eventually, their case landed before the Supreme Court, where their lawyer, former president John Quincy Adams, argued for their freedom. The Court ultimately ruled that because the international slave trade was illegal, the *Amistad* slaves were free men under American law and were allowed to sail back to Africa. Their story was told in the 1997 movie *Amistad*, directed by Steven Spielberg.

One of the great accomplishments of the Civil War was, finally, the inclusion of thousands of black troops among the Union's fighting forces. The Fifty-fourth Massachusetts Infantry formed in February 1863, almost two years into the war. More than a thousand black men volunteered to join the Fifty-fourth, including two of Frederick Douglass's sons. One-quarter of the Fifty-fourth's troops had escaped from slave states.

Robert Gould Shaw, the twenty-five-year-old son of wealthy abolitionist parents, was appointed to lead the Fifty-fourth. Shaw dropped out of Harvard to join the Union Army and was injured at the Battle of Antietam in 1862.

Ultimately, the Fifty-fourth led an assault on Fort Wagner at the port of Charleston, South Carolina. On July 18, 1863, Shaw led 600 of his men over the fort's walls. Badly outnumbered, 281 men of the Fifty-fourth were killed in the initial charge, including Shaw. The Confederates dumped all the dead bodies into one large, unmarked trench outside the fort. They sent a telegram to Union leaders saying, "We have buried Shaw with his niggers." Shaw's parents said there was "no holier place" than to be buried "surrounded by brave and devoted soldiers."

The American constitutional system worked for good and justice after the Civil War with the passage of the Thirteenth, Fourteenth, and Fifteenth Amendments. These amendments abolished slavery, granted black Americans citizenship and equal protection under the law, and gave black males the right to vote. This was revolutionary. Sure, they should have been included in the Constitution seventy-eight years earlier, but the U.S. finally did the right thing in the face of fierce opposition. That is progress.

The Fifteenth Amendment granting black males the right to vote in 1870 was largely a congressional response to the terrorist activity of the southern Democrat-supported Ku Klux Klan. Congress also passed the Enforcement Acts, making it a crime to interfere with blacks registering to vote, voting, holding office, or serving on a jury.

President Ulysses S. Grant's administration is usually remembered for the scandals that swirled around the president (without implicating him). But he doesn't get the credit he deserves for defending black civil rights, especially in fighting the KKK. Congress passed a bill, informally called the Ku Klux Klan Act, giving Grant the right to suspend habeas corpus in arresting Klansmen. In October 1871, Grant used his new authority to send federal marshals into South Carolina, where they rounded up hundreds of terrorists. Hundreds of others fled. Few substantive convictions resulted, but Grant's efforts crippled the KKK throughout the South. The Klan was forced underground and wouldn't publicly rear its ugly head again until the new century.

When Grant died in 1885, a group of black Union veterans stated, "In General Grant's death, the colored people of this and all other countries, and the oppressed everywhere, irrespective of complexion, have lost a preeminently true and faithful defender."

Other faithful defenders of black citizens in the South during and after Reconstruction include the hundreds of northern white men and women, many of them supported by Christian missionary organizations and the government's Freedmen's Bureau, who opened schools for black children throughout the South. Booker T. Washington would later write, "The history of the world fails to show a higher, purer, and more unselfish class of men and women than those who found their way into those Negro schools."

One of that class was former Union Army general Samuel C. Armstrong, who founded Hampton University in Virginia to educate black men and women and, later, Native Americans. He became Booker T. Washington's close mentor and lifelong friend. When Armstrong received a request from Tuskegee, Alabama, for a white man to organize and run a new school for black students there, Armstrong replied that he did not know a good white candidate, but he had the perfect black candidate for them: Booker T. Washington. The Tuskegee Institute became Washington's life's work.

In his autobiography, *Up from Slavery*, Washington wrote that General Armstrong was "the noblest, rarest human being that it has ever been my privilege to meet. . . . It has been my fortune to meet personally many of what are called great characters, both in Europe and America, but I do not hesitate to say that I never met any man who, in my estimation, was the equal of General Armstrong. . . . It was my privilege to know the General personally from the time I entered Hampton till he died, and the more I saw of him the greater he grew in my estimation. One might have removed from Hampton all the buildings, classrooms, teachers, and industries, and given the men and women there the opportunity of coming into daily contact with General Armstrong, and that alone would have been a liberal education."

Booker T. Washington was a pivotal, often overlooked champion of black civil rights. Though he clashed with President Theodore Roosevelt over Roosevelt's mishandling of the 1906 Brownsville incident mentioned earlier, they both took positive, if small, steps for American race relations. Roosevelt took considerable heat for inviting Booker T. Washington to dinner at the White House in 1901, a first for a U.S. president.

During World War II, the U.S. military established a flight school for black pilots at Tuskegee. Six hundred pilots went through the program, and they became known as the Tuskegee Airmen. Their stellar combat record in the skies over Europe earned the men 150 Distinguished Flying Crosses. Their success helped pave the way for President Truman to finally desegregate the military by executive order in 1948.

It took America nearly a century to unravel the tangled mess of Jim Crow laws. The Supreme Court helped in 1954 with its landmark decision in *Brown v. Board of Education*, which effectively desegregated America's schools. Three years later, President Eisenhower enforced the Court's decision by deploying twelve hundred federal troops to override Arkansas governor Orval Faubus's attempt to prevent nine black students from enrolling at Central High School in Little Rock. The federal troops remained for the rest of the school year to protect the "Little Rock Nine" as they entered and left the high school building each day.

When you look at some of the photos of the leering white crowds confronting the black teenage girls on the sidewalk outside Little Rock Central, it's amazing that within those students' lifetime, attitudes have changed so dramatically, not only about integrating schools and colleges but even when it comes to interracial marriage. Gallup polling shows that in 1958 only 4 percent of Americans approved of interracial marriage. By 2013, it found that 87 percent of Americans approved. That is progress. This should be celebrated as we continue to move forward.

Yes, America had slavery, and yes, it is shameful. But often all the left wants to talk about is the depressing, shameful part of the story. It's like they want to ignore that there is a happy ending—slavery was abolished. As Lincoln said, paid for in blood. Millions died to stop this scourge. Of course, the left argues that there hasn't been a happy ending for minorities, especially blacks—that they're still in metaphorical chains created by a society built on the backs of slaves. That is a self-defeating outlook. When will we learn from the Asians who literally built the main infrastructure of this nation while enduring terrible conditions and racist horror? It is not what happened to you historically; what matters is what you do with it now. It can either build you or destroy you. Let's find a way to hearing, healing, and helping others help themselves.

For progressives, there is little redeemable about America's decision to drop the atomic bombs on Hiroshima and Nagasaki. But once again, it's unfair to judge President Truman and his military advisors from our 2018 vantage point. It's disingenuous for modern critics to presume they would not have dropped the bombs when more than 111,000 American soldiers had already perished in the Pacific theater. Nowhere is mentioned the estimated 3 to 14 million civilian and POW deaths ordered by Hirohito or the horrors of Unit 731, which engaged in medical experiments, some of which made the actions of Nazi doctors look tame. And nearly always missing in our history class discussions of the atomic bombs is that the U.S. dropped millions of leaflets over Hiroshima and Nagasaki warning residents to flee these cities. Each leaflet explained, in what must have seemed like hyperbole, the overwhelming destructive power of the weapon that would be dropped if they did not surrender. We also took the extraordinary step of telling people to take food and water with them, as it would become scarce in that area. I have dozens of these in our vaults at the Mercury library. I have yet to meet the American of any age who has ever even heard of these leaflets, let alone seen one.

Also lost in the wider discussion are the resources the U.S. poured into Japan after World War II. For five years after the war's end, the U.S. oversaw the reconstruction of Japanese industry and government, including the writing of a new Japanese constitution. Then the U.S. handed Japan the keys and left. The result is a thriving democracy and America's closest Asian ally. Who could have predicted this miracle in 1941?

And finally, more than forty years after World War II, the surviving Japanese American family members who lost three years of their lives in internment camps were given reparation payments of $20,000 per family by Congress. It is the understanding of what, who, and why it happened that will ensure we never repeat it, and unfortunately, those details are not taught.

Here is a key point: Though it's often too little, too late, America does try to right wrongs. Though we can debate what and how much retroactive congressional action is appropriate, the fact is that despite popular progressive belief, America is not heartless.

So which are we? Good or Evil? We are attempting to be judge, jury, and executioner of an entire culture without actually looking at the full picture. Our past has been bad, and it has been good. We are no worse than every country and civilization in all of human history. We are like Winston Churchill, both hero and villain. Our job is to learn from our mistakes and grow stronger and better as a people.

But our cultural bloodlust is so intense that we don't even want to wait to hear the evidence; we focus on the bad, the injustice, and any of the good, "Well, that could have happened anywhere or even in spite of America."

In his epic book *The History of the English Speaking Peoples since 1900*, Andrew Roberts concludes:

> It is in the nature of human affairs that, in the words of the hymn, "Earth's proud empires pass away," and so too one day will the long hegemony of the English speaking peoples. When they finally come to render up the report of their global stewardship to History, there will be much of which to boast. Only when another power—such as China—holds global sway, will the human race come to mourn the passing of this most decent, honest, generous, fair-minded and self-sacrificing imperium.

30

Shaving Ockham

So for a long time the human race is sort of bumbling along, taking from somewhere around 300,000 years ago until about 1804 AD to reach 1 billion people. Progress is slow. Then the U.S. comes along, and it's another 120 years or so to get to 2 billion, another 33 more years to get to 3 billion . . . you get the idea. Today, we sit at just over 7.6 billion of us.

Of those, about 320 million are lucky enough to call the United States of America home, or about 4.4 percent of us. Yep, 4.4 percent of the world's population are our fellow citizens, the ones we keep getting outraged about all the time. What's interesting is that while we're only 4.4 percent of the world's population, we own over 25 percent of the world's wealth (much more if you count U.S. companies housing cash and assets in foreign countries), consume 33 percent of the world's energy production, hold command of all seven seas, own 48 percent of all satellites in orbit, are the only nation that has sent men to the moon (four times), and consume 41 percent of the world's chewing gum.

Okay, so, not 100 percent sure the last figure is one to brag about, but you get the idea.

In barely 120 years we grew to become the world's most powerful nation, and 100 years after that, the world's lone "superpower." We're pretty well set up for the future, too, at least as far as resources are concerned, with more than 55 percent of the world's shale oil and 65 percent of the world's uranium under our control. We have enough energy to provide power to the entire planet, including projected population growth, for the next two thousand years. Doubt that last one? Google "TerraPower Wave Reactor."

Let's see, what else . . . the bottom 10 percent of our population by way of wealth is still in the top 10 percent compared to the world's population as a whole. We have 68 percent of the world's PhDs living among our population (many of them foreign born/educated, but the money is better here).

In the #MeToo era, it's easy to focus on the very real and disgusting cases of violence against women that flood the media. But it's worth noting that violence against women is actually dropping. Violence against wives and girlfriends has actually dropped by about 75 percent since the 1990s.

While the news cameras point at Charlottesville, at Richard Spencer and his band of tiki-torch-toting buffoons, and at NFL players kneeling to protest police brutality and racism in our police departments, hate crimes against blacks have dropped by about 50 percent.

The amount of money we spend on necessities such as food, home, transportation, clothing, furniture, utilities, and gas has been cut in half since the 1930s.

Globally, the rate of children dying before the age of five has dropped by over half since 1990. This is a miracle that has gone almost completely unnoticed.

As Max Roser and Jaiden Mispy illustrate, that's like averting twenty-seven major plane crashes filled with children every single day.

The improvements cover the spectrum of horrible ailments and accidents no one wants to be associated with.

Deaths from:

Malaria down 32 percent
HIV down 50 percent

Neonatal preterm birth complications down 55 percent
Protein-energy malnutrition down 57 percent
Diarrheal diseases down 64 percent
Lower respiratory infections down 66 percent
Measles down 91 percent

As Arthur Brooks notes: "It's the greatest anti-poverty achievement in the history of mankind. And it happened within our lifetimes." The causes for this are numerous but are largely the result of the spread of capitalism, technological and medical innovation, and free trade.

Putting this miracle into perspective is incredibly difficult, especially because it doesn't have the energy of a partisan firestorm around it. So, let's insert one.

If you happen to be of the pro-life persuasion, you probably have fought hard to stop the funding of Planned Parenthood. You probably want the doors shuttered immediately. However, you would have to eliminate the number of abortions that occur annually because of Planned Parenthood more than nineteen times over to equal this improvement.

But don't worry, progressives! If you have been fighting to repeal the Second Amendment with the hopes of stopping all gun-related homicide, I have more good news. This incredible global lifesaving achievement is equivalent to more than 630 years' worth of gun-related murders.

It's such a wonderful development that you could forgive a modern society for losing track of some of the real problems that remain. Instead, we do the opposite. We are on a constant search for kneeling players, cultural appropriation, white privilege, and tweets that are slightly askew.

Now, I'm not in any way saying America is perfect. Far from it. We've done some pretty horrible things over the years; I get it. But all in all, something about this place has really worked out.

Lots of Jared Diamond–type intellectuals have tried to decipher how and why we seem to kick so much ass all the time, coming up with theories involving the luck of our geography, geology, climate, isolation from enemies, and so on. Actually, there are probably valid elements and pieces of all those arguments. I mean, I agree it's great that we have two oceans to our east and west, frozen tundra and mountains to our north, and barren deserts to the south. Note that it wasn't always that way. The thirteen colonies had enemies on all sides, but we still whipped the British, the Spanish, the British (again), and Mexico as we expanded west, and numerous Native American tribes (moral inventory!).

It's strange—we don't have a cohesive religion, ancestry, or biology, we don't have the heritage of a shared ethnic background or creed, and we're made up of every race on earth, every culture.

One thing that's always troubled me about the various conjecturing that goes on about why the U.S.A. has been so dominant for so long is that it all fails the Ockham's Razor test: The simplest explanation is generally the true one. All the origin stories explaining America's Super Powers that rely on five or ten or twenty randomly thrown-together ingredients miss the simple, plainly obvious ingredient that is by far the most logical answer: liberty for the individual.

Lots of countries have had access to lots of natural resources. Lots of countries have had protective geographical zones. Lots of places have access to two or more oceans, have rivers that cross the continent, have oil, have white people, have protection from enemies by way of space or distance.

But all those other countries didn't have a group of guys who got together and said, "We hold these truths to be self-evident . . . that all men are created equal, that they are endowed by their creator with certain unalienable rights. That among these are life, liberty and the pursuit of happiness."

Just, wow. But wait, there's more!

"That to secure these rights, governments are instituted among men, deriving their just powers from the consent of the governed."

For those of you who still think "rights" are granted to us by the government, think through the sequencing here: Man has rights, and to secure those rights, we institute government. Rights first, then government to protect those rights. See, the whole reason a government exists at all is to secure rights that we have by nature, before the government existed!

That—had—NEVER—been—said—before! And neither had this:

"That whenever any form of government becomes destructive of these ends, it is the right of the people to alter or to abolish it. . . . It is their right, it is their duty, to throw off such government, and to provide new guards for their future security."

Drops mic . . . spikes football . . . does the moonwalk.

You want to know what made America GREAT in the first place? Why we came to dominate the world so easily? Why we've enjoyed more success, more invention, more improvement, more wealth than any other nation in the history of the world? That's it. That's the big secret that nobody told you in school (because God forbid we teach our history anymore). That is the key to American greatness, the wealth and success and dominance of our people, our nation, and our culture across the world.

The Bill of Rights and the Constitution are our unum! The thing that takes us from the many of "e pluribus" to the one of "unum." The thing that binds us, that makes us a nation, a unique country in world history. That is the thing that can and should bring us back to the table.

And for those of you who have never made the connection, here is why this system of government works: it is aligned with our nature as a species.

Human beings are pretty interesting creatures. We have these still-evolving apelike brains that somewhere along the line picked up self-awareness and free will. We're inquisitive, inventive, and, because of the whole self-awareness thing (I am me and you are you), we have an ego. And by our nature, that ego needs to be developed and nurtured and fed. What feeds it?

Achievement. Setting goals and accomplishing them. Yep.

Wow. Interesting, Glenn. Tell me more.

We don't have thick fur, so we need to invent things to stay warm. We can't digest most plants, so we need to grow those plants that we can digest. We don't have wings to fly and don't run that fast, so we need to invent things to get from place to place. We don't have gills or fins, so we aren't the best swimmers, but we can invent boats, oars, sails. We don't have sharp claws or teeth, but we can invent pointy-stabby-cutty things to take care of all the rending of flesh we need to do to survive.

Getting the picture here?

To thrive, man needs to invent. To invent, man needs freedom. More freedom equals more invention. More freedom equals more trade equals more invention . . . you're getting the idea.

Man's idealized state is one of individual liberty and voluntary cooperation.

Ever wonder why socialism/statism keeps failing and America keeps crushing everyone all the time? Well, now you don't have to wonder anymore. Those systems of government are designed around a goal of "equality," not around a goal of "freedom," so they don't incentivize invention or reward achievement. Since man needs to invent to thrive and needs achievement to feed his ego, those systems of government are anathema to human beings. They don't fit us.

Now you know. Congrats. No more shade for you. No more excuses. Sorry you spent all that money going to college and nobody ever thought to mention this stuff. Could have saved you a boatload!

Ours was the first system of government that was perfectly attuned to man's nature. The Founders saw this as self-evident, very much like what Bret Weinstein says about human genders.

Look at the thing for what it is! Aristotle kindly pointed this out for us 350 years before Christ: A is A. Study the creature, use the scientific method, logic, reason, physics . . . identify the facts of reality and then apply them. For Professor Weinstein, that means that we have genders and they matter when it comes to human biology and reproduction. That is self-evident; it's obvious. It's scientifically demonstrable. Sure, the PC crowd says that he is racist, sexist, and doesn't take into account everyone's feelings, but scientists tend to be pretty A-is-A types.

As our Founders studied the creature, they saw a self-aware, thinking, sentient being with free will. And they said, Well, heck, we're forming a new government here, and it's for these people to have a good, productive life and a good, productive country, so since we're making a new government, why not implement one that fits what human beings are and protects their natural state of being?

And poof! There it is, black and white, clear as crystal! We are the entities that we are. The secret of our success is not geography or geology, it is a government that fits our BIOLOGY! Those things that make us human are immovable, unalienable from us, because they are part of us, just like our DNA. Wishing and feelings won't make you fly, won't give you gills, and won't remove your gender. That is not natural. It is also unnatural for man to be man without freedom and liberty.

America, that is our unum. The self-evident truth that unites us. That is the thing that makes the many of us one. One people. One nation, under God, indivisible, with liberty and justice for all. These are the principles that we must again rally behind, that made us great. The very elements that gave our forefathers a mutual identity, a shared set of values that held us together and transformed us into the most powerful nation the world has ever seen. It's scientifically demonstrable, because we've been kicking ass for 250 years. The formula works, and turns out it's also the antidote to Outrage Addiction.

31

Our Self-Evident Rights and Seemingly Invisible Responsibility

"We hold these truths to be self-evident" is something all of us know—what follows is what our Founders, those who wanted to break free from the tyranny of the king, all knew. For many years, I thought that all men are created equal and endowed by a Creator with certain unchangeable rights such as a right to life, personal liberty and freedom, and the right to produce and to keep that property as theirs was universally self-evident.

But it is not. Most in China would tell you that being able to have as many children as you wish and not having to ask for state approval to conceive would be a luxury. Some might even feel uncomfortable for a time in that world. It would not be "self-evident" for many around the world that you could do, speak, and work as you wished, to do as you chose and to keep the fruits of your labor. In fact, our self-evident rights are so polar opposite in some places in the world that choosing to do nothing, being what we used to call a "freeloader," would be against the highest law of the land, and an unforgivable sin or insult to the state and citizens. Many of the world's constitutions state what each citizen must do to be "in compliance."

Many people are comfortable with a system like that. In a way, I understand. There is something to the idea that I can just drop my kids off at a bus stop and pick them up later that day, and they receive a "free" education.

We are all busy, so we assign a personal responsibility to someone else who can do that job while we are away doing another job so our families can have food to eat, shelter, and, if we are fortunate enough to pursue it, our "happiness." Another perfectly reasonable and essential way we prosper together is that long ago we figured out that we can't all watch our stores all night after we finish our work or close for the day. We need sleep, so we assign or hire someone else to take on our personal responsibility of being a night watchman to keep us, and our property, safe. If we were all independently wealthy, we all would have hired our own personal security, but the cost is beyond the reach of the average store owner and certainly beyond the run-of-the-mill citizen. At first we all took turns watching over each other, as we see in every military or "on the lam" movie. "It's my turn to take the first watch. I will wake you at three." But as we became able, we all decided that the idea of staying up all night once a week sucked. So we came up with the idea of pooling our money and assigning our right of protection to what we called the police force.

It is why we as people began to gather in the first place. If we can all help share the load, we can accomplish much more. At first, it would have had to be strange, and a bit unnerving. To hire a stranger, not one of our friends or neighbors but someone new and perhaps unknown to us personally, to enforce the rules or laws of the community. Up until the last fifty or so years, it didn't take us long to get to know those people. As the new cops moved into to our neighborhoods, we quickly got to know them, and they knew us and became part of our community. No one was an outsider.

This is not the book to go into the problems this change has made just in those two examples, teaching and policing. Just those two roles gaining real distance from each of us and our neighborhoods has caused many of the problems we now face, but I want to discuss the other inherent issue when we assign our rights to another.

Put yourself back into the local township days when you were first discussing how to build a police force and the idea of hiring an "outsider." You can bet that one of the things you would ask is,

"Who is going to watch over the watcher?" You wouldn't want them to be able to come and use the power of that badge to take control of your community. Yes, you would need to write down the things they needed to look out for and to stop people from doing—to make laws—but you would also need to make sure that they never felt above those same laws.

It would have to be made clear that they work for us—not in a controlling way but simply to ensure that power never became an issue. After all, in the worst-case scenario, we would all be asleep, they could do anything they wanted, and we might not know.

Two things happened. The laws were written down, simply I am sure in the beginning. "Look, here is what we want to make sure happens: nobody steals my cow or shoots a neighbor, and when we get sidewalks, we don't want anyone to spit on them." The laws were not really for the neighbors, they were for the policemen to know what to look out for. As we grew, and people in the town saw things elsewhere that they didn't want coming into their neighborhood, they added to that list. Eventually, laws became both a warning to bad guys or to out-of-towners and lists for the cops. But something else had to have taken place.

Early on, the citizens had to make it clear that the police officer had no more power than the neighbors had when they were watching over each other. In fact, since they were now assigning this right to another, they wanted to make sure that the laws were even more limiting than those they had lived under. For instance, I know my uncle Dave could have gone into his neighbor's barn, or even house, if he felt something was amiss and the neighbor was away. Because they trusted each other and one had said to the other, Listen, while I am away, keep an eye on things. But that would not give my uncle Dave permission to go into the house and start going through the drawers and reading the neighbor's mail or papers, no matter how close they were.

Things really were different on this little street back in the 1970s, but let's just suppose there was no police force and they were still on the "I'll take the first watch" system when my uncle began to piece a few things together and came to the logical and reasonable conclusion that somehow the vacationing neighbor was responsible for the string of terrifying garden-gnome thefts in the neighborhood. What would he do? My uncle would have called everyone together to discuss his claim and what he thought might be found in the house that would prove the criminal case and ask for the rest of the neighbors' permission go in and look. If the neighbors agreed that his theory seemed not just plausible but very possible, after sincere conversation and deliberation they would act, knowing that if they did this, they might catch a thief, but they could also destroy the trust of the neighbor upon his return, and they would set a precedent that would allow for this same thing to possibly be done to them the next time they were away. They agreed, and surely someone would have said, Dave, you have made a good case, but this is a real violation of our trust in the neighborhood. We are letting you go in, but you are only allowed to look for gnomes and gnomes alone.

If he came out with nothing but did find that the neighbor had a secret collection of clown paintings that maybe they should be concerned about, everyone in the neighborhood would have lost all respect and trust for my uncle Dave. In fact, they would begin to suspect that he was untrustworthy and just had it in for the neighbor and clowns.

We cannot assign a right to someone that we ourselves do not have. We have no right to listen in to someone's phone calls or to go through their papers or search for missing gnomes, so we cannot hire someone to do those things for us. It's the same with protecting ourselves and our families with deadly force.

It wasn't until the 1970s that we called police officers or firemen "first responders." They were backup. If our home caught on fire, it was our responsibility to put it out. We as townsfolk, early on, did require everyone to have a large leather bucket of water sitting next to every fireplace or stove in case a fire broke out. Our neighbors would come to help, but we acted first.

The same with self-defense. In fact, in some towns the laws stated that if you had the chance to stop someone on your property and did not stop them, you could be held responsible for your failure to act. Many towns issued a gun to those moving in who did not own one.

However, in no town, at any time, was it lawful to simply string people up. Those who did were called lynch mobs and were not part of any decent society. No citizen had the right to take the law into their own hands unless it was in self-defense. So when they finally hired a sheriff because all of the cats were being rustled—though I am not sure what that is or if cats can even be rustled, but let's just assume they can and that this is bad. Even if the sheriff knew the defendant was the cat-rustling type, he could not play judge, jury, and executioner or he would be held for trial. He only had the right to do what the average citizen had the right to do as well.

This is important, because in both cases—gnomic cat rustling and education—we are now being told that our police or teachers are the only ones with the right to do certain things. This is not entirely true with police and certainly not true with teachers, but the mere suggestion is corrosive to our liberties.

Yes, I cannot arrest someone and put them in my homemade jail in the basement. However, if I catch someone hurting a child or animal, stealing, or breaking into my home, I can take action and call for backup. I can hold them in a locked room until police arrive if I feel my life or the lives of others are at stake. And for that same reason, I can shoot them. But only if I fear for my life. It's the exact same standard for police.

Too many times, I hear "experts" tell us that they know what is best for children. That may or may not be true. But the right and responsibility to care for and teach those children has merely been assigned to you by me and my neighbors. You do not have more authority over my children as a teacher than I have over your children as a neighbor. This is the way human rights work.

The trouble with the necessity of distributing our responsibilities is that it tends to make us apathetic about the job and blind to our role in the first place. The cop is only stopping us because we voted for people to help us design the town, and the laws that they came up with in our name state that the speed limit should be set at a certain mph on this street. The cop isn't the bad guy. When we are all seeing our roles properly, he is only acting on the authority we gave him, with the laws that we set, at our request. However, on the other side, it is easy for those to whom we have assigned the cop role to grow arrogant and overstep their role as our agent, especially since we no longer know each other.

It will not be enough to just stop being outraged, quitting cold turkey. In fact, that will be impossible. After all, we were outraged for a reason. Our lives are unmanageable. Something is deeply wrong, but our outrage wasn't helping to fix it—it was, rather, just what we did to be able to make it through the day. It made the problems into something we felt we were doing something about or had some control over. If we just stop being outraged, we will quickly fall off that wagon and perhaps be worse than we were before.

We need a plan to help reduce the chaos in our lives, to understand the difference between the things we can affect and those we cannot, and to let go of the latter.

We certainly need at least a refresher on our rights and more so on our responsibility if we are going to hold to our "sobriety," as these are the keys to restoring balance and reducing chaos.

32

The Cages of Our Addiction

*All experience hath shewn that mankind are more
disposed to suffer, while evils are sufferable than to right
themselves by abolishing the forms to which they are
accustomed.*

—The Declaration of Independence

*I am not what I ought to be, I am not what I want to be,
I am not what I hope to be in another world; but still I
am not what I once used to be.*

—John Newton

I never understood how rules could make you more free until my
anger, outrage, and lies had built a cage so tight that I had no option
other than to remain locked up. Until you have experienced the bars
that you live behind that your actions and choices built, you cannot
truly understand how sweet freedom really is. I was never in jail or
prison. When I was a kid, I think I was sent to detention once. But
I spent many years trapped in a place of my own design that I never
thought I could escape. In the end, just before my self-appointed
release, there were many days that I feared release. My cage had become the place I knew best.

Our anger, fear, victimhood, and outrage can become a warm
blanket. It begins to define us and shape our entire world view. We

actually can convince ourselves that this prison, this hell, is better than what lies beyond. We indeed will suffer while evils are sufferable rather than right ourselves by abolishing the forms, cages, lies, abusers, and so on that we are accustomed to. There is a sense of comfort in those things that we know, strangely, even if they are our jailers. It is why chaos is such a powerful tool, as men will cry out for a semblance of normalcy again, even if it involves prison bars or totalitarian rule.

What our jailers do not want us to know is that adherence to the Bill of Rights, especially when it is difficult, is the key that unlocks the cell.

DO WE ACTUALLY BELIEVE IN A "FREE PRESS"?

In the summer of 2018, the media began to feel the effects of an immoral, ignorant, and tribal society. It was that summer, to me, that signaled that without constitutional protection and reunification, the press as we now know it will be obsolete by the mid 2020s.

For a few years "fake news," which I first saw in 2008 come from the left as "faux news," signaling to America that Fox could not be trusted, had been the charge leveled against any news source or opinion on the right. However, this was quickly turned around and used even more effectively by a media opponent who refused to play by the rules: Donald Trump. He took "fake news" and made it his secondary campaign slogan. I'm surprised we didn't see it show up on red hats. Soon, both sides were claiming fake news. Facts were less important than conclusions, news less important than opinions, and principles important only if they could be used to crucify your "enemy."

Even principles were forever fluid. There have been times since the Trump election that the average citizen honestly didn't know what side they should be on, if the topic was given without the political figures or parties disclosed, because just the day before you and your political party may have had the exact opposite opinion. Those opinions were not minor. Both parties switched sides on principles on issues that were long held to be core tenets that defined, in many cases, what they stood for as a party. Each party betrayed itself, literally overnight in some cases, without explanation or discussion. You went to bed KNOWING that your side had always been on the right side of an issue and you and your party would never surrender that hill because the price you paid for it was too high. The next morning you found out that you not only abandoned that hill but were now shelling the hill. The other side, which had called that hill immoral or whatever, had now taken the hill and declared it all that you had claimed it to be, and you were now expected to fall into line and shout all of the slogans they had used.

It is hard to believe, and our children will not understand it when we once again regain our senses and admit the truth of these times, but there were days when many Americans on both sides had to turn on their cable news channel to see what side they were supposed to be on and why. Yet even more disturbing was the fact that so many did it and never vocalized how bizarre it was. Perhaps because those who did were called out by the party police as traitors.

Donald Trump used "fake news" so effectively that even some constitutional conservatives began to remain silent when the president called for reductions in free speech, or for libel trials for networks and reporters, or hand selected those reporters allowed in the press room.

President Obama put more reporters on trial or in jail than any other president since World War I. Obama targeted and even spied on members of the press, but for some reason the press mostly tolerated it from him.

Others had tried it before. Nixon had his famous enemies list, as did FDR, but in the twentieth century Woodrow Wilson was the one who scared Americans and the press the most. In fact, it was his antipress rhetoric that caused the creation of the White House press corps. To fight back, they knew that they needed to band together. However, once the president saw this, he and subsequent presidents established the White House press dinner to make the press "part of the family." By the 1930s, Edward Bernays and others had created the Council on Foreign Relations, which in his own words was the propaganda machine that would teach the press how to shape the world the way the "leaders" saw it:

> No serious sociologist any longer believes that the voice of the people expresses any divine or specially wise and lofty idea. The voice of the people expresses the mind of the people, and that mind is made up for it by the group leaders in whom it believes and by those persons who understand the manipulation of public opinion. It is composed of inherited prejudices and symbols and clichés and verbal formulas supplied to them by the leaders.

Trump would discredit the media, but the media needed very little help. They had done more damage to themselves over the preceding nine years than Donald Trump could inflict in a lifetime. For those who wanted to see the media destroyed, it was quite a Dumpster fire.

Because we were now living in a postmodern time when "there is no truth," the media and the left decided to take their own action. They began to call for their own selection process. During an interview I did with Ted Koppel, I was horrified to actually hear him suggest and defend a new license for the press. It was fascinating for me to hear this icon justify the idea of creating a "board of some sort" to decide who was "trusted enough" to tell the American people the "truth."

Who would be on that board? Would it be a government board—the same government whose wrongdoings you were trying to expose? Or would it be a media board that had already shown itself to be sleeping with the government? Would any "neutral" board that derived its power from a protective government actually ever be expected to side against its protector? When I suggested that perhaps those who were not in those circles and didn't fall prey to groupthink might have a different take on what was happening in D.C. and NYC, it quickly became clear that the Internet was the problem and that just anyone could now have a voice.

I had a very similar conversation with Bill O'Reilly in July 2018. He was calling for the wiretapping of reporters' phones to find those who were leaking information to the press and "subverting democracy." Since when is a whistleblower not protected? I strongly disagreed with both Koppel and O'Reilly. They both agreed, and if either had been taken seriously and their proposals had been put into action, one would be in jail, wiretapped, or silenced.

As I have done my research on the Bill of Rights, I have indeed gone through the original documents, drafts, and arguments that our Founders made. The First Amendment is truly remarkable and something that I just do not think more than a handful of today's powerful would ever consider, let alone write and pass. But our Founders were men as well. Flawed, just like the men and women of today. They may have passed the Bill of Rights in 1791, but some of those same men tried to subvert it in 1798.

THE SEDITION ACT

In the extremely handy *Know Your Bill of Rights* book, the authors use original sources to outline the arguments for freedom of the press. Blackstone wrote that the liberty of the press "is indeed essential to the nature of a free state." Madison described freedom of the press as one of the "choicest" of the "great rights of mankind."

But, as is still the case today, the question remained, what did that mean? How far does the freedom reach? Is ALL speech covered and protected? The old saw "You can't scream 'fire' in a movie theater" had not yet been heard, and wouldn't be until Edison invented the projector and movies. They were concerned with bigger ideas. Should someone be allowed to incite violence against the government? Could you knowingly spread false and damaging statements against others or the government? What speech would be protected, and what would not?

Charles Pinckney of South Carolina suggested in the Constitutional Convention that the liberty of the press needed to be "inviolably preserved." It failed in 1787 as Roger Sherman spoke what was then "self-evident," that it was unnecessary, as "the power of Congress does not extend to the press."

The protection of the press then fell to the states. Some states added protections in their constitutions that reflected that people could write or publish anything they wanted, but if they defamed the government, they would be tried and criminally convicted. Chief Justice of Pennsylvania Thomas McKean felt that publishing "bad sentiments destructive of the needs of society is the crime which society corrects."

William Livingston wrote in an essay that anyone who published "anything injurious to his country" should be convicted of "high treason against the state." The original Sherman framing was that it would protect the right to express one's sentiments "with decency," which at the time was understood to exclude libels personal, obscene, blasphemous, or seditious. Jefferson wanted to prosecute only those who would publish "false facts or falsehoods." He wanted no prosecution for accurate information. But many states upheld laws that freedom of the press allowed for the prosecution for seditious libel and that even truth was not a valid defense. While there would be NO censorship, every person would be responsible if he attacked the government in speech or writing, and that action could lead to criminal charges in a federal court.

Now, wait a minute. How did this group of people who began a revolution by first speaking out against the actions of their government put together a new Constitution that would put people in jail if they verbally attacked the new government, which was supposed to be run by the "consent of the people"? Sometimes history gives you answers that inspire, and other times it provides answers that only show us that people never really change. As fate had it, after the Bill of Rights passed and was ratified, very few in the press were prosecuted for criticisms of the government, which was just as bad if not worse than our press today. The federal and state governments knew that the people didn't trust the government, and what little trust they had would disappear quickly for any government that would jail its critics.

When the Sedition Act was passed in 1798, it broadened the common-law understanding of freedom of the press and required that criminal intent be proven, and it gave a jury the power to decide if the accused's statement was true, and it admitted truth as a defense. But the public had begun to be more tolerant of the press, and thus the rights began to expand to include the right to censure the government, its officials, and its policies and to publicize opinions on any matter of public concern. George Hay, James Madison, and others rejected common law, which had originated in England. Madison wrote: "It would seem a mockery to say that no laws shall be passed preventing the publications from being made, but that laws might be passed for punishing them in case they should be made."

Hay charged that the Sedition Act "appears to be directed against falsehood and malice only; in fact . . . there are many truths, important to society which are not susceptible of that full, direct and positive evidence, which alone can be exhibited before court and a jury." Albert Gallatin argued that if a citizen were prosecuted for his opinion, would not a jury composed of friends of the government find his criticism "ungrounded, false and scandalous, and its publication malicious? And by what kind of argument or evidence, in the present temper of parties, could the accused convince them that his opinions were true?"

The truth of opinions could not be proved, and thus, it was argued, allowing truth as a defense of freedom made as much sense as allowing a jury to decide on "the best food, drink, or color."

A citizen should have a right to "say everything which his passions suggest; he may employ all his time, and all his talents, if he is wicked enough to do so, in speaking against the government matters that are false, scandalous and malicious, and despite this, he should be safe within the sanctuary of the press" even if he "condemns the principle of republican institutions . . . censures the measures of our government, and every department and officer thereof, and ascribes the measures of the former, however salutary, and conduct of the latter, however upright, to the basest motives even if he ascribes to them measures and acts, which never had existence thus violating at one, every principle of decency and truth." (from Sean Patrick's *The Know Your Bill of Rights Book: Don't Lose Your Constitutional Rights—Learn Them!*, p. 16)

WOW.

This was totally novel and new. No government had ever come close to such freedom for its people. It was so radical that we still are debating it. But it is the only way a government that is actually run by the consent of the people could be consistent and true to itself. John Thomson wrote that a government cannot tell a citizen, "You shall not think this or that upon certain subjects; or if you do, it is at your own peril." This for the first time makes the citizen the master and the government the slave.

However, over time, particularly in the twentieth century and beyond, the press began to become the master itself and joined with the government to once again make the citizen its inferior and not its master. The press in this new, unspoken, progressive arrangement would become in some cases a co-conspirator or a teacher to the citizen to "educate" people about what the ruling class felt was the best option on government legislation and action. The press rarely found interest in its partnership with the average American to remain on high alert to injustice, inequalities, and infringements unless they were to expand the power of the government or destroy a political enemy or movement.

John Stuart Mill, in his book *On Liberty*, argued that the silencing of opinion is "a peculiar evil," for if that opinion is correct, then we are robbed of the opportunity of exchanging error for truth; and if it is wrong, we are deprived of a deeper understanding of the truth in "its collision with error."

PART FOUR

Reconciliation

The room is bare; it smells like excrement, blood, and sweat. Yours. You no longer even know how long you have been held here. You have long ago lost your dignity. You have wet and soiled yourself from fear. You were stripped long ago. Each day, you think, This is the day. I will make it today. I won't give in. I won't beg like a child. I won't plead or show them just how worthless I am. How do others do it? How do they stand up to this? They didn't give in. They didn't humiliate themselves like this.

> *The same routine,*
> *every time the light goes on,*
> *the door opens and a man steps in.*
> *What you have isn't this important.*
> *He must have the wrong man.*
> *You have nothing.*
> *He hasn't asked you a single question.*
> *Just the beatings.*
> *Is this how he gets his kicks? Has he been paid to do this?*
> *"What?!" you cry. "What do you want?"*
> *Your eyelid is cut. Dried blood cakes your face.*
> *It reopens. Blood flows freely, clouding your vision.*
> *The head bleeds so much.*
> *"I don't know what you want from me," you sob quietly.*
> *But somewhere inside, you do.*
> *The beating continues . . .*

33

The Long Journey Back

The fifth step is "Admitted to God, to ourselves, and to another human being the exact nature of our wrongs."

Personally, for me, it was the hardest step other than the first, admitting that I had a problem I could not conquer alone. To admit I was an alcoholic for some reason was perhaps the hardest thing I have ever done. Maybe it was because of the societal shame, but I don't think so; nor was it that I had associated alcoholics with winos and bums, although that is what confused me and slowed me down in asking for help for so long. Too long.

Two years after I had first tried to stop, my doctor told me, "Look, I don't know what you are drinking or putting into your body, but it is shutting down. You can either talk to me and we can get you help, or you can continue on this path; but if you are dead in six months, it wouldn't shock me."

His talk wasn't enough. I could stop drinking. I was in control. I wasn't weak and pathetic, even though that is what I told myself every morning in the mirror, before I stopped looking in the mirror. "You promised that you wouldn't drink yesterday. And yet you found a reason, an excuse. It was a hard day, you didn't feel well enough to start, someone put their burdens on your back and you needed the escape just one last time.

"You are weak and pathetic.

"No, today I am going to do it. I will prove that I am strong and not addicted to anything. Today, I am not going to drink."

Wash, rinse, repeat. Over and over the same words, same promise, same failure, every day of my life for four years. I wouldn't crack. I wouldn't give in. Every morning begging for mercy. Every night betraying myself and on my knees, lost in its gentle numbness.

I believe what was so terrifying was the fact that I was stripped naked, with no control and no idea what would happen next. But this is why AA works. Unless ordered by a judge or spouse, no one admits this lightly. You not only have to join, to want to join. You are so desperate to end the pain that death is your only option. Your addiction has taken everything that was truly and authentically yours away and made a mockery of it. You have been ground almost to a pulp. You literally have nothing left. Even if you still have money, a job, family, and a home, it is all worthless, because you have no control. You are worthless. All of what you have built is gone or meaningless. Everyone's bottom is different. Kitty Dukakis, I will never forget, was, in the end, drinking hair spray for the alcohol it contained. You are ashamed at what you have become. In hopes of some release, you have tried everything else: sex, money, fame—all of it empty, all of it a bigger lie than the demon before. And yet for so long, you refused to do the only thing really required to stop. "No, not that. Anything but that."

All you have to do is surrender.

For me, I imagine it feels the same as the moment you give in to torture.

"Okay, okay," you whimper, "I will give you whatever you want. Please . . . please . . . just make it stop."

My mother was an alcoholic. She committed suicide. I almost did. I guess I was more of a coward. That is the way I used to look at it. I was too afraid to kill myself.

And for that, I thank God.

Our nation is addicted to a destructive way of life. What is our bottom? We always had the respect of the world. They looked at us as leaders. They counted on us.

"Well, maybe they shouldn't have. When did I become the one who had to carry the load? When did I decide that I couldn't have fun and lie on the beach, drink a little, be a little irresponsible, and have fun?"

Respect? From them? What's that worth? They are more screwed up than I am. They are just getting away with it. Most of them are judgmental frauds. You know they are hiding their dirty little secrets, too.

But it isn't "them," and you know it. Not them. But others are there in that crowd. I have been there, in both roles. It is why at some point you double down. You are ashamed. You see the way your friends, the people you truly respect, look at you now. The ones who were counting on you, the ones who have always been there for you. You have let them down. You have lied—but they know. They haven't said anything except to ask if you were okay. It isn't that they don't have problems. It just seems that they can handle theirs, and you were supposed to be the tough one. They are the ones whom you love, because they love you. They see in you what you no longer can— someone better than what you have allowed yourself to become. This is the one that you hopefully haven't snapped at when they quietly came to you after you publicly embarrassed yourself, helped you back up to your feet, and compassionately said, "Maybe you should go home. I can drive you."

The disappointment in their eyes . . .

You will need to drink away those eyes, for a long time.

You have read enough of this book or listened to me long enough to know that my job exposes me to some dark and terrifying things. It is my job to read, listen, learn, and then warn when I must. I had to watch the video that had been smuggled out of Syria that showed a child, maybe five or six, screaming in a hallway for his mother and father. Being led forward by an ISIS member. When they entered the next room, the floor was covered with blood and bodies. There, just beyond his reach, lay his parents, dead, bloodied, and stacked like cordwood. The boy began to scream as he was lifted up onto a metal table that had been shoved up against the outer wall. So filthy, so bloody. The walls were chipped, almost an old mint green, and the flickering of an old fluorescent overhead office light. As they laid the boy down, another man put out what could almost be a shallow turkey-roasting pan. They shoved it under the boy's back and opened his shirt and held him still as his screams for Mommy and Daddy went unanswered. It was then that I realized what they were going to do and who these people were. As that was running through my head, almost simultaneously, I gasped as I realized . . . there is no anesthesia coming.

I told the man showing it to me, "Please, turn it off." It had been given to him so he could ask for my help. It wasn't me they wanted, it was my audience.

This image stuck with me for months. How many more before or since the little boy I saw? I have seen heads on pikes along the road and heads used as bowling balls. Both of those were just across our southern border.

I have seen things that I will never be able to unsee in the jungles of Thailand. In Mexico City I sat until 3:00 a.m. with women who had just been freed from captivity, listening to their stories and determination. I have held a newborn in Haiti. Her mother was a thirteen-year-old girl who had been raped up to ten times a day since she was eight. Her baby was alive only because our jump team rescued her before her traffickers knew she was pregnant; otherwise it would have ended the way the others had before. If it weren't for us, no help was coming.

When I say us, I mean Americans. We are the people the most desperate pray will come and save them. The French aren't coming. But they know that we will. Sometimes in uniforms, many if not most times not—just regular people who care and won't take no for an answer. We are the ones who have the means and can be away from our children, because most of our monsters are only shadows in the closet or the groaning of the old furnace through the vent.

And it is us who should be coming! We should be exercising our Super Power. We should be flying into the fray, with the love and the sympathy afforded to us by our system, by our invention, by the capacity afforded to us by the incredible people we can be.

They pray for us to come.

I hope, for their sake, they don't know how drunk we are, as just the thought that someone is coming is enough to keep you alive.

We sincerely do not appreciate the things we have until they are gone.

We are blind and ignorant too many times by choice. We are arrogant and unforgiving.

Because we can be and are stubborn and foolish almost to the point of being cruel because we don't ever step back to see the bigger picture or, worse yet, just sit and listen.

The fifth step in AA comes after we have been broken in half. If we were not, we would never do this step, as it requires us to be dispassionate in self-examination and more vulnerable than we've ever been. It requires us to share all that we have done with another human.

They are not there to judge you, or to excuse you. They are only there to listen. There is something healing about saying all the things you know are true but have hidden for so long. It is a release. In the end, you realize none of that matters. Everyone has something like that in their life. But you are now one of the few who admitted it, so you begin to rebuild who you are. But this time on a solid footing.

I believe that the real wounds this nation has are the ones we think don't matter. Like my mother's death when I was a child. For years, I was "fine" with it. It happened, I dealt with it, I moved on. "It is in the past, I am fine, and there is nothing I hate more than people who whine about their childhood. Stop making excuses. We all have problems." That is the way I used to feel when someone asked about my mom. You know how you may feel when someone brings up slavery? You just feel like rolling your eyes and saying, "Get over it." But you really cannot until you have reconciliation.

It seems crazy now, but I really did think I was over it. I wasn't. I had NEVER talked about it, EVER—not even with my wife. Until I began to sober up. It may seem crazy now to you, but if we are going to ever really get well and come back together, we are going to need to sit and talk. More important, we are ALL going to need to sit and listen.

We need the fifth step. What Martin Luther King Jr. called reconciliation.

It is hard and uncomfortable. But it also requires powerful strength to hold back human instinct, to avoid the temptation to pile on, accuse, judge, especially when the other is at his or her most vulnerable, to try to "win." Winning requires a loser, and if we are going to come back together, there cannot be any losers.

Had Lincoln lived, I believe we would be a very different nation today—for the better. America had just gone through its biggest fight, even before the war itself. It had been fighting the scourge of slavery for almost two hundred years. It had gotten easier, as it had happened for generations, it was just how things were, and most were not around it. The vast majority, even in the South, didn't own slaves, and almost no one wanted to talk about it. It was too horrible to address. People felt that we had paid the price in blood (600,000 dead versus 140,000 in World War II), the president was killed, and the slaves were free. Everyone was motivated to move on. And because Lincoln was dead and his corrupt vice president took over, the moment of reconciliation passed, and eventually the vengeance of the South rose again and brought with it hell and all its horrors.

It was the same in the 1960s. After almost a hundred years of Reconstruction, lies, Jim Crow, insults, and indignities, our blindness was ripped away. Kennedy was shot, Malcolm X, Bobby Kennedy, Charles Manson, Chicago riots, the freedom bus attack, church bombings, fire hoses, dogs unchained, and Altamont. It was a blood-soaked decade. After King was shot and the civil rights bill was passed, people wanted to move on, forget, and move back to easier times. We wanted to make sure we began to live up to the words in the Declaration of Independence, but no one wanted to sit down and just listen to one another. It is human nature, but we are not animals alone. If we want the privilege of being called men, than we need to do the hard work. Then, just like now, people were afraid of stirring it all up again. There is very good reason to worry. There are radical revolutionaries who have no intention of listening to MLK. But without closure, a wound this deep never heals.

Look how quickly one can exploit wounds. Just a few short years after Nelson Mandela's death, South Africa is spiraling into hate again. This time it is the blacks who are the aggressors. The new president said recently, after the seizing of white-owned land, "The time for reconciliation is over." This is what Mugabe did. His country starved to death, and his torture room and prisons were filled.

Now, no one wants to talk about it, because there are too many people with agendas. It seems like "leadership" just wants something. Blame, anger, and outrage will get us nowhere. This is where our churches have failed us, now three times. This is where this dialogue should be taking place. But the only goal is peace, a hearing, understanding, forgiveness, and unity.

People say it cannot be done. I disagree. Perhaps we haven't hit our "bottom" yet and are just not willing to sit and listen to one another.

I had dinner with the Rwandan president Paul Kagame about a year ago. Beginning in the 1990s, the two tribes that made up Rwanda began to war with one another. Neighbors who had lived side by side and were good friends suddenly were dragging each other out into the streets and raping and slaughtering those same old friends. The ethnic Hutus butchered more than eight hundred thousand people in just under a hundred days. The minority Hutus were vicious in their efforts to "exterminate the cockroaches," as was broadcast daily on radio. The cockroaches were, of course, the Tutsis. The dehuman-ization of their neighbors happened so quickly and so completely that it was breathtaking. Hutu neighbors raped entire families in the street and butchered them one by one. Hutu husbands killed their Tutsi wives.

Now, twenty years later, as the country struggled to get back on its feet, officials knew that they could not merely move on as a peo-ple and as a country. But the system could not handle the load. How could they handle the caseload, and even if they could, would that, in the end, bring peace and unity? The only thing they knew for sure was that if there were to be any hope for a future, they needed to find a way to try to bring justice to the almost two million Hutus directly involved.

The nation enacted what is called the Gacaca system of commu-nity justice. Once a week the community would gather, in a market or large building, but usually under a tree, to discuss the genocide and hear from the perpetrators. If you volunteered to come and confess, if you looked at the entire community and any remaining family of the people you killed, confessed what you did and where the bodies were buried, and asked for their forgiveness, you stood a chance. IF the family believed you, believed that you were sincere and penitent, you were released. If not, and you were convicted, your sentence was life at hard labor. For those who did not turn themselves in, the conviction rate was nearly 70 percent. For those who did and asked for forgiveness, the rate of forgiveness was 80 percent. There was no retribution or redistribution, merely recon-ciliation.

Tania and I sat and listened as two neighbors, Jacqueline Muka-mana and Mathias Sendegeya, spoke of their friendship. How the two of them are once again true friends. How they help each other, and he now even watches over her children when she needs to complete errands. She has only one child and no other relatives. He butchered all the others in the street as she watched, hidden.

The story is not unique. Megan Specia in the *New York Times* tells much the same story, quoting Mr. Sendegeya: *"We massacred them, killed and ate their cows. I offended them gravely."*

When Mr. Sendegeya was in jail, he was waiting for death, and reconciliation never crossed his mind, he said.

He reentered society through a program that allows perpetrators to be released if they seek forgiveness from their victims. While in prison, he had reached out to Ms. Mukamana through Prison Fellowship Rwanda.

"He confessed and asked for forgiveness. He told me the truth," Ms. Mukamana explained. *"We forgave him from our hearts. There is no problem between us."*

This is not an event. This is a way of life.

Today, Rwanda appears to be getting back on its feet. It has one of the fastest-growing economies in Central Africa. Rwanda has notched GDP growth of around 8 percent since 2001. The country reduced the percentage of people living below the poverty line from 57 to 45 percent in five years. Life expectancy, literacy, primary school enrollment, and spending on health care have all improved. Rwanda has also made big strides toward gender equality—almost 65 percent of those in Parliament are women, which has enabled women in the country to make economic advances. Women are now able to own land, and girls can inherit from their parents.

Currently, around 83 percent of Rwanda's population of 10.5 million live in rural areas, and nearly 70 percent of the population still works in subsistence farming. But the government wants to change this.

In the long term, the government looks to transform the country from a low-income, agriculture-based economy to a knowledge-based, service-oriented economy with a middle-income status by 2020.

The country is far from perfect, and Kagame is not the man I would want for president, but if the people are to be believed and they can build years of trust between them, they will be the model for the whole world to study.

34

The Only Thing Constant

Change is hard. I know that from my own experience. Sometimes it's absolutely necessary, though; change or die is a pretty strong motivation. As an alcoholic, when I reached bottom, when I was blacking out, it was pretty obvious that if I didn't stop drinking, my life as I knew it was over. Knowing that made change a lot easier. Easier, not easy. True change always is hard.

Letting go of my own outrage was more difficult, if possible, than stopping drinking. My well-being wasn't in any danger. In fact, change was about the only thing that could damage my career.

And then I did what I am asking you to do now. And for the same reasons: Our country is in trouble, and buying into this us-versus-them mentality—that's both sides—is making the situation worse.

I wasn't helping at all; I was doing my best, but what I actually was doing was hammering in that wedge between the two sides a little deeper. I was adding to the problem. I have grown to understand that, as the great novelist Robert Harris wrote in *Conclave*, "My brothers and sisters . . . let me tell you that the one sin I have come to fear more than other sin is certainty. Certainty is the great enemy of unity. Certainty is the deadly enemy of tolerance. Even Christ was not certain at the end."

The third step in the AA program is to "turn our will and our lives over to the care of God as we understand Him." I've interpreted that to mean a willingness to make a commitment to change; to accept the reality that you will have to give up certain behavior patterns. Among the things that make real change difficult is other people. Other people don't want you to change. For the most part, you are a supporting player in their lives; you fit in a certain role and can be relied upon to do your predictable job. But when you change, everybody in your life has to respond to that change, and suddenly you're playing a different role, you're saying different lines, and you're upsetting (at least in my case) the liquor cart. A lot of people don't want to change, and they sure don't want you to do it either. Those who are mired in their own addictions will try to drag you down; they want you with them in their misery. Your success in changing is threatening to them. It forces them to examine their own beliefs and behavior. And eventually they have to wonder, if you can do it, why can't they do it?

One person who did not embrace my decision to take a more spiritual, conciliatory tone was Roger Ailes. Roger and I never really got along; he admired my work ethic and skill, I admired his intelligence and skill, but we didn't see eye-to-eye about ethics. But Roger figured out years earlier that passion sells, and he was passionate about destroying the Democratic Party.

Roger built a great media machine, and when I joined Fox News it was already humming along beautifully and quite profitably. One day he made it very clear to me that he was not going to let me or anyone else cause any problems. After I got there, several people told me they could never leave Roger; they owed him so much. I was impressed by the fact that he engendered that level of loyalty. But I was wrong about that; as we now know, some of them literally owed him. It seemed to me he was always trying to find some way of putting me in his debt. He tried to get something on me. After the success of the Restoring Honor event in Washington, Rupert Murdoch invited me to his office, which was unusual. The rally impressed him, he told me, and he wondered what I intended to do with all that power.

"Nothing," I told him. "I didn't do it to gain power. I just wanted to bring people together and make a statement."

"So you're not running for anything?" he asked, which I thought was a curious question. In response I laughed.

For obvious reasons, I've employed a security team for several years. On occasion they've discovered that people were digging into my background. I've actually had people steal my garbage in hopes they would uncover something that would lead to a story. The biggest discovery was that I really like Chinese food. None of this surprised me. I considered it an occupational hazard. And I knew I had nothing to worry about; I've been incredibly open about my personal problems with my audience. There's no secret card I hadn't turned over myself. So I wasn't shocked when my team informed me that once again someone was trying to investigate me. But when I asked if they had any idea who was doing it, this time the answer did surprise me: "We're pretty sure it's Fox."

Weeks later I was in Roger's office to discuss something or other. "You know," he said, "this can be a pretty rough business." I agreed; I'd seen it, I said. "There are a lot of bad people out there, Glenn," he continued. Then he opened a bottom desk drawer, picked up a thick bunch of files, and put them on his desk. I've always believed it was just blank pages, but I had no way of knowing. "A lot of people have been investigating you from all sides." He paused, smiled, and added, "You have a good wife."

The hairs on the back of my neck stood up. I sat on the edge of my chair. "Yes," I said. "I do."

He continued, "It's always a shame when a man does something to hurt a woman like that."

Oh my gosh, I was ready to explode, I was so angry. Instead I said evenly, "That's exactly why it's never happened with me."

We just sat there staring at each other for what might have been thirty seconds. Then he put the file back in the drawer and finished, "I know, and that's why I think you're doing good and you're safe."

Whatever my feelings about Roger Ailes, I loved my audience at Fox. It was large, enthusiastic, and always supportive. But over time,

I began to appreciate the magnitude of the problem America is facing and that my approach wasn't helping to heal the divide. Gradually, I realized that the certainty I'd once felt had disappeared, and in exchange I'd gained what is much less valued: perspective. I learned pretty quickly that perspective doesn't sell nearly as well as certainty. I could have kept up the charade; there was a lot at stake, but to be true to myself I had to change. I had given up on both political parties and almost all politicians.

At about this time I was having a spiritual conversation with a friend of mine, a farmer, as we were driving through his wheat fields. I was discussing the doubt that had been seeping into my mind when he asked, wisely, "Have you ever heard of Ezekiel?"

"Of course," I said. In the scriptures Ezekiel is the Watchman on the Tower who was to give God's warning to the people of Israel. "What about him?"

He then quoted Ezekiel 33:6 to me: "'But if the watchman sees the sword coming and does not blow the trumpet, so that the people are not warned, and the sword comes and takes any one of them, that person is taken away in his iniquity, but his blood I will require at the watchman's hand.'" Then he glanced at me and added, "That's quite a responsibility."

I took him seriously. I had the trust of 50 million Americans a month, and I would not be the person they believed me to be if I didn't get the word out about the trouble I saw coming over the horizon. I couldn't be responsible for the way they reacted, but I am responsible for my own position. When I wavered—and there were times when I wondered whether I was doing the right thing—Ezekiel's words came back to me.

It was tough to change. Tough? That doesn't begin to describe it. There was a lot of pressure on me to continue giving people what they wanted. But I couldn't do that to myself or to that audience. It was a really strange situation; if I hadn't respected my audience as much as I did, I easily could have given them the Glenn Beck they knew and wanted. But having given up on politicians and the political parties, about the only thing I had left was my belief in the decency of the average American.

Admittedly, my audience didn't understand it at first—what's going on with Glenn?—and a lot of them didn't like it. And when I spoke out against Donald Trump, a lot of them thought, Glenn's gone crazy and sold us out! My change had affected their lives, and they didn't like it. There were some nasty responses and a lot of name-calling, which I returned. It was a low point, as I failed to listen to my own audience. I thought they had sold out, and they thought I had done the same. Neither was true. We were just talking past one another, each of us convinced that the other was wrong. To show how far I'd gone, I made the enemies list of two totally different presidents: Obama, who used the IRS as a weapon against the Tea Party, and Trump, who called me "a sad and pathetic loser."

There was a real cost to change for me. But it was something I had to do if I really believed what I was saying. It's important to point out that I didn't change my basic belief system; I didn't suddenly start to believe in Government Nanny. I'm a proud constitutional conservative. I am pro-life. I am pro–First Amendment, big pro–Second Amendment. Pro–individual Americans. I have never wavered in my support for all of those things; what I have changed is my approach. I resolved that I was no longer going to get mired in the belief that if my side doesn't defeat the other side, it's all over; that my side winning was the only acceptable result. I wasn't going to get caught in the back-and-forth bitterness.

I found myself in agreement with Yale sociologist Nicholas A. Christakis, one of *Time* magazine's one hundred most influential people in the world, who has been studying group behavior. "Why must it be the case that we love our own and hate the other?" he wondered. His research confirmed, "In order to band together, we need a common enemy." But then he added that he had also found that it doesn't have to be that way: "It's possible to treat the out-group with mild dislike or even grudging respect. Cultivating in-group distinctiveness does not require that the other side must be killed."

Getting to that point was tough. It's no secret that I earned my reputation as an extremely partisan bomb-thrower. I saw the political divide as the battle for the soul of America. While I was still at Fox, trying to figure out how serious I was about these thoughts, we got some pretty damning information about someone who was attacking me. It probably would have destroyed this person's career. Our evidence was strong enough to go with, but the story was a little cheap, a little smeary; I didn't like it because it was personal. There was a lot of pressure to release it, though, because this person was doing an effective job coming after me. In the past I wouldn't have hesitated; I would have gone after this person and never looked back. Truthfully, every part of my body was just aching to get even. I loved the feeling that I got when I let loose on one of "them." Of just allowing my outrage to take control. But I was trying to change. This was a test. This was the glass of whiskey on the bar, the rolled joint. It was incredibly hard to resist; my mind was telling me it was okay, I would start changing tomorrow. Just this one last time. Of course, that's addiction talk.

I prayed for guidance, and as I did a phrase came to mind: They're not enemies of yours, they're enemies of the truth. Do not treat them as enemies.

I got the guidance I needed. Among the historical items in my collection is a surveyor's compass owned by George Washington. He got it when he was fourteen and carried it with him through the rest of his life, on every campaign, every battlefield; he used it for every map he drew. On the morning I had to make a decision whether or not to run with this story, I put Washington's compass in my pocket. For a lot of the day I held on to it, and as I rubbed my thumb against it I found it had been worn down near its top. I realized that Washington must have done the same thing, rubbing it distractedly with his thumb. It was the imprint of the man. I felt a connection with him, and with his values: Stay true to who you are. Do the right thing, not the easy thing, not the thing you want to do; do the right thing.

I never said a word. I didn't fight back; I just ignored that person. As a result, the accusations against me faded out of the media pretty quickly. If there was a single event that marked the beginning of change for me, this was it. I had proven that I could resist the pull to satisfy my emotional need by snapping back quickly and tougher.

Pay attention to that—it's a big point. Because if I could change, if I could stop shouting at the other side over every issue and start listening to what they were saying—listening, and often not agreeing— you can, too. It was a gradual process, and as with any addiction there were times I slipped up, but eventually I was able to do it.

Okay, I hear you: Really, Glenn? Then why haven't more people changed? I have some theories about that, and actually I might be wrong. First, I think, as I've learned in AA, that people are far more afraid of the unknown than concerned with their current pain. We tend to normalize even destructive behavior patterns; we incorporate them into our lives, make the necessary adjustments, and figure out how to deal with them. I continued drinking well past my good-to-go point because I had learned how to hide it from other people; I knew when and where to drink so it didn't affect personal relationships or my career. I was able to relentlessly attack Democrats without any penalties because my audience was Republican and conservative. We figure out how to live with our problems, even if they cause pain, because we're terrified of what might happen if we change that behavior.

We tell whatever lies we need to convince ourselves we're actually telling ourselves the truth: If I stop drinking, I won't be the same outspoken person who has been so successful. If I stop being so angry at Democrats, I'll lose my audience, and I won't be able to pay the bills, and just like before I'll lose everything I have and my family. No thanks; it's easier to live with this pain.

Second, we have created our own definitions of truth. Many Americans are far more comfortable having the opinion they already hold reinforced—and it doesn't seem to matter if it's true or not—than having it challenged by a bunch of so-called facts. This is where fake news proves to be so important. Too many people refuse to research, investigate, or even question their beliefs because they may find out they aren't true. If you uncover an uncomfortable truth and you still don't change, then you have to deal with the reality that you're a fraud. That's hard to do. Nobody wants to face that void. Dealing with it might require you to do things that you don't want to do; in my case it meant shutting my big fat mouth, losing my ratings and my status, losing friends, and even having to change employment.

Or live as a happy fraud!

Several years ago, I remember, I started reading a book entitled *Blacklisted by History* by M. Stanton Evans. It was a reevaluation of Senator Joseph McCarthy, whose name has come to mean a wild witch hunt and the use of unproven claims to defame people. I always considered him a pretty bad guy. But when I got about thirty pages into it, I put it down. The author was presenting a more flattering portrait than I had expected. The theme seemed to be that Tail Gunner Joe wasn't quite the raving maniac that I thought, but actually was a guy who had uncovered at least a little evidence of Communists infiltrating the government. I decided I wasn't going to read any more until I found out more about the author; I wanted to make sure he wasn't some wild conspiracy freak. Even then, even if I convinced myself that he was a legitimate researcher, I still wasn't sure I wanted to continue reading, because there was at least the possibility that this book might challenge my opinion on what our government is, how it operates, and even whether it is fair. And I was kind of happy with my view of things.

I don't know how many people do things like this, but I'm pretty sure I'm not the only one. I was concerned that if I continued reading that book and found truth in it, I was going to end up at a crossroads. I was going to have to make a decision: I could either reject Evans's research and continue believing as I always had or admit I was wrong, admit I had new information, and then be brave enough to reset my course based on those new coordinates. There are a lot of people who'd rather not have to make that decision. I get it.

But that says something about those people. I kept reading; I wanted to add to my knowledge. If you consider yourself someone with an open mind, it's fair to ask what you've read lately. What have you learned or reexamined? What have you done, discussed, or listened to that challenged what you think you know? When was the last time you thought, "Wow, I didn't know that" or "I never looked at it that way" or, finally, "Wait; if that's true, then maybe I'm wrong about this"? Getting your information from the usual sources is safe, I guarantee that; it does nothing but confirm what you already believe.

There are people who are afraid of change. Fear has become part of our culture. We're so afraid of falling that we don't stand up; we are so afraid of failing that we don't take a chance. Instead we go to our so-called safe places. It's easier to stay in your chair than take a risk, but that chair is a comfortable trap. It isn't moving forward; it's just there. *New York Times* (I warned you) editorial page editor James Bennet described it perfectly: "We exist in an incredibly hyperpartisan environment where the media is increasingly niche-ified and increasingly partisan and picking a side and shooting back and forth at each other between media organizations. And also because Donald Trump is president of the United States, and that makes a lot of people feel really, really vulnerable and afraid. And I get that. It makes it harder for people to hear an opposing point of view or a challenging point of view with the same sense of security."

Personally, I consider myself risk-averse about things I can't control but confident about those things within my control. I've been to Las Vegas once in my life. I walked into Caesars Palace and put five dollars down on the blackjack table. I got my cards and said, "Hit me." I was done. The dealer took my money. I looked at him and said, "That was not five dollars' worth of fun." That was the last time I put cash down on the table.

But I got out of Fox to start a web television station. Nobody had done it before. We had to create the technology. Everyone said it would fail. But within two years, Google's Eric Schmidt was being interviewed in my lobby, calling TheBlaze groundbreaking. I'm not saying overcoming that fear is easy; the truth is, you're going to win some, but probably not all. Risk big, win big—do whatever homework is necessary, but don't let your fear prevent you from rolling the dice!

There are a lot of people who believe giving up an addiction means admitting you've been wrong, and they can't do that. They are so deeply invested in being right that it is impossible for them to admit they're wrong. It would be the emotional version of poking a hole in the dike, and once the ocean started dribbling in, the whole structure might collapse. Well, in some instances at least, they're wrong about being wrong; in this case it doesn't require that at all. Harvard psychologist Dan Gilbert pointed out, "Human beings are works in progress that mistakenly think they're finished." Circumstances change; sometimes people get new or additional information, and people who refuse to adapt to changing situations are stubborn but not necessarily wrong. I wasn't wrong about my beliefs; they were based in knowledge, and I have been pretty consistent. What I have tried to change is the way I express myself, and the way I respond when people who disagree with me express their opinions.

For the most part, I've discovered, people don't wake up in the morning and decide to change. They're not like Kafka's Gregor Samsa, who awoke one morning and "found himself transformed in his bed into a monstrous vermin." Generally, people change when their behavior affects their own life in a negative way, when the person they love leaves because they can't deal with the problems anymore. When they can no longer afford to feed the beast. When just getting up and facing the day seems like an ordeal. Most people won't commit to change until the pain they have to deal with is greater than their fear of the unknown.

Taking the first step, admitting to yourself that you may be on the wrong track, really is super-hard to do. Especially after you've made a real emotional investment. In 2000 I was doing talk radio in Tampa, Florida, trying to rebuild my career. I struggled for the first six months. I remember complaining to my wife that no matter what I was talking about, some so-called expert would call in to tell me I was wrong. At times I was ready to quit and go back to culinary arts and learn how to be a chef. Then the Terry Schiavo right-to-die case surfaced.

In 1990, twenty-six-year-old Terry Schiavo suffered massive brain damage when she went into cardiac arrest. To save her life, she was put on artificial life support and fed through a tube. Seven years later, after she had shown no improvement, her husband petitioned the court to have that tube removed. He claimed she would have not wanted to "live" this way. Her parents fought that application. It became a major issue.

In my mind I knew I would not want to survive in an unconscious state, dependent on a feeding tube, and I took that position. I became a loud advocate for pulling the plug. And I was right. I was sure of that. It was so clear to me that I couldn't understand how any sane person could disagree with me. Then on a Friday afternoon, about five minutes before I finished the show and went home for the weekend, a caller challenged me. He asked, "Do you consider food extraordinary medical assistance?"

I spent the weekend thinking about that. It seemed pretty obvious to me: Feeding someone wasn't an extraordinary measure. We feed people, we don't starve them to death. Okay, I had changed my mind. The question was, what should I do about it? I had invested a lot of my credibility in my opinion, and the prospect of admitting I had been wrong was not very appealing. My listeners liked certainty.

At our Monday-morning meeting I told my staff, "I have to reverse myself on Terry Schiavo." The room went completely silent. A talk show host admitting he was wrong? That was practically radio heresy. "I've been thinking about it all weekend, and I'm wrong. It's not like extraordinary measures are being taken. It's food, and her parents will take her and feed her."

After I'd finished my announcement, a producer suggested that I not talk about it, that we just move on. But I'd been pretty outspoken about my opinion. I felt I had a moral obligation to admit that I had changed. I went on the air and explained what I was thinking. I feel like I've done real damage, I said, and I need to make up for it. While at least some of my listeners didn't agree with me, they respected my honesty.

It's much better when you're wrong, or when you change your mind, to admit it. I've always believed that, unlike newspapers that bury their corrections, I should make them the lede. I know that it's difficult to do that at times, but it ensures credibility.

I understand that a lot of people, maybe even a majority of people, just can't do this. Their anger at the other side, the side that everyone can agree has caused all of our problems (which is true no matter which side you are on!) is too strong. And these people know what the real truth is: The people on the other side have to change for the good of the country! And they are happy to tell them that.

Not everybody is capable of change. I accept that. My grandfather, for example, was old-school. He was a man with strong values. He never said very much, but he had this odd quirk: At times he would just blurt things out of the blue. We were driving along one afternoon in his old pickup when he suddenly said, "I want you to listen to me. No matter what anyone says about coloreds, they are just like you and me." This was a huge leap for a person of his generation. He was trying to reach out from his place and make sure that I knew the men with dogs and fire hoses were wrong. He may not have known how to express it, but he tried. To me it is still a powerful message on never getting "stuck"—saying what others will not, and being a man who sees people for who they are, not what they look like.

Remember that this was still the late 1960s or very early '70s. But even then, his language may have been out of tune. I could have explained to him why many people would find the word "coloreds" offensive, but at six or seven, I doubt I knew. Today, however, simply using the word that was okay until last week will get you fired. Can we not look into one another's heart and see how hard we are trying? We are all new at this, and if all we ever get is bitten, we will stop reaching our hand out.

Even when people aren't riled up, it's hard to convince another person to change. That willingness has to come from inside. All I'm trying to do is show why you should be open to the possibility that there is another way of getting what we all claim we want: a stronger America that recognizes and protects individual freedoms. AA didn't convince me to stop drinking; I made that decision myself. But after I had made that decision, the tools I found in AA helped me reach my goal. The political equivalent of that was replacing certainty with perspective. Instead of being so sure I was right and diligently lecturing Democrats—which turned out to be kind of a fruitless effort, as they aren't listening any more than Republicans—I allowed myself to be open to change.

When somebody proposed something to me that might make sense, I thought, Okay, let's run it through a test. If it makes sense, I'll pay attention. Obamacare, for example. I was against it, but I wasn't against universal health care. My belief hasn't changed: I have always been against creating another giant government bureaucracy that we will never escape; I still am, and always will be. But if individual states want to create programs and show me good results, I'll pay attention to them. If a concept works, why wouldn't we do that? But only as individual states. The Constitution must remain supreme.

We know what's happening: Chamath Palihapitiya, formerly a top Facebook executive, said with some regret, "I think we have created tools that are ripping apart the social fabric of how society works. . . . No civil discourse, no cooperation; misinformation, mistruth. . . .

"So we are in a really bad state of affairs right now, in my opinion. It is eroding the core foundation of how people behave by and between each other. And I don't have a good solution. My solution is I just don't use these tools anymore. I haven't for years."

Turning it off is the extreme solution. All I'm suggesting is that we begin to meet the challenges by turning down the volume.

35

God Is Expansive—Think Bigger

I am fundamentally an optimist. Whether that comes from nature or nurture, I cannot say. Part of being optimistic is keeping one's head pointed toward the sun, one's feet moving forward. There were many dark moments when my faith in humanity was sorely tested, but I would not and could not give myself up to despair. That way lies defeat and death.

—Nelson Mandela

Let a wave of intolerance wash over you . . . Yes, hate is good . . . Our goal is a Christian nation . . . We are called by God to conquer this country . . . We don't want pluralism.

—Operation Rescue founder Randall Terry, August 1993

I like your Christ, I do not like your Christians. Your Christians are so unlike your Christ.

—Gandhi

I have come to believe and accept the fact that we need strengths beyond our awareness and resources to restore this country to sanity. A lot of the principles of AA are based on an individual relationship to God; the fifth step, for example: "Admitted to God, to ourselves, and to another human being the exact nature of our wrongs." And the sixth: "We're entirely ready to have God remove all these defects of character." And the seventh: "Humbly asked him to remove our shortcomings."

I'm a man of faith, but I'm not a big fan of religion. I ask a lot of questions that I'm pretty confident are not going to be answered while I'm alive. The biggest one, of course, being (imagine trumpets blaring here!): Is there a God? I believe there is. But I cannot prove it to you, nor can you prove He doesn't exist. So let me respect your point of view, and I would ask that you return the favor.

Civilizations have been debating that question long before we had an Internet. That just made it easier. The current debate between believers and nonbelievers is basically summed up as the Big Bang Theory versus Intelligent Design. Let's say it was the Big Bang, where the world was created in a massive explosion that spewed the universe. What caused it? What existed before it went boom? Truthfully, I don't care. On the other hand, do I really believe the world was created in seven days? Did He create using evolution? Personally, anyone who asks the seven-day question is just looking for a Twitter fight. What is a day to God? It is akin to asking whether God can make a rock so heavy that He himself cannot lift it. What is He, a bodybuilder now? Stop. I believe that God created the universe and all that is in it. What does that mean, and how did it happen? I don't know, and neither does anyone else—not the popes, not the professors.

So much of history, literature, and the Bible I didn't understand or appreciate until recently. I guess most of my life, when I would read the stories, I couldn't understand how the people could be so stupid. I mean, they were just wiped out on page 1260 for what they are now doing again on page 1281. "Morons," I always thought. Until we became those morons.

We are missing basic connections that have always brought us together. If you really want to understand the West, its culture, its systems of government, or even its art, including Shakespeare, you must read the Bible. It was the stock of everything we did, thought, and created. Almost everything we have heard our whole life came from that book, and we don't even know it.

At their wits' end; a two-edged sword; a drop in the bucket; a house divided against itself cannot stand; a labor of love; nothing new under the sun; fire and brimstone; fight the good fight; beat swords into ploughshares; it's better to give than to receive; in the twinkling of an eye; the ends of the earth; at the eleventh hour; the blind leading the blind; by the skin of your teeth; to cast pearls before swine; eat, drink, and be merry; to fall by the wayside; feet of clay; a fly in the ointment; a leopard cannot change its spots; like a lamb to the slaughter; a millstone around your neck; to move mountains; the writing is on the wall.

How can we dismiss something that most have never read cover to cover and yet its words are so deeply rooted in our culture?

Imagine now what other lasting civilization building blocks are in that book.

Even if we take the Thomas Paine approach. He didn't believe in the Bible's being an accurate history. He didn't believe in Jesus. But he believed in a higher being. Franklin told him that everything he could dream and do was because of the people who did believe in the Judeo-Christian teachings. It was the civilization that sprang from the true principles that allowed men to live free and in harmony with one another. It was the absence or distortions of that truth that caused chaos and death. It is why in the end, the man the world deemed an atheist risked his life to try to convince the followers of Robespierre during the French Revolution that they must not dismiss God.

Thomas Paine didn't need to "baptize" the French. He knew that self-governance was essential, and throughout the history of mankind, when man has faith in the Judeo-Christian concept of "God" and the humility that comes from the correct understanding of the "faith," he behaves differently and has a better chance of governing himself properly.

Without a foundation, all is fair game. What is moral? Is it more moral to kill a child with Down syndrome, as it "will have no quality of life" so others can receive food and care that we couldn't afford due to this "useless eater"? Natural rights tell us that this is what the "pack" will do with its weakest link.

If we want to leave the Judeo-Christian world, let's at least discuss what that means. To do so, we must first know what those truisms that built this world were and which ones have been distorted. There are indeed big problems, but there have also been things that have been achieved only in this culture. Which are the good parts that should be saved, and which need to be discarded?

What are we even shooting for? What is our goal, object, or pinpoint on the horizon we are now striving to reach? Man has always had hero stories. Even the box office is showing us how hungry we are for heroes. Iron Man, Thor, the Black Panther. Luke Skywalker is probably the most famous and sound of today's hero archetypes. But who are the real-life heroes whom we want to emulate and foster? Can you name one? Can you identify the traits? If you can but cannot name a man who lives up to those traits who is accepted by most, can we ever achieve that goal?

We had two archetypes that we all agreed were our ultimate men, or ideal spirit or attitude. The Western world is built around these two men: a selfless lawgiver, Moses; and Jesus, the man from Nazareth. One "perfect" and the other riddled with flaws and mistakes. But through each of them we could learn all we needed to know to grow in character and strength. Because of them, we knew the difference between right and wrong at the most basic level as well as the most intellectual. These two men were the basis for what MLK said he thought all men should be judged by: the content of their "character."

We have almost totally obliterated those images and even a basic understanding of what they meant and did. We have lost our mooring line. It is why character no longer seems to matter. Who is the archetype?

It is no wonder we are so lost. We have no North Star. There is no universally shared truth or hero stories. We are a culture that has lost its heroes, God, and even myths. As Nietzsche said to the people of the German republic as they headed toward madness: "God is dead." However, as he and others have pointed out, "When people lose their faith in God, it isn't that they believe in nothing; rather, they will believe in anything."

Churches have so distorted the message of God that most under thirty have no image of God outside a religious description. People are forgoing "God" and just trying to be better men or women than they were yesterday.

Once, years ago, I was talking to my father and I said something about God. He stopped me and said, "Before we have this discussion, Glenn, what do you mean by God?"

I didn't understand his question. At that time I was still young enough to know everything, and everybody knows about God. "What do you mean?"

"Well," he began, "if you say God, does that mean a Father God? Or does that mean Jesus and the Holy Spirit, too? When you say God, do you mean the God of Buddha? Or do you mean one that's in heaven? One that created heaven and hell? What exactly do you mean?"

He was causing chaos in my mind. Obviously I'd never considered anything like that. God is God. He's just God.

Apparently not, though. "That's the problem. We can't have a discussion about God using the word 'God' because it means too many things to too many people. You say the word 'God' to someone who's been abused by a pastor and that God looks very different. God, if you want to have a fair discussion, is first cause."

"What do you mean?"

"What started it all? All physics, all knowledge, everything breaks down fractions of a second after the Big Bang. So let's go back to one second before; what lit the fuse? What created that?"

My father was more of a deist in a way. He did not believe in praying to God for solutions, or favors, or whatever. And I guess I didn't either. I do now. I still go to church grudgingly. I am just not a fan of organized religion, and it is very different from my faith. Thank God, one doesn't depend on the other.

Ben Franklin was asked as a religious trap, "Sir, what is the American religion?" He responded: "That there is a God. He is just and will judge us. Because He is just, we should serve Him. The best way to serve Him is to serve our fellow man."

Where do I find that church? Our churches spend too much time inside their own four walls. It is time we live it.

I think this is why Christians get such a bad name. Christ's followers rarely act like him when the chips are down. A recent Barna poll, which is a faith-based pollster, found that there was NO statistical difference between the life religious people live and non. Health, marriage, honesty, theft, sex, divorce—nothing. Except service and charitable giving. Honestly, I would rather be around a liar who admitted that he lied than one who lied about lying. WHERE ARE ALL THE HONEST LIARS?

Please don't wrap political justifications around the Bible. Just come out and say it like it is. Nope, all that stuff isn't Christian behavior, but I do it or I accept it because. But then don't act all high and mighty when someone else does it.

I am a long way away from being a Millennial, but I am with them. If the people in the church aren't doing it, there is nothing there for me to learn. I can read the book on my own or find a group of people and we can go out and serve for an hour or two. That is going to bring me closer to whatever God wants me to be than sitting in a pew just talking about it. Let's make our prayers and time count.

I do make my plea every day, but it is never for anything specific; rather, it is simply to accept whatever happens during the day. It's, "Let me find meaning in whatever happens." My prayers bring me to a peaceful place within myself.

"Lord, let me accept whatever comes my way. You know what I am working toward and on; should it put me on the wrong path, close the door and change my path. Let me see the pain in others and make the time to comfort, listen, or bolster. Help me be a better man than I was yesterday. I AM open and I AM searching to see you in all people and all things today. Give me the opportunity to be reminded that I AM your servant."

So if people want to talk about God and religion, I can do that—I can sit and talk about it with them for years, and I'll have a great time with the intellectual exploration of what it all is and how it happened. I doubt we'll come up with an answer. If we do, will be it right? I don't know. Most important, it doesn't matter. Here's what I do know: I will die someday, and only then will it be revealed if there is an afterlife. But the faith that I have in my life it has made me a better man on earth. It has helped me on a daily basis to navigate sometimes treacherous waters.

The result of my exploration has been my faith. I don't know the answers to all those questions; nobody does, nobody can answer them. There is a wonderfully provocative book written by Robert Harris entitled *Conclave*. It's the story of the gathering of cardinals to elect a new pope. The cardinal running the conclave may be having his own doubts. The one thing he has come to fear more than anything else, he explains, is certainty. Certainty is the deadly enemy of tolerance. Even Christ wasn't certain in the end, which is why he wondered in his agony, Father, why have you forsaken me? If there was no doubt about it all, there would be no mystery; there would be no need for faith.

While the God question isn't going to be answered anytime soon, I have absolutely no doubt about the power and value of faith, even if trying to describe it is like picking up mercury. People tend to look at it from their own corner of the world and make it fit into their current belief system. "Faith," Dr. Martin Luther King Jr. said once, giving it the broadest definition, "is taking the first step even when you don't see the whole staircase." That is having faith, or maybe "blind faith"—believing when there is no scientific reason to do so. You believe because you believe.

That's actually reasonably close to the religious definition, which is essentially believing something is true even though there is no material evidence to support that belief. Hebrews 11:1 explains, "Now faith is the substance of things hoped for, the evidence of things not seen."

British journalist Andrew Brown focused on a nonreligious meaning, which is equally beneficial in overcoming an addiction: "What we all need is not best described as faith. It is simply more than can be proven by logic and science. We need to believe in things that are not entirely justified by reason, but that does not require us to embrace creeds that reason tells against. The non-religious do not find meaning, purpose and value by taking a leap into the unknown and transcendental. We find it in the beauty and joy of life, and in the empathy that makes us see the value in the lives of others too. These things are not facts captured by fundamental physics but nor are they religious mysteries to be taken on faith."

Both faith healing and the placebo effect, in which people actually receive some positive benefits from treatments having absolutely no scientific value, also show the power of faith. If you believe, really believe, that something is true or has value, your mind is so strong that it miraculously can make it happen. Researchers have suggested a lot of explanations for that and all of them are very interesting, but the bottom line is simply this: In many cases, faith—non-religious faith—has proven to be a strong medicine.

Faith has always played an important role in step programs to overcome addiction. But a lot of those programs emphasize the difference between faith and religion. Cocaine Anonymous, for example, refers to a "higher power" in its basic tenets, but then explains that it is up to each individual to decide what that higher power is. On its website CA makes the point that "It is easy enough to confuse the word spirituality with religion. As it relates to God, Cocaine Anonymous is a spiritual program, not a religious one."

It would have been a lot easier for me to quit drinking if I'd had some type of guarantee that something better was waiting for me when I did. You know, some kind of double-your-Jim-Beam-back if you aren't happier. But I didn't have that. So giving up my lifestyle required me to believe that going through all that was going to lead to something positive. The organization Recovery.org explains, "There is no point in dealing with the pain, discomfort, anguish, guilt, shame, and all the other emotions and feelings that recovery can bring if there is no end that makes it worth it."

My personal faith has sustained me through some difficult times. I have relied on it. It has served as a moral barometer. It enabled me to have a strong marriage. But it's different from what is taught in AA. AA is very God-oriented. In AA, the function of faith, or a belief in a supreme being, is to give alcoholics something to rely on to fill the vast emptiness created by giving up drinking. Giving up your outrage is also going to leave a void that's going to need to be filled. And it may require you to accept, on faith, that there is a real benefit to you and the country.

At another time in our history we would have had the American myth to rely on. We would have believed in the righteousness of our country and known that more was expected of us as Americans. We don't have those beliefs anymore. We know that our government is capable of torturing prisoners, we have a president who has at best a distant relationship with the truth, we know our fellow Americans can be vicious in their personal attacks. It's hard not to fight back, and there are times when we need something greater than our own internal fortitude to rely on.

We don't have those basic underpinnings we once could rely on as a guide to do things "the American way," but we still need some kind of moral foundation. We know the difference between right and wrong, between love and hate, between anger and understanding, between coldness and compassion, although too often we place them aside and focus on winning and losing, which leads inevitably to outrage. There is no winning when you fight to win. There is winning in reconciliation. There is winning in listening to one another, in being peaceful to one other. Martin Luther King Jr. was absolutely right about that: He was not trying to win anything, he was just trying to figure out how all Americans could live together, governed by the laws of the land. And through all of that he was carried by his own faith. He didn't know what was waiting on the mountaintop, but he believed that the goal was worth fighting for. King called it reconciliation. Gandhi called it love. Jesus called it the way, the truth, and the light, but in the end it is faith.

And it plays a very important role. At one point several years ago I attended a conference with one of the biggest Silicon Valley venture capitalists. This was someone heavily invested in cutting-edge technology. We were talking about predicting the future, which is essentially his business, as he bets hundreds of millions on the success of certain technologies. He is not at all religious, so you can imagine how surprised I was when he told me, "In the future, the people who are going to have a leg up on us are the people who have faith. If they have God in their life, they will find meaning in their faith. And so when they lose their job or something bad happens in their life, they will have their faith to rely on that somehow it will all work out."

I've thought about that. And I've wondered, what do any of us believe in that's bigger than ourselves? What defines us? It occurred to me that many Americans had God in their lives without knowing it; we've just changed His name. We find Him in our cars, our job, our house, fame, sex, the environment, political parties—whatever it is that regulates us and gives us permission to act. For me, it was my car. Back in the 1980s, I was successful as a radio show host in that I was able to buy a Mercedes. That car represented everything I had worked for. I loved it; it was the material embodiment of my success. My father loved it, too; he'd never owned a new car in his life, and the fact that his son could afford a Mercedes had real meaning to him. But when my life collapsed, the Mercedes had to go. I will never forget the feeling of loss, that emptiness inside, as I watched that car being towed down the block. That was me disappearing into the distance. I had allowed that car to define me. Losing it felt like I was losing everything that mattered in my life, like I was losing myself. I was left without any sense of who I was, and there is nothing more empty than that.

My father always said that the two most powerful words in any tongue are I AM. Because what you put after those words is how you see yourself; what you see, what you speak, will become what you are. It is the creative power of God. If you say I AM worthy, or I AM worthless, or I AM capable, or I AM too dumb to figure it out, that is the you and the reality that you will create.

This is something I actually think about often. How do I answer that question today? I AM . . . what? The answer changes. And as a result I know that I am changing. Try it yourself; you'll see what an incredibly complex mix of emotions, ideas, thoughts, moods, needs, and wants we all are. What have you created for yourself? I have spent too long saying I AM outraged.

I AM finding new ideas and new people to connect with on a whole different level.

The only thing that doesn't change for me is my faith. That's there all the time. Resolute, solid. My bulwark. So, when I talk about the importance of faith in giving up your addiction to outrage, I'm writing from my own experience. I didn't know when I started on this path that I would reach this point. But fulfilling the first and second steps, admitting I was powerless over my addiction and believing that a power greater than myself could restore me to sanity, required more than just surrendering to the unknown. That possibility was scary. That's when I came to understand the power of faith for me to rely on—and then rebuild on.

People don't just become addicts. It's not like making a wrong turn and getting caught on a backwoods road. It's a path you follow to fill a need, whatever it might be, inside you. Whatever you are running from, the addiction helps you get away. I don't know anyone who can just give it up without some sort of replacement. I had no idea what that might be, but I had faith that I would be led to it, that I would find it, and that somehow I would be okay.

Believe me, there were a lot of times when I doubted that. A lot of times when I came close to having a drink. That was also true when I realized I was causing dissension and outrage and had to stop. I questioned whether I was capable of giving up what I had in exchange for . . . for something, I didn't know what, that would be better. When I started on this path I had no way of knowing I would reach this place. The more faith I had that there was something waiting for me once I escaped my addiction, the easier it became.

Coming to my faith was a journey for me. Growing up as a Catholic, I was greatly puzzled by what I was told were matters of faith. I know many great Catholics, and in no way should my personal experiences reflect on them or the Catholic faith. I had to believe because I was told to believe. And if I didn't believe, oh boy, I was surely going to spend eternity burning in hell. That didn't have much appeal to me. I am not good with the heat. I live in Texas; I will not do well in hell. But when I thought about the precepts of my religion, they made little sense to me. Did Gandhi go to hell because he wasn't a good Catholic? Why did babies have to go a place called Purgatory? If I dared question any of this, they told me I was committing a sin called blasphemy. How could trying to understand my religion be considered a bad thing?

Well, I didn't have faith that these people, who were so certain, knew a whole lot more than I did. In fact, the whole concept of an all-encompassing God seemed pretty strange to me. As my father had warned me, in addition to worshipping different Gods, everybody seemed to have their own definition of God. He was in the air and in the trees, blah, blah, blah. I can see the appeal, but it still was too vague to me. I sort of muddled along for a long time, not so much wrestling with the question as ignoring it. Religion didn't play an important role in my life at that time. Then in the mid-1990s I read a letter that Thomas Jefferson had written to his nephew, Peter Carr. "Fix reason firmly in her seat," he wrote, "and call to her tribunal every fact, every opinion. Question with boldness even the existence of a God; because, if there is one, he must more approve of the homage of reason, than that of blindfolded fear."

Question with boldness! I liked that; that thought resonated with me. Question with boldness. That was a game changer for me. Right around the same time, I was reading Carl Sagan's *The Demon-Haunted World: Science as a Candle in the Dark*. In that book he used the scientific method as a way of encouraging and even teaching people how to think critically. I didn't even consider myself a Catholic any longer, but when he began criticizing the Church, I became enraged. It shocked me. I literally threw the book onto the bed.

And then I picked it up and continued reading. It forced me to at least consider the concept of God. I began reading a great variety of opinion, trying to unravel my own feelings. I read everything I could find, from Billy Graham to the I Ching. I read about other religions, remembering my father telling me that no single religion has the answers, that there is truth in a lot of religion. "God's not just passing it out to one group," he said. And what I found was that there were some universal beliefs: that all of the great religions seem to agree on certain broad principles. There was no way they heard that from each other; they all arrived at those points separately, so there was a good chance of their being true.

Among those truths is that there are natural laws, and many of them are beyond our understanding. The first, I believe, is an understanding by all living things that they are alive. A fly, for example, has no knowledge. It doesn't know there is a universe or an earth, it isn't aware that it exists, and yet when we try to swat it, somehow it senses danger to its existence and flees. Somehow a fly knows it has to protect its life. There is some internal alarm that goes off. Flowers and plants have developed defense systems to fight off the predators that would kill them. Now suppose you go into a cave and try to hug cute little bear cubs, and Mama bear rips you to shreds. No one blames the bear; instead we agree that you're as dumb as a box of rocks.

It seems to me that that is nature telling us we have a right to defend ourselves. Okay, I get it—we all have a right to life and self-defense.

Also, I began to understand that the broad purpose of all religions is to provide some sense of moral guidance. The different religions propose different systems; that makes sense, they all were created by men with their own agendas, but all of them lay down some rules. The point is that man has always felt a need for some power greater than himself to provide a framework by which to live with other people. This isn't some new concept; every civilization has had its God or many Gods, and while the rules differed, they all provided some structure for a society.

And among the other universal concepts that emerged from my research was that even though few ever claimed to have seen God, they believed He existed. They accepted the mysteries of the universe as evidence of that. Thunder meant God was angry. Abundance meant He was pleased. The fact that they couldn't prove His existence didn't make any difference; they had faith.

Faith is fundamental to life, I believe. My wife appeared in my life at the very moment I was about to start drinking again. I challenged God to send me a message if He wanted me to stay sober, but there was some bitterness in that. I had stopped drinking but didn't seem to be getting the rewards I had believed would come with that. Not only wasn't my life better, it was a lot worse. I'd lost everything that mattered to me. Then I met this wonderful woman who just kept appearing in my life. Many people would think the fact that our paths crossed several times in a brief period of time was a coincidence, but others would say it was design. Whatever it was, I fell in love with her, and after spending more than a year together I asked her to marry me. She had lifted the darkness from my spirit, and I expected her to immediately agree.

"No," she said.

What? "Are you kidding me? Why?"

At that point there were some pretty good reasons for her to turn me down. I was working as a disc jockey for a small salary, and most of that was going for alimony and child support. I was ten years older than she was, and my prospects weren't that great. But none of that was the reason she turned me down. "Because we don't have God in common," she said, "and without God, we won't make it."

But I believed in God, I told her. The truth is I believed in some concept of what might be called God, if you stretched it, but I didn't have an active faith. I summed it up as "The church just doesn't work for me."

We decided to embark on our church tour. We went religion shopping, and I loved it. We dipped into a smorgasbord of different religions and denominations. My disappointment as a Christian was my belief that somewhere it had derailed; too often it was wonderful preaching about principles we weren't living. I didn't want to listen to a preacher anymore; I wanted to see people whose lives had been changed. I wanted to see happy families, spiritual, prosperous people who were going through the same turmoil as everyone else but had it together—not Facebook together but really together. Because I wanted to incorporate that into my life.

Tania and I put no restrictions on our quest. One Saturday, for example, we went to a synagogue. I didn't understand a word of the service, but I loved it. We spent several months soul searching. And the result was that I discovered myself.

One day I got a call from my friend Pat, who had heard what I was doing and invited me to his church. I turned him down. I wasn't going to be a Mormon. Those people are nuts! "Oh," he said, "I thought you were honestly looking for the truth. I didn't know you were cutting out the things you didn't want to do."

Okay, I agreed to attend a Sunday service. When he told me it was three hours long, I said, "STRRIIIIIIKKKKKEEE ONE! Nope. You get one hour, just like the other faiths."

When we walked in we were welcomed. A little too strong, I thought. By a guy who was just too happy to see us. Okay, Plastic Man, turn that down a notch. Then, because my friend called his friends and told them I would sneak out early, we got trapped there. In the second hour we were allowed to ask questions. I knew I had them. It was the old tried-and-true get-out-of-Jesus-talk-free card. I raised my hand and whispered to Tania, "We're going to be in the parking lot in five minutes."

"Don't embarrass me," she warned.

"I have an honest question," I said when called upon. "Where's Gandhi?" One of my biggest problems with other religions was the belief that anyone who did not follow their beliefs ended up in hell. Gandhi knew about Jesus and rejected Him. I couldn't imagine anyone believing that a deity would tell one of the greatest men in history, "Yeah, did a lot of good, but you didn't join the right church, so it sucks to be you." And then he would be sentenced to eternal flames.

"Well," came the answer, "we don't know, but he's in heaven."

We stayed through the entire service. We decided to keep going until they said something that pissed me off. The person who invited us made me angrier and angrier because he insisted on being loving. We met his family. They were just as nice as he was. Behind his back I began referring to him as "Mr. Plastic Man and his amazing plastic family." And every time I said that, Tania would roll her eyes. This went on for about eight months. One week he began discussing the biblical concept of Zion.

Zion is the utopia, a place where there are no needs, no wants. The highest goal of man, I believe, is to reach that place. It seems counterintuitive that a staunch conservative believes that our highest goal sounds rather Marxist. But it actually should be everyone's goal and desire. The problem with socialism isn't the utopian desire, it is how it is achieved. "How do we get there?" he asked. "How do we build that?" Some other members of the congregation offered opinions. Finally he looked directly at me, and with tears welling in his eyes, he explained, "We have to find a way to love one another. I have to be able to find love for you—even though I don't know you. I may not even like you, I may not like the things you do, but I know who you are. You're my brother. You're my sister. And therefore, I love you."

It was clear that his words came from his heart. So much for Plastic Man; he was the most genuine man I'd ever met. Somehow, he had found a way to connect to that part of his heart. I sat for a long time, even after most other people had left; there was a warmth in my chest, the kind of warmth and excitement I'd felt when I fell in love for the first time. It felt like anything was possible. I thought, "I don't care if I have to drink chicken blood—that man found love. I want to be like him; I'm in."

I could have been stubborn and said, "You know, I don't know about this whole three-hour church thing." But what mattered to me was the truth of the fruit. A bad tree cannot bear good fruit. This was good, and I wanted this fruit. I knew, I just knew, "This will change my life." And it has, deeply and profoundly. "Utopia" does not come from a government or a church. No system that imposes by force "acts of charity" through redistributive taxes or nonvoluntary tithing will create utopia. It comes only from a change of heart. It has mine. It is why I and so many of my listeners were on the border three years ago, even when it "hurt our side." Doing the wrong thing is never right, and doing the right thing is never wrong. That simple truth seems to be harder and harder to live by with each passing day.

Now, I don't know how much of what any religion preaches or promises is true, and we won't know until we get there—or don't. Personally I am keeping my options open. God could be a space octopus, although that's not likely. I have a deal with many of my Jewish friends: When we die, we will ask, has the messiah come? If God says yes, I will vouch for you; if he says "NO," you vouch for me. I also have a deal with my atheist friends: Let's be really good people and friends, because if you are right, this may be it; and if I am right, when you get there I am going to turn out all the lights and pretend we're not home like on Halloween. But here's what I do know: That feeling I get inside when I give myself up to the possibilities is real. I don't care if it's my mind playing tricks on me—that feeling is real. And wonderful.

Something else happened, too; I changed. People can speculate on the reasons for that. I believe it was what Christians call "the atonement," but for the purposes of this book, what is important is that profound change can and did happen. Over time, I became a better man. I was no longer the guy I used to be. I didn't miss him, either.

After I embraced faith, I didn't suddenly become a zealot; I didn't stop questioning the broadest concepts or suddenly accept every claim as true. But I did change. I found what I didn't even know I had been looking for; an inner peace. Maybe it was there all the time and I needed to give it room to grow, or maybe it was new, but it was there.

I had real evidence of that. When I was drinking, I alienated some people close to me. Among them was a relative with whom I had been close. He felt that I had treated him poorly. It had not been my intention to do that, but that's what alcoholism can do. This was a person who in the past I had done quite a bit for, but at the low point of my life, when I was getting a divorce and living in what was essentially a studio apartment, he did just the opposite. He turned on me. After that I saw him only at family events. We were thrown together at a celebration, the wedding of a mutual relative. As I was standing on the side watching my daughter dancing, he came up to me from behind, put me in a neck lock, and said, "Do you know what a fucking bad dad you are? You're the worst dad in the world." As I was watching my daughter dancing. He did some other things that really made me furious. If he hadn't been a relative . . .

After Tania and I married, we would be at events and he kept his distance. He said some really nasty and untrue things about me, but what really bothered me were the things he said about Tania. I wanted to confront him, but she wouldn't let me. Instead, after one event I drove home in a rage. I was twisted inside; I was holding the steering wheel so tightly my knuckles literally were white. "Leave it alone," she told me, "it doesn't make any difference." I couldn't, though—I just couldn't. This is how angry I was: We left the event and drove almost three hours—in the wrong direction. We went north instead of south.

Once we discovered our mistake, we spent most of our long trip home talking about this situation and how destructive it was to us. But I didn't want to give up my anger. I wanted to get even somehow. But after that we began praying about it, praying for something to change. His presence was ruining our relationship with the rest of my family. Maybe that was his intention.

About two years after we were married, after ending our religious odyssey, we had to attend another family event. We were both dreading it. Tania knew what it would do to me. We went, and he was his usual self—but I had changed. I saw him differently. Afterward Tania and I got into the car and we both started crying. We actually felt bad for him. I was sort of startled by that; I was ready for anger. But it had suddenly become obvious to me how much pain he was in. Whether or not he was the instigator, it was clear he was suffering far more than I was. It was sort of a miracle. Something important inside me had changed. I had let my anger go. I don't know if I would have been able to forgive him; he didn't ask for that and I never offered, but he had lost whatever power he had once held over me.

While I can't prove it, I know that it was my faith that allowed me to deal with him in a new way. For me, the key was accepting that there was something better for me if I was brave enough to pursue it. In a sense I was fortunate; I had hit bottom both with my drinking and afterward with my life. I don't know if I could have survived if I hadn't made changes; there wasn't a lot of questioning with boldness going on. For me it was a matter of survival.

I've been incredibly fortunate; the faith that I've found has been both religious and secular in nature. I've had the support of my church, and I've also been able to beat an addiction without it. Having a church or synagogue or mosque that lays out a path for you probably makes it easier; it provides someplace inside yourself to find a shelter. Religion isn't required to beat an addiction, but faith is.

Have any people in history placed more faith in the future than our Founding Fathers? These men literally risked their lives in what most people of that time would have considered foolhardy at the least and suicide at the most. Just stop for a second here and try to imagine what they had to believe was possible—and not just believe it but have such faith that it would happen that they were willing to bet their lives on it. The idea that a loosely hung-together federation of very different types of people, with little financial or military support, could come together to defeat the greatest military power on earth was ludicrous. How would any sane person believe that?

All those men had was their faith, a belief that it was possible.

For some of them that faith was based in their religious beliefs, but not for all of them. Thomas Paine, for example, whose pamphlet *Common Sense* provided the intellectual basis for revolting against Great Britain, did not believe that God would somehow protect the righteous cause. Paine was a monotheist; he firmly believed in the existence of one God, but he disdained organized religion. "I believe in the equality of man," he wrote in *The Age of Reason*, "and I believe that religious duties consist in doing justice, loving mercy, and endeavoring to make our fellow-creatures happy. . . .

"My own mind is my own church. . . . I do not mean by this declaration to condemn those who believe otherwise; they have the same right to their belief as I have to mine. But it is necessary to the happiness of man, that he be mentally faithful to himself. Infidelity does not consist in believing, or in disbelieving; it consists in professing to believe what he does not believe."

Thomas Paine's faith was not religiously based. He didn't put his fate in the hand of God but rather in his fellow man. He believed in the essential goodness of man and understood what had to be done for men to be free, and he had the courage to move forward with it. As he wrote in *The Rights of Man*, "The World is my country, all mankind are my brethren, and to do good is my religion."

Having taken so-called leaps of faith made it a lot easier for me to believe, to trust, to have faith that breaking away from my outrage would lead to something better. What I'm asking people to do is made much harder by the reality that not only haven't you reached bottom, you're actually pretty happy with what you're doing. What I hope you are seeing is that the country has reached bottom. We don't stand for very much anymore. We're too busy fighting each other over things that will make little difference, to focus on those battles that will determine the future of this country. Asking me to provide some evidence that what I am saying is true, that this country is in trouble and we need to do something about it, before you make the leap is a profession of a lack of faith. It doesn't require any faith to move forward when you're certain of the outcome.

Whether it comes from God, your belief in God, or your personal beliefs, faith is essential. Without that hope, I don't know whether I could have gotten up off the floor of my living room. Without it, maybe I would have killed myself, because I'd made too many mistakes, I'd created problems that seemed insurmountable. But there was that reservoir inside me that gave me hope. I'm not asking you to believe in my religious faith, I'm not asking you to go to church or rely on any religious teachings; I am asking you to find that place inside yourself that allows you to find the courage to overcome this addiction.

People have told me to forget it, that this kind of plea won't work. It's too idealistic or simple. I've been told that people have become accustomed to using their political outrage to channel their emotions, that they can take out all the frustrations of their daily life on people they don't know, and do it without any consequences. No one wants to come together, they tell me; they like feeling good about pounding the other side. And they will never give that up for some sort of vague fears about the future of the country.

But I have faith that the American people are much better than that. And I have seen that faith transform me and many others. And I know what is possible.

36

Line upon Line

If my starting offer is "I get to rob, beat, enslave, and kill you and your kind, but you don't get to rob, beat, enslave, or kill me or my kind," I can't expect you to agree to the deal or third parties to ratify it, because there's no good reason that I should get privileges just because I'm me and you're not. Nor are we likely to agree to the deal "I get to rob, beat, enslave, and kill you and your kind, and you get to rob, beat, enslave, and kill me and my kind," despite its symmetry, because the advantages either of us might get in harming the other are massively outweighed by the disadvantages we would suffer in being harmed (yet another implication of the Law of Entropy: harms are easier to inflict and have larger effects than benefits). We'd be wiser to negotiate a social contract that puts us in a positive-sum game: neither gets to harm the other, and both are encouraged to help the other.

—Steven Pinker, *Enlightenment Now: The Case for Reason, Science, Humanism, and Progress*

To begin bringing our country together, we have to find those things on which most of us can agree. For example, I think most of us agree that America has always served as a symbol of freedom and hope for a better future. Go ahead, nod your head. Then I think we agree that most Americans are good and decent people, who, given the opportunity, will do the right thing. And most of you will agree that there are sensible solutions to the problems we are facing now and will face in the future—and that what is preventing us from solving those problems is those people on the other side. This problem could be solved if those people just accepted reality. It's the opposition with their lack of knowledge that makes me crazy. . . .

Well, you get the idea. The seventh and eighth steps in AA are "Made a list of all persons we had harmed, and became willing to make amends to them" and "Made direct amends to such people whenever possible, except when to do so would injure them or others." Basically, look at those people who have suffered because of your behavior and try to make peace with them.

Let me make a big statement here: In a lot of the situations we're shouting at each other about, there is no easily determined right and wrong. And more important than that, it doesn't matter. Nothing you do or say on social media is going to make an actual difference; it isn't going to solve a problem or resolve an issue. But what it will do is cause mutually destructive outrage. While you've been expressing your anger, outrage, and frustration at the inability of the other side to understand reason, so have the people you've been fighting with; in a lot of instances that's why you got so angry in the first place. And here's something else: It's possible you are 100 percent right. Every word you say may be absolutely true, and by disagreeing with that the other guy is just provoking you. You may just be responding to the crazy things the other side is saying. But as much as you don't want to admit it, the other side may not be completely crazy.

It doesn't matter. The other side is not your enemy. We are all in this together, and you have to find a way of admitting to yourself that neither side is right all the time, and, hard as it is to believe, there may be times when they are right and you're wrong. Finding the highest truth is your goal.

Let's assume you're a good person. I assume that about all of my audience. And let's also assume that you are both a patriotic American and a person of religious faith. And, as best you can, you follow the tenets of both the Bill of Rights and the Bible. In fact, when you look at both of them, you realize that in most ways they complement each other.

But there is a problem: According to Matthew 22:36–39, Jesus said that the two most important Commandments of all were "You shall love the Lord your God with all your heart and with all your soul and with all your mind. This is the great and first commandment. And the second is like it: You shall love your neighbor as yourself." I know you really try to do that; you try hard to love your neighbors and treat them with respect, but there is this one person at work who doesn't believe a word of this. In fact, this person doesn't share any of your beliefs and instead does everything possible to provoke you. You're even pretty sure he was the person who took that chocolate bar you left in the office fridge. So here's the question: If he doesn't believe any of this, why is he entitled to the benefits of that Second Commandment?

Because this is about you. If you believe, as I do, that the level of mutual outrage in this country is destroying this country, you'll take a deep breath and make a really difficult admission: It's possible you're wrong about a few things. Even if he did take that chocolate bar!

I have a friend who tells this story: At the height of the anti–Vietnam War movement, he was walking through New York's Grand Central Terminal when he saw a well-dressed commuter, briefcase in hand, standing in front of two protesters and screaming at them. He was furious; he called them traitors and Communists, he accused them of siding with the enemy, he said soldiers were dying because of their actions. He went on and on, and when he finally quieted down, one of the young protestors looked at him and said calmly, "Have you ever considered the consequences if you're wrong?"

And my friend, who was actually against the war, was stunned to realize that he hadn't done that either. He was so certain the war was unnecessary and unjust that the possibility that he might be wrong had never occurred to him. Until that moment, which he never forgot, he had just sort of assumed that people who believed differently than he did actually knew on some level they were wrong, but for their own reasons didn't want to admit it. The fact that he knew what was right was so obvious to him that it didn't seem possible that any intelligent human being could believe the opposite and think they were right. What came with that was the realization that the screaming commuter believed just as strongly that the war was right and that supporting it was his patriotic duty as my friend believed that it was wrong—and he couldn't understand how anyone could believe the opposite. It was a life-changing encounter for my friend.

I understand your desire to fight back. But we must not become what we say we are against.

We all know what's right—it's what we believe. So accepting the fact that someone can believe exactly the opposite of what you believe and be just as positive that he or she is right about it as you are is not the easiest thing to do. But admitting that you might be wrong is even harder. And there are reasons for that: Researchers have found that our political beliefs tend to get entwined with our personal identities; in other words, we become what we believe, so an attack on our political positions is perceived by our brain as an attack on our self, and the brain has been conditioned to fight that type of attack. "The brain's primary responsibility is to take care of the body, to protect the body," explained USC psychologist Jonas Kaplan. "The psychological self is the brain's extension of that. When our self feels attacked, our [brain is] going to bring to bear the same defenses that it has for protecting the body." Meaning our party affiliation has become a personal statement; it represents our values probably more strongly than at any other time at least since the Civil War. And as the two parties have grown farther apart, our party loyalty has hardened. It's reached the point where many of us see members of the opposition party not just as people we disagree with but rather as the enemy, and we react to them as we would to anything that poses a danger to us.

One of the most difficult things I've ever had to do was stand in front of a camera and admit that maybe, possibly, I wasn't completely right. It was both an intellectual and an emotional challenge.

I know it was hard for my audience to believe that I would admit that. Me? Being wrong? How could that be? I'm the guy who provides guidance. My whole job is explaining things to you. I had studied the issues, I had collected a big pile of facts, I spoke clearly and succinctly and laid it out point by point. I was a proud member of the so-called vast right-wing conspiracy—or, as I always believed, the good guys. I heard all the nasty names the left-wing media called President George W. Bush, and I defended him as they made fun of him. I was furious about that. I thought so much of their criticism was in response to the Clinton impeachment. They were more interested in getting even than concerned about the safety of the country. When we invaded Iraq, most people on the left were against it. Not me. Whether or not Saddam had WMDs, I believed he was supporting terrorists, and we had an obligation to stop him. The liberals were screaming that we shouldn't get involved, we shouldn't be nation-building, and there was no indication the Iraqi people had the will to be free. How insulting, I thought; everybody wants to be free.

So we went in and I was cheering on the sidelines. Whoa, what a mistake. It turned out you can't force democracy on anybody else; the Iraqi people didn't understand it or even want it. It was similar to a mother forcing her child to eat broccoli "because it's good for you!" And as the reality of the situation became obvious, I either had to continue to defend the president or admit that I was wrong. Unlike many politicians, I had too much respect for the American people to pretend I had taken a different position.

Admitting you're wrong is one of the hardest things for human beings to do. We're not built for it. When Galileo claimed that the earth revolved around the sun, church leaders were so outraged that in 1633 they charged him with heresy for "having believed and held the doctrine (which is false and contrary to the Holy and Divine Scriptures) that the sun is the center of the world, and that it does not move from east to west, and that the earth does move, and is not the center of the world." It didn't matter that scientists had concluded years earlier that the earth was not the center of the universe. The truth was not politically practical. Galileo spent the remainder of his life under house arrest. It took the church three hundred years—three centuries—to finally admit it was wrong.

It didn't take me nearly that long. But I also saw what was happening. The pendulum was swinging back; Obama got elected by offering hope and change. Many of us on the right were proud of America breaking a foolish and outdated race barrier, but we were concerned about his Marxist upbringing, radical friends, and something we had never before seen from a U.S. president or could even identify by name—his postmodern attitude about the West and American exceptionalism. We went after him as the left had gone after Bush. With great challenges facing us—most important, we were in the middle of a terribly draining war that was costing thousands of American lives and billions of dollars—we were reduced to petty partisan arguments. Our elected officials in Washington were doing everything possible to distract us with nonsense. And people like me were enabling them. I had a responsibility to the several million people who listened to me every day to be honest. And that meant admitting I had been wrong.

I'll tell you what I learned once I started my crusade to bring America together again: Even more difficult than admitting you might be wrong is accepting the opinions of other people without anger or hostility. That's where people like me come in: "Unfortunately," wrote Edward Wasserman, professor of journalism ethics at Washington and Lee University, "mainstream media have made a fortune teaching people the wrong ways to talk to each other, offering up Jerry Springer, *Crossfire*, Bill O'Reilly. People understandably conclude rage is the political vernacular, that this is how public ideas are talked about. It isn't."

Although we're focusing primarily on political issues, the expression of outrage certainly isn't limited to that. If you want to generate anger, just go online and type in something like, I don't think Michael Jordan is the greatest basketball player in history. Or, *Hot Tub Time Machine* is the funniest move in the last fifty years! Then wait for the response. I promise you, it won't be pretty.

It turns out that it isn't really about being right or wrong; an opinion isn't right or wrong, it's a belief. But the fighting on social media is about winning and losing, about gaining attention, about power. In the early 1980s Republican strategist and national chairman Lee Atwater figured out how to emotionally motivate voters. "While I didn't invent 'negative politics,'" he once admitted, "I am among its ardent practitioners. Frankly, I didn't care what anyone called me so long as we won. "Like a good general, I treated everyone who wasn't with me as against me."

The nonpartisan National Election Study, a survey that tracks voter preferences, found that beginning in 1980, the same time Atwater burst onto the political stage, voters began reporting increasingly negative opinions about the opposition party. Dartmouth professor Sean Westwood interpreted that data and concluded, "Partisanship, for a long period of time, wasn't viewed as part of who we are. It wasn't core to our identity. It was just an ancillary trait. But in the modern era we view party identity as something akin to gender, ethnicity, or race—the core traits that we use to describe ourselves to others." More than that, researchers have found that political identity has seeped into our daily lives. It helps determine who we associate with and apparently has made marriages between Democrats and Republicans somewhat unusual.

That's one reason a part of my audience felt betrayed when I refused to support Donald Trump.

Two years after Atwater and Roger Ailes managed George H. W. Bush's successful 1988 presidential campaign, at least partially by introducing racial fears with their legendary Willie Horton ad campaign, Atwater was diagnosed with brain cancer. Facing death, he had a revival of spirit, converting to Roman Catholicism. As a way of repenting, he reached out to many of the people he had maligned to offer an apology. In one such letter he wrote, "My illness has taught me something about the nature of humanity, love, brotherhood, and relationships that I never understood, and probably never would have. So, from that standpoint, there is some truth and good in everything."

Finally, in an article in *Life* magazine, he reached a significant conclusion, admitting, "My illness helped me to see that what was missing in society is what was missing in me: a little heart, a lot of brotherhood. The 1980s were about acquiring—acquiring wealth, power, prestige. I know. I acquired more wealth, power, and prestige than most. But you can acquire all you want and still feel empty. What power wouldn't I trade for a little more time with my family? What price wouldn't I pay for an evening with friends? It took a deadly illness to put me eye to eye with that truth, but it is a truth that the country, caught up in its ruthless ambitions and moral decay, can learn on my dime. I don't know who will lead us through the nineties, but they must be made to speak to this spiritual vacuum at the heart of American society, this tumor of the soul."

The difficulty is that it was much too late. Atwater, Ailes, and later Karl Rove showed politicians how to win. Former Democratic congressman Robert Wexler, who lost his first campaign for Congress but won his second, admitted he had figured it out. "I learned in my first campaign that whoever goes negative first wins."

Just as with every other addiction, there is a strong physiological component to your feelings of outrage. A study conducted by USC's Brain and Creativity Institute and published in *Scientific Reports* in 2017 showed that when forty self-identified liberals were confronted with political statements that contradicted their beliefs, there was increased activity in that part of the brain associated with the regulation of emotion and a decrease in activity in the region of the cortex governing cognitive flexibility. It also demonstrated increased activity in the area of the brain generally associated with emotion, fear, and anxiety. Meaning that when confronted with statements that reinforced an opinion different from ours, rather than being open to change or persuasion, our own position hardened. We are too strongly emotionally invested in being right to be open to a differing opinion.

In other words, your outrage results in actual physical changes—changes you may enjoy like a jolt of coffee or, in my case, a good drink or three after work. This confirmed the results of earlier studies that had shown, according to Emory University professor Drew Westen, the author of *The Political Brain*, "The last thing to do is to try to argue someone out of a belief when they're strongly committed to it emotionally, because what makes it so strong is the emotion attached to it, not the facts or arguments that support it."

So the emotional hold our political positions have on us isn't limited to the intellectual satisfaction of being right, and it's not really about the issues; it's not about guns or abortion, free speech or privacy, it comes from that great feeling we get from winning. That's why so many otherwise intelligent people so easily defend fake news or even obvious lies; satisfying their emotional needs is way more important to them than having a nice intellectual discussion with all of its nuances. It no longer surprises me when I speak to really smart people who refuse to condemn or even criticize Trump for his practically pathological lying; it isn't about him, it's about them. Also unsurprising is my friends on the left's inability to distinguish "fake news" from facts when its coming from someone on their "side." In the past, the kind of "alternative facts" he routinely spouts would have made it impossible for any politician to be elected; now a significant segment of the American people just doesn't care. Being on the winning side—the joy they get from watching their opponents complain in frustration—is more important to them than the truth.

This isn't a new phenomenon. When I was a teenager I picked up a copy of Dale Carnegie's 1936 classic *How to Win Friends and Influence People*. I thought it might help me relate to the radio audience I expected to have one day. This is a book that has influenced Americans from presidents to Charles Manson. "Nine times out of ten," Carnegie wrote, "an argument ends with each of the contestants more firmly convinced than ever that he is absolutely right. You can't win an argument. You can't, because if you lose it, you lose it; and if you win it, you lose it. Why? Well, suppose you triumph over the other man and shoot his argument full of holes and prove he is non compos mentis. Then what? You will feel fine. But what about him? You have made him feel inferior. You have hurt his pride."

What Dale Carnegie didn't foresee is the fact that making your opponent feel inferior would not only become a good thing, it would become the ultimate goal. But that's where we are today in political debate. When Carnegie wrote his book, just about the only way people could argue with each other was face-to-face. We knew the people we were arguing with; maybe we worked with them every day or they were friends or relatives. So we knew they weren't bad people, they were just misguided. In addition to manners, the proximity of a clenched fist caused people to hesitate before they called someone a nasty name or insulted them.

That's changed; through social media we communicate every day with people we've never met; often we don't even know their real name or, in some situations, whether they are a human being or a bot. The only thing we know about them, or it, is that they disagree with us. And there are times when they are disagreeable about it. They have the audacity to call you a name or make fun of you. That brings us to the ultimate excuse: They started it! It's human nature to easily absorb and forget compliments, but, boy oh boy, when someone hurls an insult at you, all systems are go! Some unnamed person living somewhere doing something, whom you have never met and know nothing about, dares to say, "You're a jerk!" and your entire defense mechanism goes into action. Oh, yeah? I'm a jerk? Well, you know what you are for calling me a jerk!

And so it escalates.

So how do we "make amends" to those people, as we are taught in AA? How do we treat them with respect, even when they're clearly jerks? You might start by understanding there is little chance you are going to change their opinion—unless, of course, they read this book, too. Billy Graham pointed out that "unfortunately, experience tells us that people like this seldom change; their pride gets in their way, and they can't bring themselves to admit that they alone are responsible for their failures." So, chances are, they aren't going to accept it when you do it for them.

We can start by remembering the words of Pogo, the great cartoon character created by Walt Kelly, who is credited with the warning, "We have met the enemy and he is us." Pogo is right. It isn't the other guy somewhere out there in cyberspace, it's us. It may take two to tango, but it takes only one person to change the dynamics of a relationship. That means taking responsibility for your own words. Truthfully, I never thought I'd be quoting pop star Justin Bieber, but after a racist video he'd made many years earlier surfaced, his apology was worth considering. "As a kid, I didn't understand the power of certain words and how they can hurt. I thought it was okay to repeat hateful words and jokes, but I didn't realize at the time that it wasn't funny and that in fact my actions were continuing the ignorance. Thanks to friends and family, I learned from my mistakes and grew up and apologized for those wrongs. . . . I'm very sorry."

A lot of us don't understand the power of our words. We send them out into cyberspace because there really are few, if any, consequences. We can be as tough as we wish we actually were. We can take out all our frustrations on someone we don't know. There is no clenched fist close by; pretty much the worst thing that can happen is that the other person will respond with bigger insults. So, who are you harming by your participation in this?

Listen to Pogo—he knows what he is talking about. It's yourself you're hurting, both directly and indirectly, both physically and mentally. Some people believe getting out their anger is good for them. And once in a while it might be. But living with outrage is unhealthy. Getting angry—yes, even getting angry on social media—causes your brain to release stress hormones. At the extreme, it can cause a heart attack. A small study published in the *European Heart Journal* reported that the risk of a heart attack increased substantially, especially among people who have survived previous heart attacks, in the two hours following an outburst of anger. In her book *Webs of Influence: The Psychology of Online Persuasion*, psychologist Nathalie

Nahai points out that anger causes an individual's cortisol levels to rise, "and when you are very angry you can end up in a fight or flight mode. Physically it's not good for people to be in a prolonged state of rage and anxiety."

There also is some evidence that social media hostility can transform into aggressive real-world behavior. That makes sense, and I suspect a lot of people can relate to this; after a heated political argument, including name-calling, your husband or wife or friend casually says something to you, and you snap back at them. That jerk on the Internet got you so angry that you just have to release your frustration at the first easy target.

Here's something else you probably haven't thought about: The person you were arguing with is just as angry as you are. And they may be taking it out on someone in their life, too!

Being outraged can make you less productive and sensitive in your real life. There are things many people would never think about saying in person, yet after using those words to describe a political opponent, they somehow seem to have lost their edge; they don't seem quite so offensive, and they may sneak into real-life vocabulary.

The long-term effect is what we have been discussing throughout this book: It is damaging to our country. No matter what happens, half of America is alienated. Even if you win, the country loses, and that will eventually affect you and everyone you know.

I'd like you to pause here for a few seconds and think about the last time someone who believed differently than you do was able to convince you that they were right and you were wrong; the last time you said to someone, "Thank you for correcting me. Now I understand." Let me take a guess: How about never? No matter how much you or anyone else explains or complains, huffs and puffs and yells and threatens, there still are only distant rumors that once, years ago, in a galaxy far away, someone used social media to successfully change another person's political opinion.

It doesn't work that way. Not only is it ineffective but being attacked, ridiculed, or even presented with accurate evidence actually causes people to embrace those things they believe even more tightly. Researchers studying this so-called backfire effect concluded that "corrections actually increase misperceptions among the group in question."

So here is what you accomplish when you get into a debate with someone who has a different opinion than you do: Neither one of you is going to change your opinion. Nothing is going to be accomplished.

You'll notice I haven't used the word "troll" even once yet. Wikipedia defines an Internet troll as "someone who posts inflammatory, extraneous, or off-topic messages in an online community, such as a forum, chat room, or blog, with the primary intent of provoking readers into an emotional response or of otherwise disrupting normal on-topic discussion." We've all had experience with trolls, even if we didn't know it. The Russian government understands the damage that this behavior is doing to this country and has used it successfully to further divide Americans. This has been one of the most successful propaganda campaigns in history, the largest hostile intelligence operation in our history, and we're not taking it seriously enough. Just think about this for a moment: You may well have been used by the Russian government in the attempt to divide and conquer the United States.

I was. TheBlaze was. A former employee of Russia's Internet Research Agency admitted that pro-Putin comments had been "left on sites like TheBlaze and Politico." In other words, sites on both sides of the political spectrum. A former hotel receptionist employed by the Putin government admitted that one of her assignments had been to write an essay as if she were an average American housewife and post it. When I found out about this, I called it a "shark bump," meaning that it was a test to see how easy it might be to manipulate American public opinion.

It was amazingly easy for them to do. I admitted that the Russians had become very good at spreading disinformation. And disinformation makes you lose trust in legitimate news sources. Most Americans are getting their information from social media, and discrediting all of those sources makes it more difficult for people to know what's real. In 2016, for example, an ad posted by a supposed conservative organization on Facebook invited Americans to protest the "Islamification of Texas" by participating in a rally outside an Islamic center in Houston, but a second ad directed at the Muslim community invited them to attend a "Save Islamic Knowledge" rally at the same place and time. Both organizations were Russian creations, and the result was a nasty confrontation. Total cost to the Russians was estimated at $200.

What was real? The confrontation. It was just a little taste of the ability of the Russians to use the outrage in this country to cause serious problems. Maybe after they plant phony stories that motivate angry people to burn down a city we'll finally take this threat seriously.

But all of this is made possible by the anger that is pulling us apart. All of it. In fact, Russian instigators made at least 130 documented attempts to create confrontational rallies.

So how do you make amends to people you don't know? You can't. AA encourages members to seek out people they have hurt with their behavior, but obviously that isn't possible in a social-media environment. You don't even know the people you've attacked (or who have attacked you), and in reality you can't be sure they are even people. You may have been provoked and manipulated by a bot or a Russian national following a script. But more than that, it isn't necessary or helpful to apologize to anyone. Chances are, whatever you were doing to them, they often were doing exactly the same thing to you. They were trading insults and accusations with you. We are all equally guilty in creating this toxic environment. And we all need to become part of the solution.

The muck stops here. That's the first thing on which we all have to agree.

37

Precept upon Precept

*I have a new outlook on life. I look forward to each day
with happiness because of the real enjoyment it is to me
to be sane, sober, and respectable. I was existing really
from one drink to the next, with no perception about
circumstances, conditions, or even nature's elements.
My acquaintance with God—lost and forgotten when I
was a young man—is renewed. God is all loving and all
forgiving. The memories of my past are being dimmed by
the life I now aspire to.*

Anonymous, *The Big Book of Alcoholics Anonymous*

There are a lot of programs, methods, and devices other than AA
to help people deal with addictions. You can go to rehab, take certain drugs, consult experts. There is no one solution that fits all. But
among the few things that all of them have in common is that they
focus on the future. They provide a goal, an appreciation for what is
possible. After you open your veins and get rid of the poison, then
what? You're giving up something really important to you; what are
you going to get in return? In other words, when we abandon this
outrage and begin treating the other side with respect, or at least
civility, what's the payoff?

For me, overcoming my addiction allowed me to have a healthy
relationship with my children, clarity, and the ability to move through

my career without the fear I was living with that I would be exposed. When I stopped drinking, I was able to deal head-on with all those things in my life that were causing my unhappiness, rather than covering them up with more alcohol. The result was so much greater than I would have envisioned in my wildest dreams.

For you? Look around; look outward, not inward. Appreciate everything we have here. We have so much. We have every opportunity. We have the most amazing tools and toys. We have phones and iThis and iThat and video devices and music; we have all the information contained in the British Library a click away. We are about to colonize another planet. Fewer people are killed in wars than at any other time in the history of mankind. We can replace lost limbs. We have access to the greatest artists and the coolest cars. We can attend MIT for FREE online. We can witness history live while speaking with someone on the other side of the globe. We have so much food that the WHO says that for the very first time, starvation has been replaced by obesity as a global problem. And we don't have to crap outside and wipe with moss . . . unless we WANT to!

There has never been a society like the one we live in today: The American lower-middle class actually has easy access to more material goods than Cornelius Vanderbilt could have imagined.

We don't stop that often to appreciate it. We really should take some time once in a while and admit, what a kickass system! It's broken, it's fouled up, we're doing a lot to destroy it, but geez, even in this bruised and battered shape it's pretty amazing.

Do you ever doubt how fortunate we are to be living here, in this country, now? Do you get depressed about what's going on now in Washington? Does it all just knock you down once in a while and make you wonder where we're going? Well, that's normal—we all go through it. What is important is getting back up. In early 2018 I had in my studio Nick Vujicic, who was born with no arms and no legs. When he was ten years old, he asked his father to put five or six inches of water in the bathtub so he could sit in it. His real intent was to slide down under the water and stay there. He was deeply depressed, sure he had no future. He thought death was better than the miserable life he was doomed to lead. He tried to do it, but then he thought about his parents, who would have been devastated.

When I met him several years ago for the first time, he had just started a relationship with the woman who would become his wife. He told me then that he'd grown up thinking no woman could ever love him and he would never be able to hug his kids. Today they have kids and travel around the world as he gives motivational speeches to literally hundreds of thousands of people.

He told me he discovered an amazing thing: "My kids hug me."

Let me tell you about a Chinese preacher I know who has dedicated his life to bringing Christians out of China. Several years ago at his house at Christmastime, some of the people he had helped escape were decorating; they were hanging lights, putting ornaments on the tree, setting up the crèche. Suddenly he noticed the woman whose job it was to untangle the knotted strands of lights; there she sat with a jumble of lights on her lap, weeping. When asked what was wrong, she explained, "I made these lights." Thinking he had misunderstood, he asked her again. "This was my job . . . in prison." She was now lost in a memory from the other side of earth. "I made these lights," she repeated quietly, almost to herself. She had been put in prison for practicing her faith, spending years making lights for us to celebrate something she could not. It was an amazing coincidence but served, once again, to remind me that I won the lottery by being born in America.

The Colossus of Rhodes, one of the Seven Wonders of the Ancient World, guarded the harbor to the island with a sword. It was a warning: Be careful if you come into this port, as we have the strength to crush you. Conversely, we have a woman holding a torch to light the way, saying, Welcome, come with your dream and let's build a better place for those who will come tomorrow. Even if that idea is challenged and lost or destroyed by us, it will inspire people far and wide—people who cannot live the promise in their land but keep that torch alive in them. I have a limited amount of knowledge about my own heritage. My dad's side of the family came from Germany in the 1870s. My mother's side is Danish and German. Recently, I discovered old papers from my ancestors on my father's side. They told the story of my great-great-grandfather and his brother, who had fought for the Union in the Civil War. Both of them were quickly captured and ended up in the notorious Confederate prison at Andersonville. One brother died, and the other never fully recovered and lived the rest of his life in pain.

I have a ranch in the mountains, and at the entrance is a sign reading "Beck and Sons: Committed to Integrity and Courage for Four Generations." I had it made to remind my children that we might never accomplish anything ourselves, but we can't ever forget the sacrifices our ancestors made to come here and give us the opportunities we enjoy.

Millions of people have died to free slaves and to cut the chains of those held under the boot of Nazi and Communist butchers, and yet we fight, hiding behind an avatar, with someone we will never meet about the use of the c-word by a B-list celebrity.

We cannot allow that to be our contribution and legacy.

So let's agree that even with all of the issues we're dealing with on an almost daily basis, we have a tremendous amount to be grateful for, and it's well worth fighting to protect it.

A second point on which all the various programs agree is the need for civility. I have always felt strongly that character matters. My parents taught me that. Doing the right thing matters, even if you don't always succeed. We lived in the town of Mount Vernon, Washington, in the early 1970s. Like every other small town in America, Mount Vernon was being threatened by large malls, which drew shoppers away from the local shops downtown. My parents tried to fight that by leading a campaign to re-create a more traditional downtown, replete with brick streets and faux gaslights. It created a lot of tension in our town, and, frankly, I didn't understand their reasoning. What was wrong with a big Sears coming to town? They were trying to save the town, while others thought they were trying to stop progress. There was a lot of yelling back and forth, a lot of angry people who back then didn't have social media on which to express their anger. So nothing happened, and our town died.

It took me a long time to understand and appreciate what my parents were doing. They saw a coming problem and tried to solve it, even when it would have been much easier and considerably quieter for them to sit down rather than stand up. That's one definition of character. My father, even with his shortcomings, was a man of character. He taught me the importance of integrity and honesty. Lying was about the worst thing a man could do. And he taught me that a man can change. My father is the person who convinced me, even before I started AA, that I could change. I probably never realized how much I was the product of his values. Even when my own character was shaky, when I was lying to myself as well as to other people about the extent of my drinking, I understood on some level that what I was doing was wrong—wrong for me, and wrong for the people who loved me and depended on me.

I had a similar realization pretty much at the height of my fame. I could have kept going as a leader of the Tea Party movement; that would have been the easy thing to do. I could have continued enjoying the incredible support I was receiving, even if inside I was starting to feel hollow. But I didn't. Character matters.

Character is the true expression of who we are. It is, I suppose, our best self. Behavioral-change programs are not set up to try to change your character but rather to reveal the best possible you. Most of them believe we have built up our defenses to protect our emotional vulnerabilities—the strike-first syndrome—which goes a long way toward hiding the person we want to be. So, successful addiction-breaking strategies are aimed at getting through those defense mechanisms, whether by long-term therapy or replacing them with a much healthier kind of behavior pattern. You have to fill that gap with something.

Like the military, most of these programs will break you down and then rebuild you, eliminating destructive behavior and substituting different goals. When letting go of my outrage, I kept one thought in mind: Remember who we are; remember, remember who we are.

Perhaps instead I should have been thinking, Remember who you want to be. Reach for your better angels. As I'm writing this, on my walls are pictures of George Washington, Winston Churchill, Ronald Reagan, Abraham Lincoln, and Billy Graham. In other places I have photographs of Martin Luther King Jr. and Gandhi. A man I greatly respected once told me that I should always have a picture on my desk or phone of someone I truly admire. There's an old Sufi saying, he explained, that what you gaze upon, you become. That works for me. Who is it that you really respect? Whose path do you want to follow? I guess when I was rubbing my thumb on Washington's compass that's really what I was reaching for.

For much of my life, it hasn't been easy being me. I'm a lot of contradictions, so it isn't surprising that at times my words have rolled out before I've thought them through. I've said things that I wish I hadn't said; I've boxed myself into complicated positions. But as hard as it has been being me, just imagine how much more difficult it is being my kids. Imagine bearing the brunt of the controversy your father has spewed up without having any choice in the matter. To a very small degree, that's what I experienced way back when in Mount Vernon. Obviously, my kids have had some material advantages because of my notoriety, but for them it has come at a cost. They have been with me several times when other people recognized me and just lost it, unable to control their hatred for me. Both of my kids have asked, at different times, why some people love me and others hate me. My answer was, "Because they don't really know me. I don't really deserve either. I don't deserve their adoration, and I don't deserve their hatred. But if anyone is correct, it's probably those who are angry at me, because I just didn't see their point."

All of this turmoil really affected my son. When he was about eight years old he was studying martial arts and was finally ready to earn his first belt. But when he found out there was going to be a crowd there, he decided he couldn't do it. "Are you mad?" he asked me.

"I'm not," I said, "but we've got to find a way to conquer that. You can't let fear rule your life." I took him into my office and asked him to look around. I have some wonderful artifacts there, including items owned by Rosa Parks and Hugh Stafford, the heroic commander of the Hanoi Hilton prison camp, and even a passport issued by Raoul Wallenberg. "What do you think all of the people represented in this room have in common?"

We talked about it for a while, and then he guessed, "They're all heroes?"

"Well, yes," I said, "most of them were. But why do you think I have all this?"

He took a guess. "Because they're like you? They weren't afraid?"

That response set me back a few breaths. Finally I told him, "The exact opposite. I'm guessing they were all terrified when they took those steps, but they did it anyway. I don't think heroes aren't afraid. That's mostly in the comic books. Heroes are the ones who say This may hurt, but it's going to hurt a lot more not to do it."

The next weekend he went back and earned his first belt.

Not being there for my kids in the present was the reason I sought help at AA. Stealing the future from all of our kids is the reason I abandoned my outrage. An important aspect of the AA program is having another person to rely on, a so-called sponsor ready to come to your aid if you slip. For a lot of people, their sponsor becomes a role model, a reminder of why they're going through all this, and a constant reminder that they are not alone in this. Other people have been through what you are going through and managed to make it work. When things get tough, your sponsor is the person to rely on. In this situation, we probably don't need another specific person. All you have to do is look at your kids, then take a step back and look at all of America's kids. That's why we have to do this.

A decade ago I wrote, "One day we will face our children and grandchildren as they ask us what we found more important and valuable than freedom. They will ask if our big, unaffordable homes, 'free' universal health care, and 'buy it now' lifestyle were worth enslaving them for.

"How will you answer?"

That same question may well be more relevant today than it was when I first wrote those words. But since then, we can add to that list of things we traded our kids' future for the right to express our outrage at people who refuse to embrace our position on issues. When our kids ask why America has lost its standing in the world, we can respond, "Because people disagreed with me on abortion, and I had to fight with them about it." Or health care. Or the death penalty. Or the Second Amendment. Or any of the other issues we battle daily over and will never completely resolve.

So, if you need a sponsor, if you want to calm down but just can't do it because someone you don't know just said you were dumb and you absolutely have to respond, just pause and look at your kids, at our kids, and at least ask yourself if that brief surge of emotion you're going to feel is really worth it.

It really is worse than ever. Pew Research reported in 2017 that "the divisions between Republicans and Democrats on fundamental political values—on government, race, immigration, national security, environmental protection, and other areas—reached record levels during Barack Obama's presidency. In Donald Trump's first year as president, these gaps have grown even larger. And the magnitude of these differences dwarfs other divisions in society, along such lines as gender, race and ethnicity, religious observance, or education."

Fortunately, I'm not the only person who recognizes the damage we're doing—and that there is still time to act. In his 2017 lecture "The Age of Outrage," published by *National Review*, NYU's Jonathan Haidt offers some hope. "If you want hope," he said, "you need only put this quotation up on your bathroom mirror: 'We cannot absolutely prove that those are in error who tell us that society has reached a turning point, that we have seen our best days . . .' That was written by British historian Thomas Babington Macaulay—in 1830! . . .

"Because as things get worse on campus, more people are beginning to stand up, and more people are searching for solutions."

I also get letters from people who support my position; they understand that while my stand on issues has remained consistent, my approach has changed, and most of the time they appreciate it. Most—not all. But like having an AA sponsor as a reminder that you are not alone, I am beginning to see evidence that other people are becoming as alarmed and outraged as I am at the out-of-control outrage.

A friend sent me a recent Facebook post by the well-respected New York City journalist Lynne White, who posted on her Facebook page: "My heart is beating so fast now I feel like it will explode." She continued, "When we start to personally attack each other because of our views or denigrate a whole country or perhaps a religion, we have to put ourselves in check. I am guilty of passionate feelings on all things politics, but when we hurt each other, we're doing what our enemies want." Exactly! Just ask Putin. She went on, "You can hate Israel, but not here. You can hate America, but not here! You can hate Muslims or Catholics or blacks or whites or gays or Jews, but not here. . . . When we cross a line to the hate zone, I have to say enough. Love, not hate, conquers all!"

That started a good—and reasonable—debate. A lot of people responded to that post, mainly in agreement, although clearly with some difficulty at not being able to get that final dig in. One person wrote: "Restraint is critically essential so that constructive conversations occur. If you resort to name-calling and despairing remarks toward another, the conversation stops and you are not better than what you are fighting against. . . ."

To which Lynne White responded, echoing precisely what I have been trying to say here: "We have to be aware there are consequences to the words we speak whether we see or feel them here or not. People are affected in ways we may not understand." Must say, I agree! She concluded, "Maybe we should look within to curtail the rhetoric when it crosses a critical line. Just saying, maybe we should think before we react!"

38

T. H. I. N. K.

Finally someone suggested a mnemonic that might be helpful for all of us: Before I say anything or respond—let me THINK. T, is it truthful; H, is it helpful; I, is it inspiring; N, is it necessary; K, is it kind. Is what I am about to say all of these things? If not, which one(s)? When you honestly THINK it through, say it and see if it doesn't change the conversation.

That general agreement that we have a problem and we have to deal with it now is spreading. Exactly how are you going to accomplish that? Just as there are programs besides AA that will help you beat your addiction, there are people other than myself who are offering suggestions on how to calm down the red-hot rhetoric. The most common suggestion also is the most difficult: Stay off or cut down your use of social media.

Nope, that ain't gonna happen. Social media is much too deeply embedded in our lives. To varying degrees, we all are dependent on it. It is our companion, our assistant and scheduler, a significant provider of entertainment, a primary source of news and information, an emergency notice and response system, and our main communications tool. So, no one is giving it up, and any program that makes that suggestion is doomed to fail.

Another friend of mine, aware of my concern, sent me a copy of his daily horoscope from a New York newspaper confirming that others are becoming aware of this problem and are looking for solutions: For Aries, it began, "The moon in your sign for the next few days will provide one awakening after another; though, to receive full benefits, you might try taking a day off from the Internet. If that is not possible, try three hours; and if that is not possible, have a long talk with yourself about why that is."

After you've tried to curb your use of social media, which exactly no one is going to be able to do, many experts suggest finding ways to divert your attention. Get involved, they urge; demonstrate your political commitment with activism. That makes sense; essentially, it urges people to do what Anita suggested to Maria in *West Side Story*, "Stick to your own kind." Rather than spending or perhaps wasting your time fighting with people who disagree with you, join with those people who share your opinions and work together as a group to bring them to fruition. This certainly was my experience at the beginning of the Tea Party movement. I embraced it very quickly when it started, so much so that members of that group considered me the "most highly regarded" commentator. As this idea became a reality, it occupied a considerable amount of my time and efforts; previously I had spent a lot of energy attacking Democrats. I was furious at them because of what I perceived they were doing to my country. But I had to cut way back on that criticism to help build the Tea Party. So I understand the suggestion that negative energy can be turned positive by working for what you believe in rather than against what the other side believes.

Treat others with the same respect you want from them. There it is. You don't have to treat the other side as your enemy.

We've spent a lot of pages discussing where we are today, how we got here, why we need to change, and what the consequences for all of us are going to be if we don't, but considerably fewer pages outlining the way to accomplish this. In some ways this is the reverse of AA; in AA, the first thing you do is stop drinking, and then you spend the rest of your life trying to prevent a relapse. Starting is the easiest part: Pretty much anyone can convince themselves not to have a drink for an hour or even a day, but it's the second hour and the next day that will always be the problem. For alcoholics, the measuring stick is painfully obvious: You either have a drink or you don't. Ending an addiction to outrage isn't quite as simple as wet and dry. You're still going to be passionate about politics, about current events, about the direction this country is heading; you're still going to support the candidates who best represent your beliefs—but what will change is the way you express yourself about it. It is learning how to treat those people with whom you still disagree—remember, I'm not challenging the validity of your opinions—with respect. San Francisco, for example, should be as crazy as it wants to be. That's fine; I don't live there. Seattle can be what Seattle wants to be. Texas will be Texas. This country is so much better off when we make respecting each other our bottom line.

For me, who has been the target of such venom, actually doing that was really difficult. Admittedly, I had earned a lot of that anger. I didn't respect the people who attacked me. As far as I was concerned, they didn't deserve my respect. I was fighting for the future of this country, while they were trying to tear it down.

There—there it is. That's where it all starts. Respect. Respect for yourself first, and then for other people—yes, even people you don't agree with. When I was living as a functioning alcoholic, I had lost respect for myself. I knew that I was living a lie. To be honest, I hated myself. That made it impossible for me to respect anyone else, and, admittedly, working with me was not always easy or even pleasant.

So the first thing we need to do if we are going to figure out how to get along with one another is learn how to respect the other guy. No matter how uninformed or silly or pretentious or arrogant or even angry they may be, you have to be better than them. You have to treat them with respect. I never will forget the first time I put those words into practice. I was in Alaska with a friend, walking hand in hand with one of my children. A woman saw me and came storming across the street screaming my name. My security agent, who was walking a few steps behind us, stepped in front of me. "Glenn Beck!" she was screaming. "Glenn Beck! I hate you! I hate you!" My friend took my son and kept walking. By this point I was already questioning what I was doing.

I knew it was either that she didn't understand me and what I'd been saying, or I had done something that made her feel this way—or maybe it was a combination of the two. This woman was almost out of control.

I had been reading a lot of Martin Luther King Jr. at that point, and all I could think of to say to her was, "I love you." She kept screaming, but when she paused I'd say again, "I love you." The third time I said it, her mouth continued moving but no words came out. She didn't know how to respond. Finally, she just shook her head, muttered, "Ugh," and walked away.

Maybe she didn't feel better, but I sure did. I could have ignored her, I could have responded to her with the same level of anger, I even could have laughed at her, which undoubtedly would have infuriated her even more. But "I love you" was the one response she wasn't prepared for and didn't know how to react to. To my surprise, I felt great about it. I wasn't quite sure where that had come from, but I walked away from her feeling a whole lot better about the day. By respecting her, I had disarmed her, and respected myself even more.

If we are going to save this country, we have to make a commitment to respect other people. I'm not saying you have to agree with them, or even like them. But it's important to remember the words of Jackie Robinson, who changed American society forever by becoming the first black major leaguer: "I'm not concerned with your liking me or disliking me. All I ask is you respect me as a human being."

Society is a sprawling mess; it's all those other people trying to fulfill their own needs and desires. Conflict is inherent in it. But when our ancestors made the decision thousands of years ago that we were going to gather in tribes for our own benefit, then went on to create villages and towns, then live together in cities, then form nations, we accepted the reality that the only possible way that would work was if we agreed to respect the rights of other people. We eventually codified those rights into a Constitution. We seem to have forgotten that the first right guaranteed by that document is the freedom to say what you want to say, to discuss your own opinions.

I understand words can be provocative; they can be painful.

Words give rise to emotions that demand we respond. Centuries ago, Americans would literally duel to the death over angry words; today we just strike back with more angry words.

Because social media provides anonymity, it's easy to forget that there is a person behind those words. Well, unless it's a Russian troll operation, in which case there is a political objective behind them. But believe it or not, most of the time the person who provoked your anger is dealing with many of the same stressful situations you face every day; in fact, for some people, the source provoking their anger is you!

Even if you don't respect another person's opinion or the way they express it, at least consider respecting them as a human being. There is flesh and blood behind every one of those opinions. They have the same set of emotions you do. There's a whole story, maybe even a great saga, that led them to form those opinions, as misguided as you believe they are. Those people may even root for the same sports team, like the same music, and watch the same TV shows that you do. They believe what they write or say just as much as you do. They love this country just as much you do. They want the very best for all Americans just as much as you do. And, hard as it is to believe sometimes, most of them have mothers whom they love!

Years ago, a comedian told a story that I have always liked. While I remember the story, I'm not certain who the comedian was. It may have been the wonderful George Wallace. But this politically incorrect comedian explained that there are some people in the world who are just downright ugly. And some of them don't know it, which hurts them. Because if they go through life being ugly and thinking they are attractive, they are fooling themselves. If they knew they were ugly, they could work with it and improve things. So, you would be doing them a favor by telling them. It's for their own good. So, here's my suggestion: The next time you're on a bus or the subway sitting opposite someone really ugly, do them a big favor and just point right at them so they know the truth.

Of course, if you are sitting on that bus or subway and you look up and someone is pointing at you . . .

Here's my point: Whatever you believe about that anonymous person who is provoking your outrage, that person probably believes the same thing about you, and is just as outraged as you are. Their finger is pointing at you for doing to them the same thing that irritates you. Hard to believe they can be so misguided? And then . . .

Wait a second. Are you trying to tell me something, Glenn?

Let me try it a different way. Suppose it simply is impossible for you to respect anyone who defends those positions on the issues. Suppose, as much as you try, you will never be able to respect someone so ignorant that they can't agree with you about the obvious truth. Suppose you've just had it with all of those people, and no matter how hard you try, you just can't bring yourself to respect them.

Now what? Now how are you going to fight your addiction to outrage, an addiction they are responsible for? How are you going to turn your back or walk away or resist responding online and still feel good about yourself?

By respecting yourself, that's how. That's the bottom line; that's the starting point. Self-respect. There was one thing I always avoided doing after I'd had a few drinks: I wouldn't look in the mirror. I was disgusted with myself, and the last thing I wanted to do was confront myself with reality. All alcoholics learn how to lie to themselves, but that reflection in the mirror is the truth. I can't speak for anyone else, but I do know that expressing my anger or outrage usually doesn't leave me feeling good. At times, I guess like everybody else, in my anger and outrage I've gone a little further than I intended to; I've said things out loud, or written them, that I later regretted. Where'd that come from? I wondered. Only later did I realize that I had lowered myself to their level. I should be better than that, I knew, but my emotions had overtaken my good sense.

It's always harder to walk away from an angry confrontation than to give it back bigger and badder. But "Oh, yeah?" and whatever

follows it is not really an intelligent argument. Probably the first
major self-help movement that swept this country took place in the
1920s and was called Couéism. French psychotherapist Émile Coué
believed strongly in the so-called Science of Optimistic Autosugges-
tion, which claims people can motivate themselves by repeating a
mantra over and over. In this case, he suggested people stand in front
of a mirror for twenty minutes in the morning, twenty minutes at
night, and twenty minutes twice during the day repeating, "Every
day, in every way, I'm getting better and better."

Millions of people around the world reported that this method
made them feel better about themselves. And if they believed it
worked, it did work. It turned out that the power of reinforced suggestion was stronger than people imagined. They repeated those
words loudly and firmly, and, son of a gun, when they thought about
it, they actually did feel just a little better about themselves than they
had yesterday. They didn't try to understand why it worked; they just
accepted it.

We've seen different versions of this self-help philosophy reasonably often over the last century. All of them have at their core the
common desire to make practitioners feel good about ourselves; to
respect themselves. The point being that you really can talk yourself
into certain behaviors. I suspect the reason Coué wanted people to
look in the mirror as they repeated this mantra is that he wanted
them to see themselves in a positive way. He was helping them create
a self-image that they would respect. They lived the positive attitude
in their reflection and carried it into their daily life.

As long as you continue to view discussions of political issues as
matters that have winners and losers, you are going to have a tough
time stopping. You're not going to stop in the middle of a good argument and let that SOB think they've won! Once you get started,
oh my, is it tough to stop.

But is that really the person you want to be? Do you really want
to be someone who becomes outraged when other people don't agree
with your beliefs? Really? Listen to me now: You are not responsible

for anyone else's behavior; you are responsible only for your own actions.

When I look in the mirror today, I stand up tall and think, You know what, I probably could lose a couple of pounds. But I like the person who is looking back at me. He may not be right about everything, but I know he is trying hard to be the best possible me.

Look in the mirror. Make that commitment to be the you that you will most respect. But if you need some words to say, you might try this quote from Abe Lincoln: "I am not bound to win, but I am bound to be true. I am not bound to succeed, but I am bound to live up to what light I have."

You've now begun to break your addiction.

39

On Saving the World

*It is hard to give up the easy wisecracking jeer that
divides and destroys. It is hard—very hard—to have
worked sincerely and wholeheartedly for a cause and to
have lost. Most of all, it is hard to put aside personal
prejudices. And yet we must put these things aside.*

—Stephen Vincent Benét

I know what it feels like to be loved and despised. Trust me, love is
better. I also know that reconciliation is possible, because I've seen it.
In 2017 I was in a reasonably large meeting at Netflix. As I sat there,
a woman came into the room, saw me, and practically froze. Uh-oh,
I thought, I know what happens next. I could see instantly that she
hated my guts. She was seething, and looked around the room as
if she'd been set up. It was clear that she would like nothing more
than to fillet me very slowly. Fortunately, I was there with one of my
agents, who knew her.

When she sat down, he reached across the table and said to her,
"Okay, okay, I know what you're thinking. Just give him twenty minutes. Just twenty minutes."

She glared at me, her look saying quite clearly, *I know everything
I need to know about you.* "Okay," she agreed, just to be polite.

Twenty minutes later we were posing together for photographs.
It wasn't that we suddenly agreed on issues—we didn't really talk

about specific issues—but rather that she figured out that I wasn't her enemy. By the end of that meeting, she was asking me how she might heal a rift with a member of her family with whom she was no longer talking. Her point was, I guess, that if I could help her get beyond her hatred for me and what she believed I represented, then I might have some pretty good advice on how people whose disagreements have driven them apart can get along.

Let me make this clear: I am not singing Kumbaya. I am not saying we can all get along. I am neither naïve nor an idealist. Admittedly, there are rifts in my own life, wounds I haven't been able to heal. So, I recognize that I'm not going to be able to bring the country together in some sort of 300-million-American hug. But we can get it started. We can make millions of people consciously aware of this problem and its dangers and cause many people to reassess their own actions. We can make people at least pause when they are about to express their outrage and wonder, What's the gain for me? Who is my attitude really benefiting?

The last steps of AA's program are "Sought through prayer and meditation to improve our conscious contact with God as we understood Him, praying only for knowledge of His will for us and the power to carry it out" and "Having had a spiritual awakening as the result of those steps, we tried to carry this message to alcoholics and to practice these principles in all our affairs."

Basically, these final two steps require you to understand that overcoming your addiction is possible, but it requires strength to do it, and that this entire program can be applied effectively to all areas of our lives. But immediately following these steps comes the reminder that it isn't easy or simple, and there might well be missteps and false beginnings along the way. Many of us exclaimed, "What an order; I can't go through with it," according to the *Big Book of Alcoholics Anonymous*. But authors "Bill W" Wilson and Aaron Cohen continue, "Do not be discouraged. Not one among us has been able to maintain anything like perfect adherence to these principles. We are not saints. The point is that we are willing to grow along spiritual lines. The principles we have set down are guides to progress. We claim spiritual progress rather than spiritual perfection."

I was lucky. To supplement the AA plan I also had access to the Mormon Addiction Recovery Program. This is also a twelve-step faith-based program. And while in many ways it is similar to the AA program, it has the added benefit of a tremendous support group. Because our numbers are comparatively small, our social groups tend to be highly concentrated. This is a blessing and a curse. So while in AA you are assigned a sponsor, in my faith's program there are a lot of people nearby you can call on for support or help. When dealing with "shame," anonymity can be important. In this case, our shame is the same. We dropped the ball and took the easy path. Hopefully it was sufficiently painful for us to want to try to come together. Having people readily available makes a difference. Try to find a friend to do this with you.

My Glenn Beck Coming Together to Save America Program incorporates all the things we've been discussing in this book while mirroring AA and other recovery programs. Actually, I just made up that name; you can call it anything you'd like. My program isn't very rigid and requires absolutely no allegiance to any political position or religion. While I feel that the actual twelve steps are crucial to overcoming true addiction, for the purposes of this book I have tailored the steps to fit our goal of coming back together. And, admittedly, there is nothing especially original in it; it is similar to those programs. I've done that because we have decades of evidence that this technique works.

If you want it to.

The first step is both the easiest and the most difficult: 1) Admit you have a problem.

In this instance, though, it probably is more accurate to say it this way: Admit *we* have a problem. Some addictions are personally debilitating. They interfere with your life. Getting high on outrage isn't so obvious. It doesn't prevent you from functioning; it is easily integrated into your normal life and isn't even something you feel a need to be embarrassed about—in fact, you probably even enjoy it. You may even get off on telling other people about your epic duels with one of them. None of that is unusual. It's not even the same kind of denial so commonly found among alcoholics and drug abusers. I know all the lines: I got this one. I can stop anytime I want. I'm not hurting anybody. I'm just having a little fun.

And then, as it gets a little more serious, we find ways to justify it: These people don't know what they're talking about. These people are destroying this country. Who does this guy think he is, writing stuff like that about me? I can't let anyone call me that.

As an addiction recovery program explains, "Even though people's addictions are different, some truths, like this one, never vary—nothing begins without an individual's will to make it begin. . . . Some people recognize the need to be free from addiction but are not yet willing to begin. If you are in that situation, perhaps you can begin by acknowledging your unwillingness and considering the costs of your addiction. You can list what is important to you. . . .

"Then look for contradictions between what you believe in and hope for and your behavior. Consider how your actions undermine what you value."

If you're still not ready to admit that you, personally, have a problem, take one big step back. Can you admit that we have a problem? Are you satisfied with the direction our country is heading? If you are, you're in the minority. In fact, Americans overwhelmingly believe the country is heading in the wrong direction. Not a single legitimate poll since 2010 has shown that a majority of Americans are optimistic about the future. Not one. This isn't a referendum on President Trump; these polls also include the entire eight-year Obama administration. They reflect the general dissatisfaction felt by Americans.

So, even if you remain reluctant to take this first step for yourself, at least acknowledge that we are on the wrong track, and as a patriotic American you have a responsibility to help turn the country in the right direction.

The second step is, why do we need to take action now? That

requires us to 2) Understand and accept the potential consequences of taking no action.

We are at the beginning of a technological revolution that is already changing our world. It is both exciting and frightening, but it offers incredible possibilities if we are prepared to take advantage of them. But that requires being able to make bold decisions, and right now we are so divided that we can't agree on anything. If our representatives can't even agree on how to fix our aging, existing infrastructure, how can they possibly make the difficult decisions necessary to prepare this country to move boldly into the future?

Rather than using the new technology to reach out to the world, we are locking ourselves into echo chambers. We click on stories that reinforce our world view, not on those stories that challenge us. We see, read, and connect to those who agree with us or make us feel good, making it easy to believe the worst of people who think differently than we do.

America is the most powerful country on earth, and what has made us that for the last century is our ability to unite around our common principles. We have used American ingenuity to create a better life not just for our citizens but for people around the world. It was an American who figured out how to mass-produce products, it was Americans who went to the moon, it was an American who dreamed of and created new forms of entertainment. When we are united, we are a mighty force.

But right now we're not united. As Lincoln pointed out, "A house divided against itself cannot stand." Empires rise, empires fall. We've seen it happen throughout history. These modern Kondratiev waves follow technological cycles: the Industrial Revolution. The Age of Steam and Railways. The Age of Electricity, the Automobile, and Mass Production. The Age of Telecommunications and Information. And now, we have begun a new cycle, the Digital Age. These upheavals are predictable, even though people refuse to acknowledge that. Do you think Alexander the Great believed his empire would last only decades? Do you think the Romans, the most advanced civilization history had ever seen, believed their empire was just a brief blip in time? Do you think people living in England at the height of the British Empire believed the sun would eventually set on them?

Consider the possibilities. If we don't figure out how to move forward together, it *can* happen here. We are being economically challenged every day. Our way of life is threatened and attacked every day. We are being lulled into passive acceptance by mind-numbing devices. We are being manipulated by others for their gain.

The philosopher-poet Ralph Waldo Emerson warned us, "The future belongs to those who prepare for it." And as far as I can determine right now, that isn't us. As I've written, I consider myself an optimistic catastrophist. I see both the possibilities and the perils that are waiting for this country. But if we refuse to deal with the real dangers that we are facing today and instead continue to participate in meaningless diversions, I fear for the future of our country. We may struggle along as we have been doing lately, or, as other countries have done, we may turn to a person who proclaims that he or she has the answers and all we have to do is put our trust in him or her. The more we bury our heads in our devices, the more divided we are, and the easier we make it for others to replace us as world leaders—others who don't share our principles.

We are facing real problems, and no one is looking for answers. We have the greatest time in front of us or the worst time in front of us—it's our choice. But we owe it to the people who built this country and we owe it to our children to understand that we absolutely have to take action right now to begin healing the national divide.

The best way to start overcoming your addiction to anger and outrage is to 3) Find places of agreement.

There are bedrock principles on which Americans do agree; in fact, these are the things that define us as Americans. More important, they are enduring values. They have been tested through time. Take a look at the issues that most often infuriate you, that divide us; I guarantee these are not the same issues that divided Americans in the past, and they won't be the same issues Americans will deal with in the future. They are mostly transient problems that will be solved by progress or compromise, or will simply disappear to be replaced by a whole new set of controversial issues to fight over.

But all Americans can find places where we agree, starting points to remind us that we are one people united. We are, even at the worst of times, "unum," one people united. We understand that the concept of America is unique in history, and it is our job to make this experiment a success. We can agree once again with Jefferson that "We hold these truths to be self-evident, that all men are created equal," and that we have God-given natural rights, and that among them are life, liberty, and the pursuit of happiness. We can all agree on the individual freedoms enumerated in the Bill of Rights, even if sometimes we don't agree on the interpretation of those rights. We can find great areas of agreement on practical matters: In this world it is necessary to have a large, strong, modern military to protect the country. It is essential that all Americans, whatever their gender, race, religion, national heritage, or abilities, be treated equally.

We all agree to be governed by this cranky old system. We agree to live under the rule of law. We abide by national customs and traditions, we celebrate the same holidays and individual events and honor the same heroes. We suffer together in tragedy and mourn together. We take pride in the same types of accomplishments, from school graduations to workplace honors. We understand that our fathers and forefathers fought for a set of ideals and gave us a gift that we have to protect.

We need to look at those things that once brought us together. The Declaration of Independence. The Bill of Rights. The principles that we all agreed on long ago that define who we are as Americans. Relying on them has led to the success we have enjoyed for the last two centuries, and they remain as valid as when they were written. They have brought us together in the worst of times; they have united us. They have reminded us that we are, all of us, on the same team.

None of this is complicated. It's just a reminder that in these contentious times we do agree on fundamental things far more than we disagree on issues. And it is essential that we remember the person on the other end of our outrage most probably shares some of our beliefs.

We can find those areas of agreement in our daily lives, too. We might all be pissed off that our street is full of potholes, the streetlamps don't work, and the sidewalks are broken. But blaming them for breaking the sidewalk isn't going to get that sidewalk fixed. Getting angry that someone else was careless and broke the sidewalk isn't going to make it safer. We can agree that we are all better off if the sidewalk is fixed. We can't fix the whole sidewalk, but we can repair the sidewalk in front of our own house. That's the best place to start. And maybe, just maybe, a neighbor will see you doing it and decide, You know what, that makes sense. I'm going to fix my sidewalk, too! Instead of harping on our differences, we should be focusing on those things we can all agree on and can work together to solve.

Every recovery program or self-help program includes some version of 4) Take a moral inventory.

Both AA and the Mormons suggest, "Make a searching and fearless inventory of yourself"—although the Mormons suggest you literally write it down. Essentially, this means taking that good long look in the mirror and accepting responsibility for your actions. The theologian Reinhold Niebuhr said it best in his now-famous 1943 "Serenity Prayer": "God, give us grace to accept with serenity the things that cannot be changed, courage to change the things which should be changed, and the wisdom to distinguish the one from the other."

A key element of this involves listening to yourself as well as to other people. Most of us have gotten pretty good at listening to the words of other people and finding the flaws and mistakes they make. It's pretty easy to figure out exactly where they're wrong. But as I've learned too often, I'm just hearing; when I enter a conversation with someone I "know" is wrong, I actually stop listening. They have nothing to teach me. They need to listen to me, because I have the only right answers.

What actually happens in these so-called debates is that neither side is listening for anything other than a few seconds of silence so they can jump in and tell the other why they are wrong. When both sides believe there is nothing to be learned by listening to the opposition, we begin to dismiss them and ridicule them. Gradually the rhetoric is ratcheted up, and we begin to dehumanize the other side. We may even begin to hate those who disagree with us and believe that if it wasn't for people like them, America would be a safer, more prosperous, and happier place.

Here, once again, is my reminder: The other side is thinking the same thing.

This thoroughly modern advice is based firmly in ancient history. Although often associated with Socrates, the injunction "Know thyself" can be traced back to ancient Egypt. It has been said to be the beginning of wisdom, as it is impossible to judge anyone else without having an understanding of yourself.

Making a moral inventory requires you to listen to your own words and admit to yourself where you might have gone too far or even, oh my, not been quite as right as you believed. Okay, I'll say it: admit you might be wrong. How you proceed to do this is your decision; you don't have to write it down, but it is vital that you examine your own contribution to this mess we've made together. The Mormons suggest you examine the thoughts, feelings, beliefs, events, situations, and circumstances that trigger an emotional response. They might include "sadness, regret, anger, resentment, fear, and bitterness." I'll throw in frustration, pissed-off-edness, and all the rest of the emotions that culminate in outrage.

None of us, deep down inside, want to believe we play a role in this problem, but unless we are willing to take an honest look at ourselves, we will only continue this downward spiral.

While several programs rely heavily on religious beliefs to help people overcome their addictions, that isn't necessary in this program. But it is important that you 5) Have faith that doing this will make a significant difference in your life and in the future of this country.

Faith most often denotes a religious connection. There are significant questions that can't be answered by facts, evidence, or logic, so we place our trust in God. Rather than being bewildered by our inability to find provable answers, we accept the existence of a higher power as a catch-all. While religious faith is certainly welcome, it isn't the only kind of faith to which I'm referring. By referring to faith, I am also asking you to believe that it is necessary for us to follow this path and that there is something of great value waiting at the end.

In this instance, we can draw on history. We can look at our past and see how strong we have been when we worked together, and how tragic the outcome has been when we were divided. We can also look at the lessons of other civilizations that collapsed after being divided. So while it is admittedly impossible for me to predict the future, I am certain we are at a crossroads, and the decisions we make today will reverberate through our lives and those of our children and grandchildren. One of those roads is simply an extension of the road we're on right now; we know for sure that it's bumpy and that there are big potholes waiting in the darkness, and the farther we go on it, the worse it is going to get. The other road is . . . well, we don't know for certain, but we do know it is smoother than our current path and probably leads to a better place.

Faith also has in it the element of hope. Hope and faith aren't quite interchangeable; hope is what we want to happen, while faith is what we believe will happen. I hope, for example, that you have faith that by following this program we will ensure a better future for all of us. Hope and faith together provide a basis for optimism. The Reverend Robert Schuller once advised, "Let your hopes, not your hurts, shape your future."

There are other elements that compose what we call faith. Among them are confidence and security. Having real faith, really believing that following the right path leads directly to a "promised land," both instills confidence and provides a great sense of personal security.

As I have written, I have no idea what will happen, if anything, after I close my eyes for the final time. But what I do know, without any question, is that my faith makes me a much better person in this life. I do believe very strongly that healing the political divide that has turned us into warring camps is absolutely necessary if this country is going to survive in any recognizable form.

That is the faith we all need to have.

On a practical note, if we are to once again come together as Americans, we are going to have to learn how to 6) Determine the facts and deal only with facts.

We are facing a new challenge that is making it far more difficult for us to find those areas of agreement. We are having to separate what is true from what has become popularized as "alternative facts" or "fake news." These politically motivated attacks on reality read and sound as if they were accurate, but they're not. They are false statements made to sow confusion and create chaos. There is no such thing as an "alternative fact"—but as we have seen, they do their job. They muddy reality. While the emergence of social media and cable news stations has allowed false information to be spread so much more quickly and widely, its use for political gain is as old as recorded history. Euripides warned in 408 BC, "When one with honeyed words but evil mind persuades the mob, great woes befall the state."

Fake news is the comfy bedfellow of alternative facts. Fake news is a phrase tossed into the public debate in an attempt to make it even more difficult for people to figure out what's real and what is simply made up. Calling something fake news without providing any support is a means of casting doubt on often legitimate stories. It's a way of dismissing things that may be completely accurate and truthful.

Few people had a better understanding of the necessity of dealing with facts than the late mystery writer Agatha Christie, who wrote in *Death on the Nile*, "[People] conceive a certain theory, and everything has to fit into that theory. If one little fact will not fit it, they throw it aside. But it is always the facts that will not fit in that are significant."

Few things, if any, have done more to create this current situation, to damage this country and threaten our future well-being, than this attack on the truth. It's why other countries—Russia at the forefront—have spent so much effort and money to spread fake news.

"Facts are stubborn things," John Adams wrote, "and whatever may be our wishes, our inclinations or the dictates of our passions, they cannot alter the state of facts and evidence." Until now. Today, with the clever use of Facebook, Twitter, Pinterest, YouTube, Instagram, and all the other modes of common communication, we can easily service the dictates of our passions with just a few words sent to gullible people.

It is your duty as an American citizen to separate facts from the half-truths, exaggerations, and lies that permeate our lives. Without being able to do that, there is no hope of any real reconciliation between the right and left. We have become so accustomed to being lied to that we struggle to believe any politician, and we no longer hold them to the truth. Our sources of news have been undermined to the point where there is no longer a single newspaper or TV or radio station that has the trust of both sides of the spectrum. But the fact remains that we can't get this country back together without relying on factual information.

So how can you determine what is factual and what is an "alternative fact"? Facts come from reliable sources. Here's a pretty good way to determine whether you can trust a source: If you always agree with reports from a source, it probably is partisan and simply tells you what its algorithms have determined you want to hear. A reliable source is one that identifies the people and places where its information comes from, generally reports information from more than one source, uses reliable statistics, and at times makes you furious because it is reporting something you don't like. Also, as difficult as it might be, listen to the friends or relatives who don't agree with your political stance. They aren't going to be wrong all the time. And, finally, understand the difference between a fact and an opinion. The most popular cable supposed-news channels have become successful by blurring the lines between the two. An opinion generally should be based on a collection of facts, but it isn't factual. It is what you think, rather than what you know.

Knowing the facts of an issue or a situation arms you with the knowledge you need. I promise you, raising your voice louder than the other guy or writing increasingly clever insults is not a substitute for knowing the facts of an issue.

There is another common factor found in every recovery program: If you're serious about accomplishing your objective, at the very beginning you have to 7) Set realistic goals. No one stops drinking in one day. In fact, it probably is accurate to say I continue to stop drinking every day. While we celebrate years of sobriety, in AA we always take it one day at a time. We stop drinking; we don't stop being alcoholics.

That same way of thinking is true for all addictions. You aren't going to change your behavior in a day or even a week. It's a process of small steps that eventually add up to a new approach to the same old things. I don't want to make the ultimate goal too big: I guess my immediate goal would be for us to not kill one another. That, I believe, is something we can easily accomplish.

The real question you need to ask is what you want to accomplish. While I don't know for sure, I sort of doubt that getting yourself so angry that you're ready to burst at the stupidity of people who refuse to listen to you is your ultimate objective. It would be considerably more reasonable to state that you want to bring people to your point of view. Assuming that really is your goal, there probably isn't a big chance you're going to be successful; the other side is dug into their position just as deeply as you are. Screaming louder and tossing more clever insults at them probably isn't going to change a lot of minds. But what might work is a calmer tone, an approach in which you try to listen with the objective of reaching some sort of compromise. Michael Kinsley, who formerly hosted the CNN show *Crossfire*, once suggested that he wanted to create a show titled *Ceasefire*, which would focus on areas of agreement and strive to find common ground.

Okay, now that we know we can achieve a goal, let's look at some other strategies that make sense. Some programs advocate keeping track of your behavior to see if patterns emerge. Many dieting programs, for example, start by having you write down everything you eat over a period of time. It might make sense to at least try to determine precisely those things that provoke the strongest reactions from you, or what issues or people cause you to respond. What issues push your buttons? The more you can understand what it is that engages and sometimes enrages you, the more likely it is you'll be able to deal with it.

In some cases, outrage just becomes your generalized type of behavior. You've become an angry person. You enjoy the online fights and try to provoke them. The problem is that if you get mad at anything, you'll get mad at everything. It becomes both your approach and your attitude. You start by going into your default position— outrage. Not only isn't it necessary, it's counterproductive. Outrage isn't going to help you accomplish any goals, and, like other addictions, it will eventually affect your personal life. For people with health issues—high blood pressure, for example—it might even be physically dangerous.

Psychotherapist and author Gary Trosclair suggests that before engaging in political debate, you should "set your priorities clearly: Do you want to prove that you're right, or to feel better and be effective for your cause?"

Start by setting achievable goals. Limit the time you spend on the Internet. During discussion of an issue, find one claim made by the other side that you agree with. Try to make one positive comment about them. Stick to facts; "So's your old man" will not win any debates. Trosclair also advises choosing to take constructive actions (such as joining with other people to accomplish a goal), pointing out, "Each time you do any of these, you break the psychological and biological cycles that keep reinforcing your anger. Addictions don't go away immediately, but with time you can build new neural circuits that override the old ones."

Here's the toughest one for many people: Admit something

you've said or written is wrong. The reaction to doing that might surprise you. A Tufts University study demonstrated that people "viewing a concession created a more positive reaction to the ideological opponent." In other words, if you're willing to give a little, the other side is more likely to listen to you. According to the *Atlantic*, "Watching a concession did make people more likely to say they understood the viewpoint of their ideological opponent, and were open to opinions expressed by the opponent. . . . Don't forget to throw in a to-be-sure sentence; it may sound like a concession, but it could wind up helping your cause, especially if your cause includes not seeing America consumed by bitter acrimony."

One reason AA and other step programs have proved to be so effective is that they are loosely structured. The how-to aspects of these programs allow each person to find his or her own way to achieve their goals. The steps are broadly defined and open to at least some interpretation. While programs like AA have been established to entirely eliminate a specific behavior—don't drink—in this case we simply are asking you to modify your behavior. There is no need for you to eliminate it. The key is to examine and analyze your existing behavior patterns and find those places where you can change them.

Right after the 2016 election, a San Francisco woman named Justine Lee cofounded an organization named Make America Dinner Again. I had her on the show one afternoon. The objective, she explained, was to bring together people with opposing political viewpoints for civil discussions over a warm, friendly meal. Lee asks guests to follow some simple commonsense rules: "Try not to make judgment statements. Don't say, 'You're bad,' 'You're wrong,' 'You're crazy.' Try to put this into 'I' statements, so 'This made me feel . . .'" The first exercise at dinner is to find one thing they have in common. They might be from the same area or root for the same team; they might have friends or acquaintances in common. It turns out that when you dig, it's possible to find those common areas. The obvious goal is to humanize each person so he or she is seen as an individual, not a label. That gets us to 8) Don't label people.

Labels and stereotypes are the worst type of shorthand. They too easily attribute beliefs and behaviors to people who may not fit into a group and make it easy to oppose them. If you tell a liberal, for example, that someone is a member of the NRA, they will instantly believe they know what that person believes. Tell a conservative that someone contributes to the ACLU, and they will know they have nothing in common with that person. I've been labeled, but it was out of necessity. To succeed in this business I had to be positioned a certain way. I became a product. I remember thinking when they told me we had trademarked my name, I'm a product? Ick! I started taking myself far too seriously. And I also remember thinking that because of the way I was presented, my audience had certain expectations that I had to meet.

I was still at CNN, for example, when I met the great magician Penn Jillette, and he didn't want anything to do with me. He made some nasty remarks. Several years later he apologized to me, telling me, "I hated the sound of those words coming out of my mouth. It was shocking to me. But I hadn't healed from 9/11." Eventually we became respectful friends who truly admire each other.

But because I was labeled a conservative, people made all kinds of assumptions about my stand on issues. Some of them were true, but a lot of them weren't. Friends of Penn Jillette couldn't believe that he went on the air with a racist, bigot, and homophobe, which they assumed I must be. That's beyond absurd. It turns out that there are many shades of conservative, just as there are different types of liberal.

That rush to judgment—immediately labeling people—is so deeply ingrained in all of us because at times our survival depended on it. Predator or prey? Stand or run?

More recently, it has become an economic necessity. Corporations long ago figured out how to exploit labels. It goes all the way

back to the silent-movie Westerns in which the good guys were identifiable because they wore white hats, while bad guys wore black hats.
That made it easy to know whom to root for. Here's something I
guarantee: Your side is wearing the white hats. Political labels have
exactly the same purpose. If there were no liberals, for example, Fox
wouldn't have an audience. As long as we remain divided, those entities that profit from this division will continue to thrive.

The problem with this is that labels dehumanize people. It makes
it easy to attack them for positions they may not even hold. One of the
techniques Make America Dinner Again uses is to have each person
interview another dinner guest—and then tell that person's story to
the group in the first person. That forces people to think of others
as individuals, while labels make it easy to demonize an entire group.
And when we make broad and sometimes unfair generalizations, we
are opening the door for a lot worse to come through that door. Former vice president Joe Biden set the tone when he told Democrats, "I
believe that we have to end the divisive partisan politics that is ripping
this country apart. And I think we can. It's mean-spirited, it's petty,
and it's gone on for much too long. . . . I don't think we should look at
Republicans as our enemies. They are our opposition. They're not our
enemies. And for the sake of the country, we have to work together."

Federal law enforcement agencies use a little-known technique
when tracking fugitives. They know that eventually most people are
going to go online. It turns out that most of us are creatures of habit,
and when we go online we visit the same sites, often in the same
order. If authorities gain access to a person's computer, they can identify those sites and that order. When someone goes online and visits
those sites, the fugitive's Internet provider notifies authorities of that
computer's location. That strategy has proved to be successful in several high-profile cases. The reason it works is that most of us are that
cliché—the creature of habit. We tend to live somewhat predictable
lives, repeating comfortable patterns. But overcoming your addiction
to outrage is going to require you to make some changes. It will require you to 9) Open yourself to new possibilities.

There are times we get stuck in a rut. It's just easier, and emotionally safer, to stay there. But when you do that, your mind and spirit stop growing. I've been a big gambler with my career. I could have stayed happily ensconced at the Fox network, making loads of money, for a long time. Instead, I got out of there to start a web television network, something no one had done before. When we decided to do it, the technology didn't even exist. Looking back, it was a crazy thing to do. But I was growing stagnant at Fox; maybe I was using different words, but essentially I was repeating myself day after day. I decided to roll the dice. I've always believed that if you risk big, you can win big—or lose big, but at least roll the dice.

More than a century ago, Frederick Jackson Turner published an essay entitled "The Significance of the Frontier in American History." Essentially, he wrote that the American character was shaped by continuing to expand our horizons. He also believed that a civilization starts dying when it stops exploring, when it stops changing and growing. Fear of the unknown plays an important role; for many of us, it's what prevents us from opening ourselves to those new possibilities.

I like to pose this question to people when I talk about changing their behavior: What's the worst that can happen? That usually causes them to fumble around for some kind of answer. That answer is rarely satisfying. I point out to them that there is one thing we do know: What they are doing now isn't accomplishing their objectives. And there are other things we know for certain: Losing or modifying your political outrage isn't going to cost you your family or your job. It isn't going to enable the other side to "win." It isn't going to pose a danger to the future of this country.

Conversely, what's the best that can happen? It could reduce the level of hateful rhetoric and stress. It could allow us to talk to each other and perhaps find some areas of compromise. It could actually allow this country to move into the future as a united country.

By continuing to exhibit the same behavior, you're not accomplishing anything other than enjoying a temporary and meaningless high. You've got that addictive dopamine and adrenaline surging through your veins, but eventually you're going to need more and more of them to maintain the same level of fulfillment.

Take a step in a different direction. Dip your toe. Visit a website popular with the other side. Walk down a different block. Listen to a popular song you've never heard before. Whatever it is, break out of the mold you've built around yourself. Remember, taking this step doesn't require you to admit that you're wrong. It isn't necessarily your stand on the issues, it's the way you think about and address your political opposition that needs to be changed. I happen to like the quote probably wrongfully attributed to Scottish lord Thomas Dewar, of the whiskey family: "Minds are like parachutes—they only function when open."

The final and often the most important aspect of the AA recovery program, as well as pretty much every other program designed to end an addiction, involves finding someone to offer assistance to you when you need it, and requiring you to offer that same assistance to others. In AA it is the last step, and the step that keeps your recovery fresh and working. It can start with a friend or with being a sponsor for someone who is struggling, but it needs to end up a part of who you are and a way of life. "Share this message with others and practice these principles in all you do." In this program, we can call it 10) Be generous of spirit and share your discoveries with others.

The objective is to reunite America by giving up our national outrage. You are not going to be able to do it all by yourself, but we aren't going to be able to do it without you. We're all in this together. This has got to be a Team America effort, but it starts one person at a time. Working with other people reinforces your own commitment while also bringing it to the attention of others. I talk about my addiction. I tell people I'm an alcoholic. By doing that, I am making a public commitment to stay sober while also sending a strong message to other alcoholics that it's possible to beat their addiction. Spreading the word helps you keep your own word. Maybe the next time you're in the middle of a heated debate, you might pause and ask whoever is on the other side if they want to do something worthwhile. Few people are going to refuse. Then suggest they join in figuring out how to spread the message: Fight for your beliefs in a civil way. Respect each other. Respect yourself. And then join in spreading this word.

It is the ultimate reinforcement, and the only way this can be effective. Here's what you and the other person have in common: Both or all of you care deeply about the future of this country and care passionately about these issues—otherwise, you wouldn't be in the middle of a debate. You'd be watching TV, playing a video game, or listening to music, but you wouldn't be trying to sway other people to your political stance. We don't have to make dinner for each other, but a few friendly words to a stranger will go a long way.

I chose the phrase "Be generous" specifically because I am so confident that this program is so important to all of us that by sharing it, you are giving out something of real value. But at the same time, as an American, you will also be giving something back to this country.

It doesn't require 100 percent of Americans to participate; it doesn't even require a majority. A movement can make a significant impact with as little as 20 percent participation.

Here is what I'm asking: think. That's all; the next time you dive headfirst into a political discussion and your blood starts flowing and your voice begins rising and gets a little strident, think.

Postscript

Think about what you gain and what you lose by holding on to your outrage.

Think about the state of our nation today.

Think about what will happen in the future if this political outrage continues to grow.

I have no doubt about the ability of Americans to heal this divide; if there is a will, there is a way.

I know that on December 8, 1941, this nation came together to defeat the Axis Powers.

I know that on September 12, 2001, this nation united in our determination to meet the challenge of radical Islam.

My fervent hope is that we don't have to wait for another such moment before we realize we are all in this together and act for the common good to make sure we are truly the United States of America.